Borges, Desire, and Sex

# Liverpool Latin American Studies

*Series Editor:* Matthew Brown, University of Bristol
*Emeritus Series Editor:* Professor John Fisher

1. Business History in Latin America: The Experience of Seven Countries
   *Carlos Dávila and Rory Miller (eds)*

2. Habsburg Peru: Images, Imagination and Memory
   *Peter T. Bradley and David Cahill*

3. Knowledge and Learning in the Andes: Ethnographic Perspectives
   *Henry Stobart and Rosaleen Howard (eds)*

4. Bourbon Peru, 1750–1824
   *John Fisher*

5. Between Resistance and Adaptation: Indigenous Peoples and the Colonisation of the Chocó, 1510–1753
   *Caroline A. Williams*

6. Shining Path: Guerilla War in Peru's Northern Highlands, 1980–1997
   *Lewis Taylor*

7. South American Independence: Gender, Politics, Text
   *Catherine Davies, Claire Brewster and Hilary Owen*

8. Adventuring Through Spanish Colonies: Simón Bolívar, Foreign Mercenaries and the Birth of New Nations
   *Matthew Brown*

9. British Trade with Spanish America, 1763–1808
   *Adrian J. Pearce*

10. Colonial Tropes and Postcolonial Tricks: Rewriting the Tropics in the novela de la selva
    *Lesley Wylie*

11. Argentina's Partisan Past: Nationalism and the Politics of History
    *Michael Goebel*

12. The Reinvention of Mexico: National Ideology in a Neoliberal Era
    *Gavin O'Toole*

13. Armies, Politics and Revolution: Chile, 1808–1826
    *Juan Luis Ossa Santa Cruz*

14. Andean Truths: Transitional Justice, Ethnicity, and Cultural Production in Post-Shining Path Peru
    *Anne Lambright*

15. Positivism, Science, and 'The Scientists' in Porfirian Mexico: A Reappraisal
    *Natalia Priego*

16. Argentine Cinema and National Identity (1966–1976)
    *Carolina Rocha*

17. Decadent Modernity: Civilization and 'Latinidad' in Spanish America, 1880–1920
    *Michela Coletta*

**Liverpool Latin American Studies, New Series 18**

# Borges, Desire, and Sex

Ariel de la Fuente

LIVERPOOL UNIVERSITY PRESS

Cover image: Raphaelle Peale, American (1774–1825). *Venus Rising From the Sea—A Deception*, ca. 1822. Oil on canvas, 29⅛ × 24⅛ inches (74 × 61.3 cm). The Nelson-Atkins Museum of Art, Kansas City, Missouri. Purchase: William Rockhill Nelson Trust, 34-147. Photo courtesy Nelson-Atkins Media Services/Jamison Miller.

First published 2018 by
Liverpool University Press
4 Cambridge Street
Liverpool
L69 7ZU

Copyright © 2018 Ariel de la Fuente

The right of Ariel de la Fuente to be identified as the author of this book has been asserted by him in accordance with the Copyright, Design and Patents Act 1988.

All rights reserved. No part of this book may be reproduced, stored in a retrieval system, or transmitted, in any form or by any means, electronic, mechanical, photocopying, recording, or otherwise, without the prior written permission of the publisher.

British Library Cataloguing-in-Publication data
A British Library CIP record is available

ISBN 978 1 78694 150 3

Typeset by Carnegie Book Production, Lancaster
Printed and bound by CPI Group (UK) Ltd, Croydon, CR0 4YY

*To the memory of my father*

*To my mother*

*To the memory of Marcela Duprat*

*To Cecilia, Malena, and Agustina*

"En toda vasta obra suele haber rincones secretos"

>Jorge Luis Borges
>Prologue to Manuel Mujica Láinez's *Los ídolos*

"Love's mysteries in souls do grow,
But yet the body is his book"

>John Donne, "The Ecstasy"

"Es por el cuerpo que se llega al alma"

>Jorge Guillermo Borges*, *La senda*

"Combien des jeux très lascivement agréables
naissent de la manière honnête et pudique de
parler des actes de l'amour!"

>Michel de Montaigne, *Les Essais*

"Que otros se jacten de las páginas que han escrito,
a mí me enorgullecen las que he leído."

>Jorge Luis Borges, "Un lector"

---

* Jorge Guillermo Borges was Jorge Luis's father.

# Contents

| | |
|---|---:|
| Acknowledgements | viii |
| List of Abbreviations | ix |
| Introduction | 1 |
| 1  On Borges's Sexuality | 19 |
| 2  Biography in Literature and the Reading of Desire and Sex in Borges | 35 |
| 3  Borges's Erotic Library: The Poetry Shelf | 48 |
| 4  Sir Richard Burton's Orientalist Erotica: *The Thousand Nights and a Night* and *The Perfumed Garden* | 84 |
| 5  Schopenhauer and Montaigne, Philosophy and Sex | 109 |
| 6  Desire and Sex in Buenos Aires: Borges's Poetry on the *Arrabal* | 129 |
| 7  Stoicism and Borges's Writing of Women | 145 |
| 8  "Emma Zunz": Sex, Virtue, and Punishment | 173 |
| 9  "La intrusa": Incest and Gay Readings | 187 |
| Conclusions | 206 |
| Works Cited | 209 |
| Index | 219 |

# Acknowledgements

The Department of History and the College of Liberal Arts at Purdue University have supported the research and writing of this book, for which I am sincerely appreciative. I have also fundamentally benefitted from the expertise and professionalism of the staff at the Humanities, Social Sciences, and Education Library, in particular the staff in the Interlibrary Loan Department, whose unfailing dedication made possible for me to consult all necessary materials. I equally thank the Harry Ransom Center, at the University of Texas (Austin), for giving me access to their Jorge Luis Borges's Collection. I am also appreciative of Carmen Vasco, Inés, Silvia, and Sonia Fernández Moreno and the journal *Variaciones Borges* for their copyright permissions and of Donna Ferullo for her gracious advice regarding these matters. I am deeply grateful to Chloe Johnson, Commissioning Editor at Liverpool University Press, for her commitment to this project.

Many colleagues generously offered their knowledge and support and I am certainly indebted to them for any virtue this book may have: I thank Jeremy Adelman, Víctor Aizenman, Germán Alvarez, Daniel Balderston, Mariela Blanco, Pablo Brescia, Barbara Brown, Susan Clawson, Susan Curtis, Chuck Cutter, Paul Dixon, Nils Jacobsen, Guillermo Martínez, Alberto Rojo, Laura Rosato, Marcia Stephenson, and Dawn Stinchcomb.

It would have been impossible to bring this book to completion without the kindness of my cousins Alma Saravia and Eli Eitan, and the friendship of Gustavo Paz, Luis Alberto Lozano, Fernando Boro, Ananth and Vidhya Iyer, Claudio and Claudia Aguilar, Stacey Smythe and Avi Kak, Marcelo Carignano and Claudia Guerin, Carlos Gambirazio, Ruth Abramovitz, Esteban Fernández Juricic and Gabriela Sincich, John and Kim Reisman, Dave and Char Warner and the "Grill Nighters".

This book is dedicated to the people to whom I owe everything in my life: to my parents, for their love and generosity; to Marcela Duprat, who gave me the opportunity to discover beauty in the world and "bonté" in human beings; to Malena and Agustina, for their endless love; and to Cecilia, whose literary insights and unfailing patience made the writing of the book (as of the rest of our life) a shared adventure.

# Abbreviations

"Auto"  Jorge Luis Borges. "An Autobiographical Essay," in *Critical Essays on Jorge Luis Borges*. Jaime Alazraki (ed.). Boston: Hall and Co., 1987, 21–55.
BES  Jorge Luis Borges. *Jorge Luis Borges en Sur, 1931–1980*. Buenos Aires: Emecé, 1999.
BH  Jorge Luis Borges. *Borges en El Hogar, 1935–1958*. Buenos Aires: Emecé, 2000.
BLL  Jorge Luis Borges. *Borges, libros y lecturas*. Laura Rosato and Germán Alvarez (eds.). Buenos Aires: Biblioteca Nacional, 2010.
BOW  Jorge Luis Borges. *Borges on Writing*. N. T. Di Giovanni, D. Halpern, and Frank MacShane (eds.). New York: Allen Lane, 1973.
BP  Jorge Luis Borges. *Borges Profesor: Curso de literatura inglesa en la universidad de Buenos Aires*. Martín Arias and Martín Hadis (eds.). Buenos Aires: Emecé, 2000.
Cartas del Fervor  Jorge Luis Borges. *Cartas del fervor: correspondencia con Maurice Abramowicz y Jacobo Sureda (1919–1928)*. Edited with prologue and notes by Joaquín Marco, Carlos García, and Cristóbal Pera. Barcelona: Emecé, 1999.
CS  Jorge Luis Borges. *El círculo secreto. Prólogos y notas*. Buenos Aires: Emecé, 2003.
CSM  Jorge Luis Borges. *Cuaderno San Martín*. Buenos Aires: Cuadernos del Plata, 1929.
CV  Jorge Luis Borges. *This Craft of Verse*. Cambridge: Harvard University Press, 2000.
ET  Jorge Luis Borges. *El tango: cuatro conferencias*. Buenos Aires: Sudamericana, 2016.
FBA  Jorge Luis Borges. *Fervor de Buenos Aires*. Buenos Aires: Imprenta Serantes, 1923. Edición de autor, sin foliación].

| | |
|---|---|
| *IA* | Jorge Luis Borges. *El idioma de los argentinos*. Madrid: Alianza, 1999. |
| *ILN* | Jorge Luis Borges. *Introducción a la literatura norteamericana*. Buenos Aires: Editorial Columba, 1967. |
| *Inq.* | Jorge Luis Borges. *Inquisiciones*. Madrid: Alianza, 1998. |
| *LE* | Jorge Luis Borges. *Luna de enfrente*. Buenos Aires: Editorial Proa, 1925. |
| *LDS* | Jorge Luis Borges. *Libro de sueños*. Buenos Aires: Random House Mondadori, 2013. |
| *NRSVA* | *The New Oxford Annotated Bible with the Apocrypha.* The New Revised Standard Version (third edition). Michael Coogan (ed.). Oxford: Oxford University Press, 2001. |
| *OC* [1974] | Jorge Luis Borges. *Obras completas*. 4 vols. Buenos Aires and Barcelona: Emecé. 1974–96. |
| *OC* [2009] | Jorge Luis Borges. *Obras completas*. 3 vols. Critical edition annotated by Rolando Costa Picazo and Irma Zángara. Buenos Aires: Emecé, 2009–11. |
| *OC* [2010] | Jorge Luis Borges. *Oeuvres Completes*. Jean-Pierre Bernes, editor. Paris: Gallimard, 2010. |
| *OCC* | Jorge Luis Borges. *Obras completas en colaboración*. Buenos Aires: Emecé, 1979. |
| *TME* | Jorge Luis Borges. *El tamaño de mi esperanza*. Madrid: Alianza, 1998. |
| *TR1* | Jorge Luis Borges. *Textos recobrados (1919–1929)*. Barcelona: Emecé, 1997. |
| *TR2* | Jorge Luis Borges. *Textos recobrados (1931–1955)*. Buenos Aires: Emecé, 2001. |
| *TR3* | Jorge Luis Borges. *Textos recobrados (1956–1986)*. Buenos Aires: Emecé, 2003. |
| *WWR* | Arthur Schopenhauer. *The World as Will and Representation*. E. F. J. Payne trans. New York: Dover, 1969. |

# Introduction

One of the personal traits that defined Jorge Luis Borges in the eyes of his friends and other contemporaries was his troubled sexuality. Estela Canto, who maintained a close romantic relationship with Borges in the 1940s, said that "la realización sexual era aterradora para él."[1] Dr Miguel Kohan Miller, the psychoanalyst who about the same time treated him for his "impotencia sexual," also observed that Borges, "como toda persona que tiene una disminución de su potencia sexual, [vivía] acosado por el problema de la sexualidad."[2]

This emotionally overwhelming condition significantly shaped Borges's literary experience: he often read, thought, and wrote about desire and sex. Yet, in a modest and reticent writer like Borges, this aspect of his work is not usually apparent. This is the case, for example, in the essay "Edgar Allan Poe," published in the newspaper *La Nación* in 1949, in which Borges offered a critique of the American author. The title of the article does not allude to sex, and the text does not seem to be concerned with it. Borges begins the essay in this way:

> Detrás de Poe (como detrás de [Jonathan] Swift, de [Thomas] Carlyle, de Almafuerte) hay una neurosis. Interpretar su obra en función de esa anomalía puede ser abusivo o legítimo. Es abusivo cuando se alega la neurosis para invalidar o negar la obra; es legítimo cuando se busca en la neurosis un medio para entender su génesis.[3]

At first glance we may think that here Borges proposes that Poe's personality and emotional troubles may help explain his work (as well as those of the other authors). But that would be barely an elemental approximation that still leaves us essentially clueless about the rationale that guided his interpretation of the American author. To comprehend all that is implied

---

1 Canto, *A contraluz*, 98.
2 Goldaracena, "Las inhibiciones del joven Borges."
3 Borges, *TR2*, 263.

in the opening of the essay, we first need to ask what was the "neurosis" common to Poe and the other writers? The answer, which requires us to investigate well beyond Borges's literature, allows us to learn a fundamental fact: all four authors suffered from sexual impotence.[4] This alone opens a whole new window into the text of the essay and tells us that we need to read it in relation to Borges's own sexuality. To comprehend the essay we also have to dispel the fog of vocabulary that stands between the thinking of the writer and the reader: the author speaks of "anomaly" and "neurosis," general terms that point toward the psychological dimensions of the problem but that allow Borges to dodge the word "impotence," too explicit and embarrassing for a newspaper in the modest Argentina of the 1940s. Thus, when an elusive poet who suffered a socially stigmatizing condition surrounds "anomaly" and "neurosis" with the figures of Poe, Swift, Carlyle, and Almafuerte, those two words take on a different meaning. That is, Borges does not fully reveal the key sexual fact that guides his interpretation of Poe (and other writers) and, instead, gives us a riddle to solve. To get to the bottom of what Borges meant in this essay we must also be aware of the hostile reception of his early work and how his impotence was a factor in it. In the 1930s some Argentine writers, who believed in the old prejudice that assumed that there was a direct proportional relation between the sexual potency of an author and his creativity, had used Borges's impotence to "invalidate or deny" his literature.[5] Here, then, Borges responded to his literary enemies by inverting the false premise: he proposed that, on the contrary, the "neurosis" from which some authors suffered could be very productive and at the origin of their literature. Finally, and to fully understand the implications of Borges's paragraph, we also have to keep in mind one of his enunciative strategies: he often used the life of other authors to speak about himself.[6] In other sections of this essay, for example, he presents Poe's trajectory from failed poet to innovative short story writer in a form that obviously paralleled his own. In the same vein, then, while proposing impotence (and sexuality more generally) as a "legitimate" interpretive key for Poe's literature, Borges was also talking about the relationship between his own life and work.

This essay is a good example of the difficulties that reading sex in Borges's literature poses. Perhaps the main obstacle for the comprehension of this text is that he does not use the word "impotence," which renders his sexuality invisible to most readers—invisibility that in the case of this essay (as happened with many of his other texts) has been compounded by a problematic publication history: the essay first came out in a newspaper in 1949 but it was only included in a book in 2001, and therefore remained

---

4 On Swift's, Carlyle's, and Poe's sexual impotence, McLaren, *Impotence*, 102, 121, 133; on Almafuerte's, Borges, *TR2*, 195.
5 I explain this problematic side of his early critical reception in chapter 1.
6 I explore this aspect of his writing in chapter 2.

largely unknown to previous generations of specialists and still occupies a very marginal position in Borges's canon today.

The largely invisible presence of sex in Borges's texts has led critics to assume that he could not read, reflect, or write about his troubled condition or about sex more generally. In a 2011 review essay in the *Times Literary Supplement*, a critic pointed out Borges's "striking ... avoidance of the erotic" in his sonnets;[7] in a recent study on literature and urban culture in Buenos Aires the author assures us that Borges could not speak about himself, particularly on sexual matters;[8] similarly, a 2006 biography underscores "the infrequency of references to women or sex" in his literature;[9] and other students of his work define him as a "mojigato" ("prude"), who could not accept sex and avoided speaking about it.[10]

The assumption that Borges would not read, think, or write about sex is pervasive and materializes in forms that are not always as explicit as the comments quoted above. For example, in Beatriz Sarlo's *Borges, un escritor en las orillas* (1995) and Alan Pauls's *El factor Borges* (2004), two insightful and influential critical readings, the asexuality of Borges's literature is taken for granted and, therefore, the two critics do not even consider the possibility of eroticism in his work and literary experience.[11] The same preconception guided the annotation of the critical edition of his *Obras completas* (2009–2011). In the substantive notes prepared by the editor to inform readers about the authors cited by Borges, it is virtually impossible to find anything that may allow us to learn that Algernon Charles Swinburne, Dante Gabriel Rossetti, Paul Verlaine, Richard Burton, Marcelino Del Mazo, and others wrote erotic literature. As an example, in a very long and detailed explanatory note on Swinburne,[12] the editor omitted Borges's characterization of the English writer as a "gran poeta erótico,"[13] which clearly shows how and why he read him. Thus the unquestioned assumption that Borges is an asexual writer prevented the editor from, literally, reading Borges's interest in sex, even when he was explicit about it.

This is not limited to the "academic" or "official" Borges. The blog *Oye Borges*, which publishes a lot of criticism and information about the author and attracts thousands of fans on the internet, has organized the repertoire of the topics it covers into more than 200 categories: some of them are obviously

---

7 Schifino, "Slow Nightfall," 4.
8 Bergero, *Intersecting Tango*, 397.
9 Wilson, *Jorge Luis Borges*, 40.
10 Aguilar and Jelicié, *Borges va al cine*, 126.
11 One of Pauls's chapters investigates Borges's "Política del pudor" but, as the title suggests, he treats it as a general aesthetic choice and discursive strategy (he contrasts it, for example, with Borges's denunciation of "color local") but, somewhat paradoxically, he does not consider it in relation to sexuality or eroticism in Borges's literature.
12 Borges, *OC* [2009], I, 459–60.
13 Borges, *OCC*, 844.

important ("Borges and English Literature," "Borges and Mathematics," etc.), others not so much ("Borges and the Astrological Map," "Borges and the City of Paraná," etc.). Yet, among those 200 categories there is not even one on, say, "Borges and Erotic Literature" or "Borges and Sex."[14]

Borges's reputation in this respect goes back to at least the early 1930s, when he was not yet a narrator and had not published most of his work, including the "metaphysical fantasies" that would make him famous. Back then, hostile critics referred to him and his poetry and essays using expressions such as "prefiere helarse," "emoción anestesiada," or "expresión frígida,"[15] all of which hinted at an absence of sex in his life and work; a reading of his early poetry and criticism that, as I said before, was based on an unjustified assumption about the relationship between male sexual potency and literary creation.

This perception of Borges's literature somehow took hold, to the extent that in 1949 Estela Canto felt compelled to address this aspect of what she called Borges's "mito." In her review of *El Aleph*, published barely three months after the book came out, she rejected the dominant view of Borges as an "escritor frío, deshumanizado, analítico" and hoped that the new volume of short stories would refute the "mito" of Borges's "presunta frialdad."[16] (Borges himself eventually endorsed—not without a venomous qualification of his former lover—Canto's reading of his work. He told his friend Adolfo Bioy Casares: "A veces Estela es muy inteligente. Fue la única persona que advirtió que en mis cuentos hay emoción. No puede escribirse sin emoción").[17]

But in spite of Canto's efforts the "myth" about Borges's "coldness" did not disappear. In the following decades other factors contributed to this generalized reading of his work. The second half of the twentieth century, the period when Borges rose to global recognition, was a time of liberalization of sexual mores, which implied a significantly higher tolerance for more explicit expressions of desire and sex, including pornography. This shift of cultural expectations and change of sensibilities regarding public and artistic expressions of eroticism left readers of the late twentieth and early twenty-first centuries ill equipped to read the literature of a reticent man who thought that "la mejor poesía erotica no es obscena."[18]

Borges's canonization has arguably created another impediment to read desire and sex in his work. It is what some have called "the purity of the eminent";[19] that is, the assumption that "great figures" are different from the rest of us and that, among other things, they could have never stooped to sex. In the case of Borges, this assumption has probably been compounded

14 As of April 25, 2016.
15 Doll, "Discusiones con Borges," 34.
16 Canto, "Jorge Luis Borges," 94.
17 Bioy, *Borges*, 766–67.
18 Bioy, *Borges*, 1157–58.
19 Williams, *Shakespeare's Sexual Language*, 9.

by the image of a frail octogenarian interested in metaphysics, since that is how most of us remember him today.

Of course, there have been a few exceptions to this dominant perception of a divorce between Borges's literature and sex and eroticism. Almost three decades ago, Julio Woscoboinik's insightful *El secreto de Borges: Indagación psicoanalítica de su obra* (1988) was perhaps the first major effort to explore some sections of Borges's literature in relation to his family and sexuality. More recently, Edwin Williamson's biography *Borges: A Life* (2004) has given Borges's amorous failure with poet Norah Lange a pivotal role in the creation of his literature. Also, in articles and book chapters, Daniel Balderston, Blas Matamoros, and Humberto Nuñez-Faraco have explored questions such as homoeroticism, homosexual panic, and desire in Borges's work.[20]

It is the contention of this book that, contrary to what criticism has generally assumed, desire and sex have occupied a significant place in Borges's oeuvre and literary experience. As we have seen, Borges himself thought that the production of his literature was intimately linked to his well-documented impotence that, along with other sexual preoccupations, became the point of departure or provided material for the more or less explicit reflections, insights, and references to sex in his literature. In his writings he re-created and addressed, with different degrees of interest and extension, questions such as desire and the sex act, casual and venal sex, incest and homosexuality, and his relationships with women, and he reflected, more or less explicitly, on the written expression of eroticism. Also, as we will see, he was an ardent reader of erotic literature, a fundamental dimension of his literary experience that, to the best of my knowledge, has not been systematically explored before. This project has demanded the rereading of some of his classic short stories, such as "Emma Zunz," "La secta del Fénix," or "La intrusa," but it has also asked for the investigation of some "rincones secretos" in Borges's "vasta obra";[21] that is, it has required the interrogation of less visible stories, poems, and essays like "Pedro Salvadores," "Endimión en Latmos," or "Edgar Allan Poe." This study, I claim, adds another, largely unnoticed, layer to our comprehension of Borges's literature and figure.

This book is deeply indebted to the insights and the research contributed by Woscoboinik, Williamson, Balderston, and others in the works mentioned but it has also been made possible by the important changes that have occurred in the field of Borges criticism in the last 15 years or so. Referring to the study of Borges more generally, Daniel Balderston said in 2009 that "Tengo la extraña sensación de que, a pesar de los miles de estudios que hay sobre la obra de Borges, apenas ahora lo estamos comenzando a leer

---

20 Balderston, "Dialéctica," "Pudor"; Matamoros, "Yo y el otro"; Núñez-Faraco, "Lovesickness."
21 Borges, *OC* [1974], IV, 514.

en serio."[22] One of the reasons for this is that since approximately 1999 (the year of the centennial of Borges's birth), an enormous amount of previously unpublished, unknown, or out-of-print texts and documents by Borges or related to his literature has been published. This material includes essays, poetry, correspondence, transcripts of classes, conferences, interviews, private diaries, the marginalia in some of his books, postcards, writings by his father, etc. In addition, although a great deal of manuscript materials pertaining to Borges are still in the hands of secretive investors and collectors and generally off-limits for scholars, the last few years have, nonetheless, witnessed the publication of critical editions of some of them. In terms of quantity alone, the number of words written or spoken by Borges published since the turn of the century is probably equivalent to (if not larger than) the material that was in print at the time of his death (1986). That is, today, the corpus of his writings far exceeds his *Obras completas,* and the latter are no longer enough to understand and explain Borges. Just as a simple example, my study of Borges's reading of the erotic poet Dante Gabriel Rossetti could not have been possible in 1999 or even in 2006: the section on the English poet fundamentally relies on the transcripts of Borges's classes at the University of Buenos Aires published in 2000,[23] and on Adolfo Bioy Casares's Boswellian diary *Borges* that came out in 2007.

The availability of previously inaccessible or unknown material has been compounded by the existence of new instruments that allow more thorough investigations (such as the online Borges index at the Borges Center of the University of Pittsburgh) and by the ever-expanding research of scholars and forums such as the journal specializing on his work, *Variaciones Borges.* The synergy created by the combination of these multiple factors has been enormously productive and therefore allowed us to pose more refined questions and to carry out more informed and deeper readings of his literature. In 2011 Argentine critic Gonzalo Aguilar sensed the changes in the field and the possibilities that they created. He pointed out that there is a side of Borges that so far can only be suspected in some of his "perversas elucubraciones," but that critics have not yet explored: there is a Borges, he said, "que todavía está por descubrirse."[24]

"Discovering" the unknown Borges, though, has also demanded the asking of different questions, and I have been helped to imagine them by a scholarly trend that has recognized the shaping energy of desire and sex in the work of artists and writers. Among them, Helen Vendler's *Wallace Stevens: Words Chosen out of Desire* (1984) remains a subtle reading of an elusive poet who shares some characteristics with Borges. Recently this trend has become more visible in works such as Stanley Wells's *Shakespeare, Sex, and*

---

22 Balderston, *Innumerables relaciones,* 13.
23 Borges, *BP.*
24 Aguilar, "Por qué Borges."

*Love* (2010); Laurence Dreyfus's *Wagner and the Erotic Impulse* (2010); and *Éros Hugo: Entre pudeur et excès* (2015).

Because of its specificity and complexity, the problem under study invited a heterodox exploration unconstrained by the expectations of current theoretical and methodological canons. As a historian I have been attentive to the particularities of Borges's life and literature and as I worked in this project I was persuaded that the questions raised allowed an interdisciplinary approach. For example, recent developments in the fields of speech pathology and psychology as well as studies on male sexual impotence have been very helpful in understanding Borges's biography and sexuality,[25] and opened the possibility of reading desire and sex in his literature in other ways (more on this in chapter 1).

In the same vein, in addition to the extensive Borges scholarship and the studies on desire and sex on other writers that my work relies on, in this literary investigation I have also taken the liberty of listening to creative writers, whose views on the production and explication of literature are, paradoxically, often absent from literary studies. The reading of this less visited corpus of criticism has made apparent the multiple intersections between history and literature and thus alerted me to the contributions that historians can make to literary studies. Because this has been a fundamental aspect of how I, a historian, thought about the project and how I worked, I will spend a few pages on this matter.

To a significant extent my inquiry was guided by the reflections on literature that I found in three critical genres practiced by creative writers. First, and most obviously, I benefitted from essays on a variety of topics by authors from several traditions and different times; in them I found a wide range of modes of reasoning, and, perhaps more important, their styles of exposition, usually clear and mindful of the reader, constituted attractive examples for the communication of criticism.[26] Second, I also gained valuable insights from transcripts of classes and lectures taught by, among others, Borges himself and Vladimir Nabokov, whose "spoken essays" provided models of practical explication of texts while highlighting relevant critical questions.[27] Finally, the correspondence of writers has been another critical genre in which the writers

---

25 Iverach et al., "Anxiety and Stuttering"; Iverach and Rapee, "Social Anxiety Disorder"; Eliacheff and Einich, *Mères-filles*, "Étendre la notion d'inceste"; McLaren, *Impotence*.

26 In addition to the essays by creative writers that I note in this section and throughout the book, I would like to highlight A. S. Byatt's and Paul Valéry's, whose penetrating analysis and effective prose became for me models in criticism. See for example, the essays in Byatt's *Passions of the Mind* and Valéry's *Varieté* (I–V).

27 I also learned, among others, from Paul Muldoon's Oxford lectures on poetry and Julio Cortázar's *Clases de literatura: Berkeley, 1980* (see below). The expression "spoken essays" is from V. S. Pritchett's blurb on the cover of Nabokov's *Lectures on Literature*.

have frequently addressed some of their fundamental literary preoccupations and, thus, their letters offer us the opportunity to become better readers (in particular, the letters of Robert Burns and Gustave Flaubert proved very illuminating).[28]

In these three critical genres, writers explicate and interpret texts, raising questions that consistently point toward the comprehension and reconstruction of the creative process. For example, Francine Prose has argued in favor of *Reading Like a Writer* (2006); that is, reading in a way that allows us to understand how the writer arrived at her text. In this respect she is a very good example in a long tradition of authors interested in the question, a tradition that goes back, at least, to Edgar A. Poe's "The Philosophy of Composition," whose purpose was to show "the *modus operandi* by which [his own poem "The Raven"] was put together."[29] This was also the overarching critical preoccupation of writers like Flaubert and Nabokov: the French writer advised a friend who wanted to master literature, "lisez les grands maîtres en tâchant de saisir leur procédé," and the author of *Lolita* believed that in the course of an explication of a text "we shall watch the artist build his castle of cards and watch the castle of cards become a castle of beautiful steel and glass."[30] Of course, as Borges lucidly warned in "La génesis de 'El Cuervo' de Poe" (1935)[31] and "Pierre Menard, autor del Quijote" (1939),[32] the mission left to us by the author of "The Raven" can never be carried to precise completion because it is impossible to unearth each of the minute choices made by the writer. Yet, we can certainly aspire to a sketch of the creative process that led to a text (which, as Borges said, was what Poe actually did).

As Nabokov's metaphor suggests, one of the challenges posed by any explication is that a writer's procedure or the purpose of a text is not readily apparent and is covered by layers of reflection, rewritings, and choices, in which the author has consciously and unconsciously suppressed a significant proportion of the evidence of his own work. Aware of this reality, Henry James said that the "general intention" of a writer was a "buried treasure," camouflaged and blended in his work "like a complex figure in a Persian carpet."[33] Poets too think that the goals of interpretation are difficult to reach because they are hidden and blurred by form and the skills of the author that made it possible. In *Who Is Ozymandias? and Other Puzzles in Poetry* (2011), John Fuller reminds us about "the crucial habit of riddling" and "concealment" in poetry, which implies that the interpretive "key [is always] behind

---

28 Other collections of correspondence that helped me become a more attentive reader were those of Voltaire, Charles Baudelaire, and Robert Louis Stevenson.
29 Poe, *Poetry*, 1374. Italics in the original.
30 Flaubert, *Correspondance*, 335; Nabokov, *Lectures*, 6.
31 Borges, *TR2*, 120–23.
32 Borges, *OC* [1974], I, 444–50.
33 "The Figure in the Carpet," in James, *Selected Tales*, 292, 295.

a poem."³⁴ Poet Jorge Boccanera proposes a similar relation between what is apparent and what may help comprehend a text: the book in which he tries a biographical reading of famous Latin American love poems is titled *La pasión de los poetas* but subtitled, more precisely, *La historia "detrás" de los poemas de amor.*³⁵

If the intention of an author, a method of composition, or the meaning of a poem, are hidden, camouflaged, or riddled, the task of criticism is to uncover them. Borges, for example, thought that "el gran crítico debe *descubrir* una verdad que estaba *oculta*, dar una interpretación nueva."³⁶ Propositions like this one highlight the kindred qualities of the historians' and critics' thought processes and overall aims and remind us that their main difference is in the subject of their inquiry but not in the nature of the latter. Explication and interpretation of literature, then, call for *investigative criticism*. It is not a coincidence that he who wanted "to *retrace the steps* by which his conclusions [in 'The Raven'] have been attained"³⁷ was also the author of "The Murders in the Rue Morgue," the first modern detective short story where the analyst reconstructed the "creative process" of a crime. Of course, the analytical method used by the main character Auguste Dupin in the short story ("*retracing the steps* by which particular conclusions ... have been attained")³⁸ was identical to the one employed by Poe in his famous essay; moreover, the epigraph he chose for the founding text of the detective genre refers, precisely, to a "puzzle" in literary criticism that was worth investigating and could potentially be solved.³⁹ Nabokov too saw himself as a Dupin of literature: his course was, he said, "a kind of detective investigation of the mystery of literary structures,"⁴⁰ a predisposition shared by Fuller, who recently has called critics "detectives of poetry."⁴¹

Literary criticism is, then, a problem-solving discipline that may "often sound like a law court" where "different views must rely on evidence to settle the matter."⁴² But, as in a court case, in criticism or history the "truth" is only an argument, an arrangement of facts or an interpretation whose "veracity" is determined by its ability to persuade the reader.⁴³ And the persuasive capacity of an interpretation in the arts or the humanities,

---

34 Fuller, *Who is Ozymandias?*, 7, 11.
35 Emphasis added.
36 Bioy, *Borges*, 391. Emphasis added.
37 Poe, *Poetry*, 1374. Emphasis added.
38 Poe, *Poetry*, 403. Emphasis added.
39 "What song the Syrens sang, or what name Achilles assumed when he hid himself among women, although puzzling questions, are not beyond *all* conjecture," by Sir Thomas Browne, Poe, *Poetry*, 397. Emphasis in the original.
40 Nabokov, epigraph to his lectures.
41 Fuller, *Who is Ozymandias?*, 34.
42 Fuller, *Who is Ozymandias?*, 32.
43 Grafton, *The Footnote*, 16, 232–33.

says philosopher Jorge Gracia, depends on its aim and the evidence that corresponds to that aim.[44] If, for instance, our goal is to interpret Borges's work purely from our own personal experience, we may need to give the reader as much information about us as about Borges's text, and the aspects of the latter that we highlight may or may not be those that the author himself or other readers considered relevant; in such a case, too, any finding about Borges's life will, most likely, be meaningless. However, if the aim of our interpretation is authorial—that is, if we want to propose an explanation of "the intention of the author"—the interpretation requires "very tight criteria of a historical nature," and, therefore, "we must work hard to find clues, both within [the work] and outside of it."[45] Poetry critic Helen Vendler has made a similar argument: albeit mediated by "self-expression ... poetry is [a] projection of fact" and therefore, its explication requires knowledge of its "historical and cultural bases", she says.[46] Thus, if a biographical interpretation of Borges's literature can only be tentative and provisional (like any other interpretation), it still can aspire to present an argument whose persuasive ability largely relies on evidence, both textual and historical. Therefore, in this book I have made evidence a fundamental aspect of my argument.

Not unlike a historian, the critic, thought T. S. Eliot, should put "the reader in possession of facts which he would otherwise have missed."[47] But which facts? First, the biographical ones, which may be fundamental for an interpretation. For example, when Robert Burns wanted to explain one of his own pieces to a reader, he told him: "The story of the Poem, like most of my Poems, is connected with my own story; and to give you the one, I must give you something of the other."[48] For the Scottish bard, then, the circumstances of his life were both the key and the point of departure for an interpretation that culminated in the clarification of the meaning of the poem. But the flow of information in a biographical interpretation can go the other way too. In his explication of Latin American love poems, Jorge Boccanera reminds us that the poem itself is a "testimonio de una pasión," a biographical document that can help fill the inevitable voids in the emotional biography of an author. Therefore, in his explanation, "el esbozo biográfico aparece ... *completándose*

---

44 Stavans and Gracia, *Thirteen Ways*, 87.
45 Stavans and Gracia, *Thirteen Ways*, 87, 90. In the passage quoted, Gracia discusses a photograph; he presents similar arguments for other artistic expressions and literature in his *Painting Borges*, chapter 15 (in particular 199–202); chapter 17 on his proposition of the "Conditional Limits View" of interpretations (235–36) and the limits of interpretation (246–50). Gracia says that "[t]he legitimacy of interpretations depend on the kind of interpretation, and the kind of interpretation depends in turn on the general, specific, and particular aims it pursues," 248.
46 Vendler, *Wallace Stevens*, 80.
47 Eliot, *Selected Essays*, 20.
48 Burns, *Selected Letters*, 165.

con el poema de amor."⁴⁹ In this dialectical proposition, then, the explanatory power between biography and text is more equitably distributed: while the former contributes to the interpretation of the poem, the latter helps us understand the life of the author (of which literature is a part).

The work of the critic must also offer the reader the textual "facts" that will make the explication persuasive. But since the specific text that the critic intends to interpret is itself part of a wider authorial work and literary experience, the analysis of that particular story or poem may require reading it in relation to other sections of a writer's project and the sources that influenced him. In his Oxford lectures, Paul Muldoon has argued for "placing a text in its social context, but in terms of its relation to other texts."⁵⁰ Thus, the textual evidence that will serve to explicate a poem on, say, the idea of cyclical time, will most likely emerge from the variants among its different published versions, the essays, lectures, and interviews where the author explored that concept, and the literary and philosophical sources that influenced him. Therefore, the production of textual evidence requires close reading (more on this later) not only of the piece that we want to interpret but of the many pertinent pages found in the work of the author under study, and in the readings that influenced him.

The latter, the reading of Borges's literary and philosophical sources, has also been fundamental for the development of this book. It is difficult, sometimes even impossible, to comprehend an author's literary experience, the evolution of his ideas, and what he attempted in his texts without having a direct knowledge of the works that helped him think and create. That is, investigative criticism is also source-supported explication, a commonsensical but not always honored methodological point (as Abdelfattah Kilito has insightfully concluded, even behind Shahrazad's orality there was a huge library worth considering).⁵¹ Reading *all* of what Borges read is, needless to say, a Utopian project but, more modestly, we can aspire to converse with the authors relevant to the zones of Borges's literature that we want to understand. Given the vastness of Borges's readings, this is still an ambitious proposition for which there are no shortcuts. Not even the excellent study of his marginalia can make up for it because it is evident that the annotations in his personal copies are not equivalent to what he read in them (throughout his own work, conferences, conversations, etc., Borges refers to or quotes sections of books where there are no marginalia).⁵² Manuscripts do not save us from this challenging adventure either. For example, most of the

---

49  Boccanera, *La pasión*, 14. Emphasis added.
50  Muldoon, *The End*, 27.
51  "Au commencement, une bibliothèque," Kilito, *L'œil*, 14–15, 25–26; for this methodological point see also his witty fictional essay "La seconde folie de Shahriar" in his *Dites-moi le songe*.
52  See Borges's marginalia in, for example, Saint Augustine's *La ciudad de Dios* (BLL, 42–44) and compare it with his comments on the book in Bioy, 325; similarly, see

publicly available and known manuscripts of his short stories do not reveal the evolution of the ideas and form of the text because, as Michel Lafon has convincingly argued, Borges had "l'habitude de composer ses textes mentalment";[53] Balderston too has pointed out that only exceptionally did Borges take notes and draft ideas before he started to write the story itself.[54] Therefore, when it comes to influences on the subjects and concepts that gave form to a story, the evidence offered by manuscripts is not significantly different from what we can find in its published version (what, however, they do offer are the many variants of expression or composition of sentences that Borges tried).[55] In other words, there is no way around the reading of what Borges read. But that is precisely the enormous pleasure of studying the reader who said, "Que otros se jacten de las páginas que han escrito, / a mí me enorgullecen las que he leído."[56]

As the historian does when he investigates the private correspondence of a figure of the past or when he disentangles the words of a defendant from the language of the court clerk who wrote them down, the critic also relies on close reading. Texts, as Francine Prose reminds us, are written "one word at a time,"[57] and it is often at this level that we have to operate to be able to notice and establish the relationship between texts proposed by Muldoon. Sometimes this relationship takes the form of an unexpected textual parallel between two authors or until then unknown literary influence that is revealed by a few words that work as telltale evidence. That is, the object of close reading is not to dwell on details for their own sake but to identify fragments of larger phenomena. Talking about the "evidential paradigm"

---

    his annotations on the volumes of John Donne's poetry (*BLL*, 116–18) and compare them with his references and quotations in *OCC*, 822 and Bioy, *Borges*, 633.

53  Borges, "Introduction," in *Deux Fictions*, 34.

54  "Conozco apenas dos ocasiones en las que [Borges] anotó ideas antes de comenzar a escribir el texto en sí," Balderston, "Una lógica simbolica," 14.

55  Here it is important to underline a significant difference between manuscripts of fictional texts, such as "Emma Zunz," and those of critical works, as, for example, *¿Qué es el Budismo?* (1976) (in *OCC*, 717–81): while the fictional texts usually contain no traces of literary sources, the critical texts do contain relevant references about the readings that informed Borges's thoughts for each particular text; see the catalog of the exhibit *Borges, el mismo, otro*, 31–32, 83–87. Among the manuscripts of short stories that I have had access to, the one of "La secta del Fénix" seems to be an exception that confirms the rule: in the first section of the story, which actually reads like an essay, Borges did record references to the *Encyclopaedia Britannica* and other works, the sources for the allusions to antiquity made in that section; however, there were no such references in the second half of the text, the more "fictional" section of the story (the manuscript in a "Cuaderno" held in a private collection). I thank Víctor Aizenman, Laura Rosato, and Germán Alvarez for sharing their experience and insights regarding this question.

56  "Un lector," Borges, *OC* [1974], I, 1016.

57  Prose, *Reading*, 3.

that governs research and explanation in the arts and the humanities, historian Carlo Ginzburg has argued that in a text or a painting "apparently negligible details could reveal profound phenomena of great importance" and that "slender clues" may be "indications of [for example] the world view of a social class, a single writer, or an entire society."[58] Thus, a few words may show us the presence of a reading that, in turn, may suddenly open a window into previously unnoticed intellectual practices or literary experiences of the author under study; and, concurrently, a large number of small findings that close reading has the ability to produce may also allow us to see things differently: textual details may look irrelevant when isolated from each other but their accumulation may reveal a whole new reality, as the many individual points in a painting by Georges Seurat allow us to see a landscape. "Il n'y a pas de minutes en matière d'art," thought Charles Baudelaire.[59]

As I have argued in the preceding pages, in the course of exploring Borges's creative process and attempting interpretations, engaging in research and practicing close reading, I could not but sense the multiple points of contact between history and literature. Others, long before me, have certainly had a similar experience: in "The Aspern Papers," for example, Henry James describes the protagonist and literary sleuth as "a critic, a commentator, an historian."[60] That is, my study of Borges has not discovered the investigative nature of criticism, but it does propose a renewed argument on behalf of an often-neglected approach in current literary studies. Thus, I hope this project not only explicates Borges but also shows what history can contribute to criticism and, at the same time, reminds historians that literature is an old but still open frontier that, perhaps more than in the past, offers opportunities for them.

The understanding of the argument advanced in this book requires at least some awareness of the cultural expectations and institutional context framing literary expressions of eroticism in Argentina and Latin America during the first half of the twentieth century, the period when Borges developed as a writer. Studies on erotic literature as a genre in Argentina are almost non-existent and we lack comprehensive anthologies which would provide more clear points of reference to place his writings in context. Yet, even if tentative, an approximation to this question is necessary.

First we may need to remember the obvious: that in spite of the exceptional quality of his literature, Borges did not escape being influenced by his own time. His personality, individual experience, and *Arte Poetica* certainly shaped the modesty and reticence of his expression of desire and sex but these qualities were also inevitably the consequence of the predominant cultural expectations of the time. Borges's criterion regarding the inclusion of sex

---

58 Ginzburg, "Clues," 124.
59 Baudelaire, *Écrits*, 312.
60 James, *Aspern Papers*, 59.

in literature and the form that it had to take could not be entirely different from the one guiding other writers of the period, including younger and, apparently, more relaxed ones, like Julio Cortázar. It is instructive to hear the latter speak about the "problema grave" of eroticism in Latin American literature. In the classes that he taught at Berkeley in 1980 (when he was in his mid-60s and Borges had already turned 80), he said that

> En América Latina el problema del erotismo en la literatura ha sido *muy dramático* porque se puede decir que *hasta –creo- 1950* las situaciones eróticas en las novelas y en los cuentos se han expresado siempre *de manera metafórica*...Hasta por lo menos 1950 *aun en los escritores nuestros más liberados...se nota que cuando llegan a los pasajes eróticos se sienten incómodos*...y eso está revelando muy claramente hasta qué punto el peso de *los tabúes y las represiones* del pasado *se sigue manifestando todavía*.⁶¹

To support and illustrate this critical assessment he shared his own experience as a writer:

> personalmente les puedo decir que para mí también ha sido y *es todavía* [1980] *muy difícil*... [hay] determinadas *situaciones* y determinados *vocabularios que directamente no se pueden escribir porque* detrás está la idea de que *no se deben escribir*. En *Rayuela* [1963], para citar un libro que yo escribí en los años 50–60, hay con alguna frecuencia situaciones eróticas pero *ninguna está tomada de frente*. En la mayoría de los casos *me sentía muy bloqueado y muy preocupado* cuando llegaba a esos momentos y...en la mayoría de los casos *utilizo sistemas metafóricos*, diversas imágenes que el lector comprende pero que de todas maneras son imágenes que no utilizo en otros momentos del libro que no son eróticos: *mi lenguaje cambia, en ese momento soy consciente del tabú y lo acepto*. Eso me molestaba, me preocupaba y me dolía, pero *no era capaz de salir de ahí*.⁶²

In Argentina and Latin America there were "vocabularios que directamente no se pueden escribir porque … no se deben escribir,"⁶³ that is, when it came to body parts and sex, naming and explicitness were not allowed. Cultural and social taboos forced authors to write "de manera metafórica"⁶⁴ and pushed them to explore a wider range of rhetorical resources. But the resulting allusive and more indeterminate language somehow blurred meaning and pixeled images and, thus, the line between aesthetic choices and self-censorship was difficult to locate. These norms were observed not only by modest or conservative writers but also by the most "liberated" ones. Revealingly, Cortázar acknowledges that even in the case of *Rayuela*, the formally transgressive novel that captivated the Latin American progressive youths

---

61 Cortázar, *Clases*, 252. My emphasis.
62 Cortázar, *Clases*, 254. My emphasis.
63 Cortázar, *Clases*, 254.
64 Cortázar, *Clases*, 252.

of the 1960s and 1970s, these norms had cornered him into self-censorship ("soy consciente del tabú y lo acepto ... me dolía, pero no era capaz de salir de ahí").⁶⁵ He believed that in Latin America these cultural constraints had framed the expression of desire and sex until the 1950s but pointed out that to some extent this was still the case in 1980 ("el peso de los tabúes...se sigue manifestando todavía").⁶⁶

When writers' expressions did not sufficiently respect taboos, they risked censorship. As far as I know, there is not a systematic study of literary censorship in Argentina and Latin America for this period, but a couple of cases may help us sense the professional and institutional context that also conditioned and shaped expressions of eroticism. The first of them, a little-known episode that concerned poet Idea Vilariño in Uruguay, allows an understanding of how far the taboos mentioned by Cortázar extended, and the varied forms that censorship could take. In the early 1950s, Vilariño got into an intense and tempestuous love relationship with the already renowned novelist Juan Carlos Onetti, a short-lived experience that, however, would occupy an important place in her poetry. In "El amor" (1955), for example, without mentioning Onetti, she speaks of the emptiness and disappointment that followed the end of the relationship:

> Hoy el único rastro es un pañuelo
> que alguien guarda olvidado
> un pañuelo con sangre semen lágrimas
> que se ha vuelto amarillo.⁶⁷

However tame it may read today, this poem brought Vilariño some problems. When she submitted it to *Marcha*, the progressive literary magazine that she and her former lover were regular contributors to, the editor objected to the third line. What apparently troubled him was not the traditional allusion to her lost love ("lágrimas") nor the more problematic but still acceptable one to the loss of virginity ("sangre") but the physiological reference to sexual intercourse and orgasm ("semen"). The incident shows that when an author's aesthetic choices or self-censorship had not been enough to suppress explicit references to body and sex, editors and colleagues could take in their own hands the policing of eroticism in literature ("[Hay] vocabularios que directamente ... no se deben escribir," said Cortázar⁶⁸). The enforcement of norms was inevitably contentious and could have professional consequences: for example, after the objection by the editor, Vilariño stopped contributing to the prestigious publication.⁶⁹

---

65 Cortázar, *Clases*, 254.
66 Cortázar, *Clases*, 252.
67 Vilariño, "El amor," *Poesía completa*, 210.
68 Cortázar, *Clases*, 254.
69 The incident is referred to by Guerriero, *Plano Americano*, 59 and Boccanera, *La pasión*, 264.

In other instances, the transgression of the norms could put in motion censorship by the government and have more serious repercussions for the writer. This was the case of Raúl Barón Biza and his novel *El derecho de matar* (1933).[70] The overall purpose of the book was to discredit the fascistic regime that ruled Argentina in the early 1930s and, in particular, to expose the corrupt oligarchy associated with it. In the novel, the immoral Argentine elite is driven by sexual desire and drowned in sensuality and, therefore, the narrative exhibits frequent moments of eroticism. Although there is no nudity or scenes of sexual intercourse, the text does mention the "coitus" and the "clitoris" and frequently includes passages that intend to convey a sense of decadent desire, such as:

> El escote atrevido, casi siempre exagerado, dejaba al descubierto el nacimiento de sus senos, ánforas de alabastro tibio, que se adivinaban macizos tras la tenue seda.[71]

When the novel came out, passages like this and other sexual references were considered "repugnantes obscenidades," copies of the book were confiscated, and its author arrested and indicted for breaking article 128 of the Argentine Penal Code that stated: "Será reprimido con prisión de quince días a un año el que publicare, fabricare o reprodujere libros, escritos, imágenes y objetos obscenos."[72] Although Barón Biza eventually extricated himself from his legal troubles, the damage was enormous: he was stigmatized and "for [the next] thirty years his name became synonymous with 'pornographic literature.'"[73]

The findings presented in the preceding paragraphs should not lead to definitive conclusions. I do not mean, for example, that at all times during the twentieth-century Argentine and Latin American societies were equally recalcitrant nor that all comparable expressions of eroticism inevitably met with the same reaction.[74] However, the nature of the evidence does give us a rough idea about the normative boundaries that were at work and allows to imagine that the cultural expectations and institutional realities that the cases demonstrate somehow also shaped Borges's reading and writing on desire and sex. For example, the existence of Article 128 in the Argentine Penal Code and its harsh enforcement in the publicly known case of Barón Biza in 1933

---

70 This paragraph on Raúl Barón Biza is based on Ferrer, *Barón Biza*, 161–202.
71 Quoted in Ferrer, *Barón Biza*, 183.
72 Quoted in Ferrer, *Barón Biza*, 162, 164.
73 Ferrer, *Barón Biza*, 182.
74 In spite of the chronology proposed by Cortázar, the publication in Uruguay of Delmira Agustini's *Los cálices vacíos* (1913) or Nicolás Olivari's *El gato escaldado* (1929) (which was awarded a prestigious literary prize by the city of Buenos Aires that year), among others, suggest that the tolerance for eroticism in literature might have been higher in the 1910s and 1920s than it would be during, say, the period 1930–1960.

may *partially* explain why three years later Borges did not include in "Los traductores de las 1001 noches" (1936) any explicit reference to the most titillating erotica that he read in Sir Richard Burton's *The Thousand Nights and a Night* and, instead, only hinted at it (a suppression that, in turn, led critics to miss his experience as a reader of erotic literature).

It is time for a couple of clarifications. I have already described how the reading of Borges has not escaped the assumption of "the purity of the eminent," a preconception that implies that he who dares to ignore it must certainly be polluted by prurience. However, I think that there cannot be prurience in research, because nothing is off limits in any project in which the ultimate goal is to understand the object of study, in this case an author's life and literature, or—as John Donne more elegantly put it—"Love's mysteries in souls do grow, / But yet the body is his book."[75] This takes me to a second question: how to write about sex? Not being a creative writer, I have accepted that good allusive language is out of reach for me and, therefore, I have largely limited myself to use the words that the dictionary provides and that correct usage allows, which inevitably implies a precise and explicit vocabulary: I call sex, sex. In addition, I have not pixeled sources (to do it would be to distort evidence), nor refrained from asking controversial questions when it was logical to do it, even if I knew I did not have the answer. This is a book that seeks to understand Borges and was written with the hope that the intellectually curious will be interested in it.

In chapter 1, I give an overview of what is known about Borges's personality and sexuality. Its purpose is to provide insights into the experiences and preoccupations that somehow reverberate through his writings. In chapter 2, I consider whether it is possible to read his sexuality into his literature. I also propose forms of finding and reading desire and sex in a modest and reticent writer like Borges. In chapters 3 through to 5, I present Borges as a reader of erotic literature, a subject that has not been systematically explored before. Because Borges was the derivative writer par excellence of the twentieth century, the study of the erotic shelves of his library gives us the opportunity to think about the relationship between his sexuality, his readings, and his own literature. We will first look at poetry, then at the Orientalist erotica translated by Sir Richard Burton, and, finally, at philosophy. In chapter 6, I expand on the dominant readings about his poetry on the *arrabal* and, thus, I revise their assumption: I propose that the working-class neighborhoods on the outskirts of Buenos Aires were also the landscape of casual and paid sex where he often confronted (or he imagined he did) his own troubled sexuality. Chapters 7 and 8 are closely linked: in chapter 7, I study how Borges has written fictional and real women and argue that Stoicism, a philosophical doctrine so far neglected in relation to his work, was fundamental to it; in the following chapter, I try this general approach on Emma Zunz, the most

---

75 Donne, "The Ecstasy," *Complete*, 55.

conspicuous of his women. Finally, in chapter 9, I propose a biographical exploration of "La intrusa" and both revise the influential trend of gay readings and offer an alternative to explain Borges's treatment of homosexuality in this short story.

CHAPTER 1

# On Borges's Sexuality

In this chapter I give an overview of what is known about Borges's personality and sexuality. Its purpose is to substantiate his experiences and establish a relationship between them and the preoccupations that reverberate through his readings and writings. Although most of the facts shown are already known, here I bring them together and I reorder them following the results of new research on stuttering, on male sexual impotence, and on incest, which have made it possible to rethink some of the facts and events in Borges's life.

Stuttering and Sexual Impotence

Perhaps the place to start is to remember that Borges stuttered.[1] Although his speech problems have been noted by students of his life and literature, they have rarely been linked to other aspects of his personal experience, such as his social relations or sexuality. Yet, psychoanalyst Dr Miguel Kohan Miller, who treated Borges in the 1940s, said that "el enfermo que sufre de … una inhibición para hablar … por lo general sufre de varias inhibiciones," and that "la impotencia sexual de Borges … era una forma de impotencia general"; thus, he explained, his therapy aimed at helping Borges with both his "impotencia verbal" and his "impotencia sexual."[2]

Recent research in speech pathology has also identified a relationship between stuttering and social anxiety disorder. Many adults who stutter are "characterized by increased fear of negative evaluation and anxiety in socially evaluative or new/strange situations."[3] People afflicted by this condition usually suffer anticipatory anxiety in speaking situations and fear embarrassing themselves in public speaking and when they meet new people; they also have heightened anxieties regarding the expectations of others and exhibit poorer emotional functioning. According to these studies, stutterers

---

1 Rodríguez Monegal, *Literary Biography*, 347; Williamson, *A Life*, 38, 45; Woscoboinik, *El secreto* [1988], 203, 204–5.
2 Goldaracena, "Las inhibiciones del joven Borges."
3 Iverach et al., "Anxiety and Stuttering," 223.

with social anxiety typically experience teasing and bullying in school, they become educational and occupational underachievers, they have a hard time becoming financially independent, possess low self-esteem, tend to evaluate mildly negative social events in a catastrophic fashion, and experience physiological arousal (such as sweating and shaking) in social situations; sometimes they also entertain suicidal thoughts.[4]

It is possible to match these research findings with Borges's personality traits, behavior, and even certain events in his life, although we should not expect the evidence found in interviews, literary texts, documents, and other such papers to be formulated in the clinical reasoning and language of the research referred to above. Certainly no contemporary of Borges would have said that he experienced "fear of negative evaluation and anxiety in socially evaluative or new/strange situations," but writer Alberto Hidalgo spoke of his "timidez salvaje y mayúscula"[5] and Ricardo Guiraldes observed that when Borges was introduced to new people he hesitatingly extended his "manos pequeñas y tímidas que retira ni bien las da."[6] Similarly, like many stutterers, Borges had a problematic experience in formal education: he started later than most children and he eventually became the victim of bullying in school. The explanation that Borges gave for it revolved around the class differences between him and his proletarian classmates, but it is quite logical to think that his stuttering must have been a factor in it.[7]

This anticipatory anxiety in public speaking situations and fear of embarrassment often translates into speech block. Borges's fiascoes in this respect became legendary. There is evidence of his incapacity to speak in public (even reading from a text) at least as early as the 1920s. One of the most notorious of those situations of public humiliation occurred in 1936 when he was unable to read a speech especially prepared for the celebration of the Fourth Centennial of the foundation of the city of Buenos Aires that was to be broadcast (a decade later Borges addressed this issue in his therapy with Dr Kohan Miller and eventually overcame it).[8] As in the case

---

4   Ibidem; Iverach and Rapee, "Social Anxiety Disorder."
5   Quoted in Vezzetti, *Aventuras de Freud*, 240.
6   Letter from Ricardo Guiraldes to Valery Larbaud, Sept. 8, 1924, "Jorge Luis Borges … tan corto de vista que tememos siga el camino de su padre que está ciego a los 44 años. Tiene unas manos pequeñas y tímidas que retira ni bien las da … Una sensibilidad llena de lastimaduras," quoted in Blasi, "Güiraldes," 246.
7   Borges, "Auto," 26; Williamson, *A Life*, 46, 51.
8   According to his mother's testimony, the text was finally read by Pedro Henríquez Ureña, Borges, *TR2*, 140–55; the situation would recur several times, Woscoboinik, *El secreto* [1988], 204; Kohan Miller said that Borges "no estaba en condiciones de hablar [en público], ni siquiera leyendo"; as part of the treatment, the psychoanalyst took him to "Radio Antártida [...] para que dijera algunas palabras por radio, leyéndolas, y no pudo hablar. No pudo, porque él tenía la sensación de que había miles de oyentes detrás del aparato y él no se podía sustraer del miedo al oyente," Goldaracena, "Las inhibiciones."

of other stutterers, his anticipatory anxiety also produced the physical and motor symptoms associated with the disorder: in addition to speech block, he experienced trembling and sweating: before one of his public speeches, Kohan Miller remembered, Borges "había estado transpirando y temblándole las manos del miedo tan tremendo que tenía."[9]

Like those who stammer and suffer from social anxiety, Borges also exhibited a low self-esteem in matters involving personal relationships and social situations. For example, when Estela Canto proposed having sex, he was surprised that she would even be interested in him and asked her: "¿entonces no me tenés asco?"[10] (Here it may be helpful to make a distinction: while the evidence of his low self-esteem as a man and in his relationships with women is clear, his self-perception as a writer reveals a notable confidence in the exceptional quality of his literary work, as we will see in various passages of this book.)

As the studies in speech pathology cited before explain, children who stutter and suffer from social anxiety frequently have negative experiences in their school years. Not surprisingly, as adults they confront occupational difficulties, and usually they start to work and achieve financial independence later than most people. In this respect too, Borges's case conforms to research findings: he did not have a steady job and source of income until his late thirties. The accepted explanation of this unusual fact has been that when he was a young adult his parents decided that he would be a full-time writer and that he would not need to worry about making a living.[11] It is a plausible justification, but one wonders if in this decision there was not an unspoken acknowledgement of Georgie's inability to function in a work environment and the intention of shielding him from his own condition: the family was not rich and seems to have needed him to work. Finally, another typical trait of adults afflicted with stuttering and social anxiety disorder is that they may entertain suicidal thoughts. According to some students of Borges's life and work, he apparently considered committing suicide at least once, probably between the 1930s and early 1940s,[12] a situation that he seems to have fictionalized in his short story "Veinticinco de agosto, 1983" (1983).[13]

An attentive look at Borges's personality and behavior, then, shows that they fit well in the profile proposed by recent research on adult stutterers who suffer social anxiety disorder. My purpose here is not, of course, to diagnose him (for which I do not possess any qualification—much less to do it post mortem!). My intention is simply to call our attention to an underlying

9 Goldaracena, "Las inhibiciones."
10 Bioy, *Borges*, 49. Helft also found out that "Borges se rebaja y se desvaloriza frente a una mujer que lo rechaza," *Postales*, 85.
11 Borges, "Auto," 26, 43–44.
12 Helft, *Postales*, 8; García, *El jóven Borges*, 183–85.
13 Borges, *OC* [1974], II, 377–80.

condition that seems to have fundamentally shaped his personality and influenced his life experience, including, probably, his sexuality.

Borges suffered, as has been well documented, from sexual impotence. When in the mid-1940s Dr Kohan Miller treated Borges for this problem, he observed that the writer had "temor al sexo."[14] Estela Canto, who about the same time engaged in a close relationship with Borges, directly experienced Borges's incapacity for intimacy:

> nos besábamos y nos abrazábamos, pero él nunca había intentado ir más allá, ni siquiera cuando estaba excitado —y se excitaba como cualquier hombre normal. La realización sexual era aterradora para él.[15]

Both testimonies make sufficiently clear the nature of Borges's sexual impotence: he could be aroused "como cualquier hombre normal," but the sexual act in itself was "terrifying," which prevented him from having sexual intercourse and, thus, from consummating sex. Bioy Casares's annotations in his private diary essentially confirm the words of Kohan Miller and Canto: in 1963 he noticed that, although Borges got emotionally involved with women, contrary to their expectations, he did not have sex with them.[16] And in 1967, when at age 68 Borges married Elsa Astete Millán, the author himself revealed his condition to Norman T. Di Giovanni, his American translator: "I told [Elsa] I could never have intercourse with her, because I am impotent. And she *agreed* that we would have a platonic marriage."[17]

According to the standard narrative of Borges's life, his sexual impotence was the consequence of a traumatic sexual initiation with a prostitute.[18] There are at least two versions of this episode. In one of them, Estela Canto said that when the family lived in Geneva, his father became concerned that at age 19, Georgie was still a virgin and, therefore, he arranged a visit to a prostitute and forced his son to go to her place:

> Le dio una dirección y le dijo que debía estar allí a una hora determinada. Una mujer le estaría esperando. [Georgie] estaba abrumado [...]. Una idea le cruzó la mente: su padre le había ordenado acostarse con una mujer que él, Georgie, no conocía. Si esa mujer estaba dispuesta a acostarse con él

---

14 Canto, *A contraluz*, 114.
15 Canto, *A contraluz*, 98.
16 Bioy, *Borges*, 963. Bioy also recorded Canto's perception of Borges's troubles. In 1953, at the Bioys's, she "agressively" psychoanalyzed Borges and interpreted that he felt "espanto por la cópula," Bioy, *Borges*, 94.
17 Di Giovanni, *Georgie and Elsa*, 236. Emphasis in the original.
18 On the traumatic circumstances of Borges's sexual initiation: Rodríguez Monegal, *Literary Biography*, 113; Vázquez, *Esplendor*, 50; Williamson, *A Life*, 66; Vaccaro, *Borges*, 72–73; Mastronardi, *Borges*, 75. As an explanation for the cause of his impotence, Rodríguez Monegal, *Literary Biography*, 113; Williamson, *A Life*, 66; Canto, *A contraluz*, 113, 116, 117; Mastronardi, *Borges*, 75; Helft, *Postales*, 45.

era porque había tenido *ya* relaciones sexuales con su padre. [...]. Tal vez no haya sido cierto, pero fue lo que él creyó. Él no tenía ninguna duda al respecto.

Aparte de la brutalidad del hecho [...] allí estaban las imágenes que surgían en su mente. La mujer que se le ofrecía era una mujer que él iba a *compartir* con su padre.[19]

Borges was not able to have sex and "Quedó doblemente humillado. No había podido cumplir la orden de su padre; era un incapaz, un impotente."[20]

The other version was told by Donald Yates, a Borges scholar who gathered it from the author himself. According to Yates, Borges

> un día conoció a una mujer que lo trató amablemente y que parecía estar dispuesta a un encuentro sexual. Hicieron los arreglos necesarios y, tal como Borges lo consignó, su debut sexual tuvo lugar en la habitación de un edificio sobre la plaza Dufour; fue una experiencia irresistible. Sin embargo ... poco después ... descubrió que su padre había arreglado el encuentro con la mujer [...] Borges se quedó pasmado cuando comprendió que la mujer que le había ofrecido su cuerpo había tenido, sin duda, intimidad con su padre también. Pareció sugerir que lo que le produjo la crisis nerviosa no fue el acto sexual en sí mismo, sino la conmoción de enterarse de que su primera experiencia sexual había sido secretamente arreglada por su padre, y no fruto de su propio mérito, como él había creído.[21]

There is a significant difference in the two testimonies: while one says that Borges was unable to have sex, the other states that the sexual act in itself was an "experiencia irresistible." What to make of this contradictoy information? Although the first version is consistent with most of the solid biographical evidence that we have about his impotence, we should not rule out the second one. As I have argued in the introduction (borrowing from Boccanera), sometimes biography can be "completed" by a poem, and this is such a case: "Endimión en Latmos," which Borges explicitly said was autobiographical, re-creates a rewarding sexual experience in his youth and thus lends credibility to the second version. I analyze this poem in chapter 3. However, the two accounts also coincide in some important respects: the fact that Georgie's sexual initiation was arranged by the older Borges and that the son suspected that the woman had also had sex with the father.

Regardless of the specifics proposed by the two versions, all the evidence suggests that it was a traumatic experience. Two decades later, in 1940, Borges would blame his emotional troubles on this event ("perhaps I have

---

19 Canto, *A contraluz*, 116. Emphasis in the orginal.
20 Canto, *A contraluz*, 117.
21 Quoted in Helft, *Postales*, 158–59.

died ... twenty years ago in a venal bedroom in the heart of Europe"),[22] and in 1986, a few weeks before dying at the age of 86, he still resented it:

> je conserve un souvenir détestable de ces circonstances triviales qui m'ont beaucoup perturbé. Je suis alors entré dans une grande dépression. Je pleurais tout le temps et ma famille a dû quitter Genève.[23]

As I said before, in the standard narrative of Borges's life, the Geneva episode has served to explain his sexual impotence. However, we could consider the possibility that the stuttering that afflicted Borges since childhood and the social anxiety disorder that he apparently suffered could have been more important in molding his sexuality than a single traumatic event. As we have seen, Dr Kohan Miller himself established a relationship between Borges's speech problems and his sexual troubles, and although research on stuttering does not propose a specific correlation between social anxiety disorder and sexual impotence, it does show that those affected by the former usually experience "increased fear of negative evaluation and anxiety in socially evaluative or new/strange situations" or that they are "characterized by significant fear of humiliation, embarrassment, and negative evaluation in social or performance-based situations."[24] Sex is, of course, a "socially evaluative" or a "performance-based situation," and certainly, given the extended prejudices and expectations regarding men and sex in the first half of the twentieth century, it was even more challenging for a young man like Borges. Surely, a very negative first experience must have compounded his problem but most likely it did not create it. Actually, this is also suggested by the extent of the father's involvement in the event: he probably perceived Georgie's difficulties in establishing relationships in general (including with women), which might have prompted him (wrongly) to give his son the shock therapy that we now know backfired.

In addition to his sexual impotence, eventually Borges also had to confront another related problem: at least since the early 1930s his condition ceased to be a purely private matter and became common knowledge in small literary circles, which on some occasions was used to stigmatize and publicly humiliate him. It is necessary to look at a few of these disagreeable incidents for two reasons: they allow us to understand how much his contemporaries knew about his condition and how that knowledge influenced their judgement of Borges's literature. Perhaps the worst incidents in this respect were the ones involving the fascist poet Alberto Hidalgo, who during the 1930s sought to expose Borges's emotional and sexual troubles. In 1933, in his daily column in the fascist newspaper *Crisol*, Hidalgo said that Borges himself "confiesa

---

22 Yates, "Behind," 323. See also Helft, *Postales*, 96, 164.
23 Borges, *OC* [2010], II, 1434. The note corresponds to Borges's poem "Reliquias" (1983) which evokes this episode. The information was collected by J. P. Bernès in a conversation with Borges, held in Geneva, in 1986.
24 Iverach et al., "Anxiety," 223; Iverach and Rapee, "Social Anxiety," 69.

haber tenido sólo dos terrores en toda su vida: la policía y las mujeres. [...] en cuanto a las mujeres actúa como si no existieran."[25] However reprehensible Hidalgo's behavior was, the reference to Borges's fear of women essentially corroborates testimonies such as Kohan Miller's and Canto's and shows how informed other writers were about the nature of his troubles. The following year Hidalgo would use his column to attack Borges again. In a comment on Borges's prologue to Elvira de Alvear's *Reposo* (1934), Hidalgo said:

> Borges nunca se tira a fondo. Les saca el cuerpo a los compromisos [...] escribe sobre ellos [libros escritos por mujeres] al revés de como lo hace la generalidad [de los hombres], y nosotros. Si a nosotros una mujer nos pide un prólogo, lo comenzamos quién sabe cómo. Borges pasa de largo. Féliz él, o desgraciado. [...] es un gran crítico, del tipo de esos que no se casan con nadie.[26]

The text is full of double entendres: Borges cannot initiate a relationship with women or engage in foreplay ("prólogo ... Borges pasa de largo"), avoids sexual relationships with them ("les saca el cuerpo," "no se casa con nadie"), and suggests he cannot have sexual intercourse ("nunca se tira a fondo"). Hidalgo would repeat the insults once more in his *Diario de mi sentimiento* (1937), in which he reminded Borges that, years earlier, one night he had lent Borges some money so he could take a taxi and drive a woman home:

> Ud. pudo irse con la chica, solos los dos, y juntos, dentro del auto y bajo la noche. Y de seguro que no pasó nada. ¡Nunca pasa nada entre Ud. y una mujer![27]

Although Hidalgo's base attacks served to vent personal resentments, they were also political: Hidalgo was anti-Semitic and in the pages of *Crisol* he had already insulted Borges because he was an "escritor judío."[28] In this context, then, the exposure of Borges's real sexual troubles sought "to demonstrate," resorting to old anti-Semitic stereotypes, that he was a weak and effeminate Jew.

In the case of other writers, however, their awareness of Borges's sexual impotence did influence their criticism of his work. Until now comments by critics such as Enrique Anderson Imbert and Ramón Doll in the early 1930s have been explained primarily as aesthetic or political negative reactions to Borges's avant-garde and cosmopolitan literature; however, and without denying those factors, a careful reading of their comments reveals that their political and aesthetic disagreements took for granted that male sexual potency and literary creation went together (an old nineteenth-century

---

25 Quoted in Greco, "El crisol," 369.
26 Ibidem, 369–70.
27 Hidalgo, *Diario*, 335.
28 Quoted in Greco, "El crisol," 364. Hidalgo was wrong also in at least another respect: Borges was not Jewish.

prejudice sanctioned, among others, by writers such as Balzac and Zola),[29] and their judgements were articulated in language and images that subtly alluded to Borges's sexual impotence. Thus, in 1933 Anderson Imbert said that Borges's essays were no more than "un puñado de reflexiones *sin vigor* ... observaciones *anémicas* ... no he encontrado página recia, viva, templada bajo el *fuego de convicciones ardientes*, regada con la *sangre caliente* de una personal *concepción* del mundo"; "Sus libritos, *engendrados sin sangre y sin fuerza en sus entrañas* mal alimentadas, van apareciendo año tras año, pero *muertos*. ¿El remedio a este mal? No es el suicidio,"[30] (which also suggests that as early as 1933 there were rumors of Borges's suicide attempts). Similarly, in the same year, in his comments on *Discusión*, Ramón Doll said that Borges's writings lacked emotion because "él prefiere *helarse las entrañas* ... toda su expresión [es] *frígida*, donde la emoción es espiada y luego *anestesiada* deliberadamente ... no encontraremos en su prosa sino un *yermo* intelectual *sin jugos vitales y sin aliento*."[31]

This more-or-less extended public knowledge of his sexual impotence among other writers had consequences for Borges. It definitely took a toll on his self-esteem and deepened the guilt with which he lived his condition. This is what suggests, for example, a passage from "El indigno" (1970). In the short story, the figure of the Jewish protagonist is largely defined by its contrast with some questionable aspects of Argentine ethics and normative masculinity (which he ends up rejecting because, not without irony, he feels "indigno" of them). In a typical Borges's gesture, the characterization of the young man includes a thinly veiled self-portrait which alludes to the generalized opinion about his person and sexuality:

> Todos nos parecemos a la imagen que tienen de nosotros. Yo sentía el desprecio de la gente y yo me despreciaba también. En aquel tiempo, y sobre todo en aquel medio, era importante ser valiente; yo me sabía cobarde. Las mujeres me intimidaban; yo sentía la íntima verguenza de mi castidad temerosa.[32]

In the guise of Santiago Fischbein, Borges shows us the shyness that impedes a man's sexual realization with women ("las mujeres me intimidaban"), the shameful modesty and fearful impotence ("la íntima verguenza de mi castidad temerosa"), the acknowledgement of his reputation with men like Hidalgo and others ("todos nos parecemos a la imagen que tienen de nosotros. Yo sentía el desprecio de la gente"), and the self-hatred ("yo me despreciaba también") caused by sexual failure. Not coincidentally Borges wrote very similar lines in "La secta del Fénix," a story whose subject is precisely the coitus and where

---

29 McLaren, *Impotence*, 120.
30 Anderson Imbert, "Encuesta," 28, 29. My emphasis.
31 Doll, "Discusiones," 34–35. My emphasis.
32 Borges, *OC* [1974], I, 1030–31.

he also refers to his sexual impotence, the social stigmatization he endured, and the guilt it caused him.[33]

One final comment about Hidalgo's attacks and critical readings such as Anderson Imbert's: they occurred early in Borges's career and when he had not yet produced most of his literature. It is worth asking then: did the fact that he knew that the others knew about his troubles shape his writing? To what extent, for example, was it a factor in his choice of reticence and decorum in the expressions of desire and sex? It is very difficult to find reliable evidence to answer these questions convincingly, yet it may be helpful to remember that this awareness of the public knowledge of his condition (and the shaming that went with it) was in his mind while, say, he rewrote or suppressed poems or, even more important, when he was writing his best literature.

The fear that coitus provoked in Borges goes a long way to explaining important manifestations of his literary life. On the one hand, as we will see in chapters 3, 4, and 5, as a reader he was consistently interested in the re-creations and reflections on sexual intercourse written by philosophers, travelers, and, especially, poets. On the other, as a writer, he devoted a whole story to it ("La secta del Fénix") and wrote about it in numerous other ways that we will look at throughout the book.

Desire and Casual and Venal Sex

In spite of the fear that the consummation of sex caused him, and his difficulties in having sexual intercourse, there is evidence that Borges intensely desired women and was aroused by them. Estela Canto said that he "se excitaba como cualquier hombre normal" and that when "[Borges] me apretaba entre sus brazos, yo podía sentir su virilidad"; Canto also told of his attraction to a red-headed woman who was, Borges said, "una de las mujeres que más me han excitado"; moreover, he underscored, "Solo estar a su lado me excitaba."[34] Similarly, Kohan Miller noticed that "a pesar de su problema, sentía placer orgástico [sic] al escuchar ciertas voces femeninas al teléfono" and concluded that his "sensibilidad resonaba a nivel genital."[35] But at the same time Borges felt uneasy and guilty about his desire. For example, he asked Estela Canto whether she thought his sensibility was "normal"[36] and, in the same vein, he told Bioy that when he was romantically interested in a woman he could feel "el deseo físico," which, however, was "molesto."[37] María Esther Vázquez, who was his girlfriend in the early 1960s, also said

33 I analyze this short story in chapter 5.
34 Canto, *A contraluz*, 170.
35 Woscoboinik, *El secreto* [1991], 260.
36 Canto, *A contraluz*, 170.
37 Bioy, *Borges*, 992.

that Borges "era el hombre que se avergonzaba de las necesidades de su cuerpo ... se despreciaba por los oscuros deseos que le encendían la sangre."[38]

In spite of his troubles, during his youth Borges engaged in casual sex and continued to attend brothels.[39] In 1921, money won in the casino allowed him to

> triompher 3 nuits de suite au bordel [avec] une blonde sumptueusement cochonne et une brune que nous appelions La Princesa et sur l'humanité de laquelle je m'enivrais comme sur un avion ou un cheval.[40]

Although we do not have to exclude the possibility that in this letter written to a friend, the young Borges may have been bragging, evidence like this also suggests that he had found ways to enjoy sex. On the other hand, the fact that he went to brothels might reflect that, at least at this early age, he still had the will to put himself to the test and that he probably thought he could overcome his problems.

After his return to Buenos Aires, in the 1920s and 1930s, visits to brothels formed part of his social life with literary friends. Yet, instead of the victorious Borges that emerges from the letter quoted above, the few clues that we have about this period suggest a somber experience that somehow coincides with the reputation that we have seen he had among his colleagues. Manuel Peyrou, one of his friends, said that

> A Borges no le gustaron nunca las prostitutas. Yo creo que iba con nosotros [a los prostíbulos] más por amistad, por no estar a contramano con el grupo, que por interés.[41]

Contrary to the evidence contained in the letter quoted earlier, which reflects an episode in the life of a 20-year-old man, Peyrou's comment comes from a later period and seems to reflect the sentiments and behavior of an older Borges who had already struggled with his problems for years and for whom paid sex had lost any glamour it might have had before (if at all: Borges seems to have feared sexually transmitted diseases).[42] Independently of what

---

38 Vázquez, *Esplendor*, 337.
39 For example, in 1920, when he lived in Madrid, "iban [con un amigo] a una pensión donde vivían unas chicas amigas ... [que] los tocaban y masturbaban," Bioy, 1441.
40 Letter to Maurice Abramowicz, Barcelona, March 2, 1921, Borges, *Cartas del fervor*, 146.
41 Woscoboinik, *El secreto* [1988], 198. This side of literary life in the Buenos Aires of the 1920s was re-created by Leopoldo Marechal in his *Adán Buenosayres* (1948), which included Luis Pereda, a character who was a barely disguised Borges.
42 Bioy, 1384. In his conversation with Bioy Casares, Borges indicated his approval of the 1935 law that closed the officially authorized brothels in Buenos Aires, because "los prostíbulos [eran] focos de blenorragia y sífilis." Fear of infectious diseases might have marked Borges since early childhood: one of the reasons why he was initially home schooled was that his own father did not want to expose his children

the evidence quoted before specifically tells us about Borges's predicament, it is clear that for him, as for many men of his generation, casual and venal sex were a common experience; it should not surprise us, then, to find that the majority of explorations and re-creations of sex in his literature are of this nature.[43]

Borges often fell in love with women. He experienced numerous rejections (among others with Norah Lange) but with some he managed to establish what Bioy called "noviazgos blancos"; that is, more or less close emotional relationships that apparently did not include sexual intercourse and that were usually short-lived ("Una mujer que le dura un año o dos con amor blanco dura mucho").[44] A 64-year-old Borges himself talked about this pattern: "Así es toda mi vida ... una cadena de mujeres."[45] The "chain of women" included, among others, Cecilia Ingenieros, Estela Canto, and Wally Zenner (the last two, dedicatees of his short stories) but also several others whom Borges typically invited to collaborate with him in book projects: Margot Guerrero (co-author and editor of two books), Silvina Bullrich (co-editor of one book), Alicia Jurado (co-author of one book), and María Esther Vázquez (co-author of two books).[46] Late in life Borges married twice. The first marriage (to Elsa Astete Millán), which he entered into with fear and hesitation, turned into a conflictive relationship and ended in divorce after three years (1967–1970). Eventually, in 1986, two months before his death at 86, Borges married María Kodama (co-author of one book).

## Incest

Borges witnessed and lived the intersection of kinship ties, love, and sex in ways that apparently disturbed him and made him think, read, and write about it. His father was a philanderer especially attracted to women who were relatives and friends of his wife, who was aware of these affairs but pretended they did not exist. This side of his family life definitely left him bitter: "*Dulce Hogar*, oximoron," Borges said to summarize his father and mother's sexual and emotional life.[47]

But more important, we have seen that his father was involved in his sexual initiation and that what shocked Borges was the realization or the

---

to contagious diseases in a public school (presumably, the fear of tuberculosis), Woscoboinik, *El secreto* [1988], 41.
43 For references and anecdotes about brothels and prostitutes that often formed part of Borges's and Bioy's conversations, see (only as examples but not as a complete list), Bioy, *Borges*, 265, 1039, 1068, 1117.
44 Bioy, *Borges*, 963.
45 Bioy, *Borges*, 991–92.
46 Bioy, *Borges*, 457.
47 Bioy, *Borges*, 1422; "una o dos veces Georgie me dijo que su padre había tenido historias amorosas con otras mujeres," Canto, *A contraluz*, 91.

suspicion that he was sharing the woman with his father. While in Geneva another similar situation apparently occurred: Georgie fell in love with his young literary friend Helen von Stummer, but he must have felt that he also had to compete with his father (as during his sexual initiation) because Helen seemed to have liked the older Borges more than the younger one.[48] Psychologists have called attention to the "devastating effects" that this type of relationship may have on the people involved and have categorized the situation in which two consanguineous individuals (two siblings, a mother and a daughter, a father and a son, etc.) share a sexual partner as an "incest of a second type."[49] According to this explanation, these relationships are traumatically "unlivable" because they "create [an emotional and sexual] rivalry between two persons already allied by the strongest possible tie: kinship."[50] As we will see in other chapters, Borges read and dwelt on literature that explored these types of relationships and, more importantly, he wrote about it: the short story "La intrusa" precisely depicts an incest of the second type in which two brothers (the "older" and the "younger," as Borges also calls them) sexually share a woman, which, indeed, has devastating effects.

In addition, Borges established an unusual and emotionally close relationship with his mother, of whose exceptionality Borges was aware (he lived with her until she died when she was 99 and he was 75).[51] The relationship was facilitated (although obviously not created) by the reconfiguration of the Borges household in the 1920s and 1930s. In 1928, Norah Borges (Georgie's younger and only sibling) married and left home, and the father, whose blindness and illness prevented him from working, died in 1938. His mother, Leonor Acevedo de Borges was a strong-willed and socially ambitious woman who devoted her life to "lo que ella consideraba la realización de su vida: el triunfo literario de su hijo."[52] Leonor's involvement in her son's career went from taking notes for him up to designing his strategies to achieve recognition and success ("indicaba a su hijo los pasos a dar para el progreso de su carrera").[53] She also maintained tight control over Georgie's emotional and romantic life,[54] and as Borges grew older and was unable to establish

---

48 Bioy, *Borges*, 1421; García, "Borges y Hélene von Stummer," I and II.
49 Eliacheff and Heinich, "Étendre," 5; a more extended treatment of the question in Eliacheff and Heinich, *Mères-filles*, 151–56. In the explanation of the authors, the incest of the "first type" would be the sexual relationship between two consanguineous persons: father/daughter; sister/brother, mother/son, etc.
50 Eliacheff and Heinich, "Étendre," 7–8. On the devastating effects of "sexual rivalry," see also Heinich, "L'incest," 947–52.
51 When he was about to marry Elsa Astete, he told Bioy "pocos hijos han estado junto a su madre sesenta y siete años," Bioy, *Borges*, 1204.
52 Canto, *A contraluz*, 91; "su sed de figurar era tan intensa …," Canto, *A contraluz*, 103.
53 Canto, *A contraluz*, 91.
54 "A madre sólo le gustan las mujeres que sabe que a mí no me gustan. Ahora [1964]

mature relationships with women, the tie between mother and son became stronger ("tras una serie de sucesivos fracasos sentimentales, el pacto de sangre se robusteció. Leonor Acevedo ... pasó al primer [plano]").[55] His first marriage, when he was 67, was essentially decided and arranged by Leonor, who apparently wanted to pick the woman who would take care of Georgie after she died (his mother was 91 at the time). Yet, in spite of forcing her son to marry, she promised him that she would remain close, which apparently comforted him ("madre dice que tratará de estar conmigo lo más posible").[56] By all accounts, the relationship was overwhelming, and the son never managed to effectively challenge his mother's strong will.[57]

When Georgie traveled or was separated from Leonor, even for a few days, he corresponded with her and, revealingly, he did it in ways similar to the communications that he maintained with Estela Canto: in both cases he wrote "equally passionate" postcards (not letters) containing language usually reserved for romantic relationships ("te extraño cada momento," "Yours ever").[58] In 1974, a year before his mother died, Borges dedicated his *Obras completas* (the work of his whole life and that meant his literary canonization) to her. For Estela Canto, the dedication, whose text opened as a "confesión" and closed as a conversation that excluded any other person ("aquí estamos hablando los dos"), truly showed who was the fundamental relationship in Borges's life: "La dedicatoria de las *Obras Completas* demuestra en todo caso que las otras dedicatorias de los diversos poemas y cuentos, a mujeres que amó o a amigos que le ayudaron, son nombres de fantasmas, figuras sin sustancia."[59]

Biographer Alejandro Vaccaro has concluded that "Borges tenía un matrimonio con su madre ... que en realidad sólo excluía el sexo. Vivieron juntos, compartieron economías y se prestaron un apoyo mutuo como cualquier otra pareja."[60] When it comes to the facts, the balance drawn by the biographer is convincing; however, the explanation seems to miss the inherent asymmetrical power of such an arrangement when it involves a mother and a child, and does not consider the negative consequences that it has for the latter. Perhaps we can have a more comprehensive understanding of Borges's relationship with his mother if we think of it as a "platonic incest" or "incest without the sexual act," which according to psychologists usually occurs between mothers and children. In these cases "the psychological and

---

le gusta Alicia Jurado pero, cuando había algo parecido a un flirt entre Alicia y yo, me hablaba mal de ella," Bioy, *Borges*, 1002.
55 Canto, *A contraluz*, 231.
56 Bioy, *Borges*, 1204.
57 Canto, *A contraluz*, 106, 231; Borges told Bioy: "madre es muy dominante," Bioy, *Borges*, 1002.
58 The observation and expression are Helft's, *Postales*, 132.
59 Canto, *A contraluz*, 90.
60 Quoted in Villena, "Borges tenía un matrimonio."

affective couple can be formed without the existence of a strictly sexual relation."[61] The relationship implies the exclusion of the father from the more common family triangle, which in the case of Borges was facilitated by Jorge Guillermo's death.[62] "Platonic Incest" is typically a "pathology" of maternal love,[63] and frequently entails what psychoanalysts call "narcissistic abuse" in which, as seems to have been the case with Leonor Acevedo, "the gifts of the child are exploited to fill the unsatisfied aspirations of a mother that is supposedly devoted to the child."[64] The facts of the relationship suggest that we could also look to this relationship for the origin of Borges's sexual and love troubles: according to psychologists, these types of mother-child relationships "may have consequences as pathological as those created by a frustrated love experience."[65] As we will see later in the book, his mother's love, sex, and the question of incest preoccupied Borges; it oriented some of his readings and left a mark on his own texts.

## Homosexuality and Homophobia

We have seen how stuttering and social anxiety, a traumatic sexual initiation, and an overwhelming mother-son relationship all might have contributed to Borges's sexual troubles. But the fact that he suffered from sexual impotence inevitably raises another question: studies on this problem have pointed out that "the inability of some men to perform sexually with women might be read as an indication of male homosexuality."[66] Was this Borges's case? I have found no evidence of erotic attraction toward any specific man (as there are with women) or that he was ever engaged in any homosexual relation. Certainly the absence of information in this respect could reflect, in part, the bigger methodological difficulties implied in identifying and documenting a "love that dare not speak its name"[67]—as would be the case too with any other culturally or legally forbidden relationship like, say, incest.

As is well known, though, Borges privileged male-male relationships in his social life and established close intellectual friendships with other men (most notably with Adolfo Bioy Casares).[68] Some of his texts and testimonies let us

---

61 Eliacheff and Heinich, "Étendre," 9; see also Eliacheff and Heinich, *Mères-filles*, 58–71. For a clinical description and explanation of this type of situation see Naouri, "Un inceste."
62 A situation that nowadays "is facilitated by the massive numbers of divorces, that make the absence of the father normal," Eliacheff and Heinich, "Étendre," 10.
63 Eliacheff and Heinich, "Étendre," 11.
64 Eliacheff, "Incest maternel."
65 Eliacheff and Heinich, *Mères-filles*, 389–90.
66 McLaren, *Impotence*, 112.
67 Oscar Wilde's allusion to homosexuality in one of his trials, see chapter 9.
68 Borges invited several women to become co-authors of books of criticism or anthologies which, as several of them publicly stated, reflected Borges's ideas and knowledge

sense the way he felt and reasoned about the preeminence of male intellectual bonds over male-female relationships. It shocked him, for instance, to see that in a novel, an author "Increíblemente" was more interested in "una señorita que un heresiarca,"[69] which, he thought, resulted in a dull plot. In the same vein, the importance of intellectual engagement among men explained for him the emotionally fulfilling nature of male homosexual relations over heterosexual ones in Ancient Greece, where "las mujeres eran iletradas; por eso el amor con ellas era sólo carnal, a diferencia del amor entre hombres."[70]

It is also logical to think that his sexual impotence with women must have raised in him the fear of homosexuality, and the evidence suggests that it did. All the circumstances around his sexual initiation seem to indicate that the older Borges worried about Georgie's masculinity, and at least one of the versions says that the latter failed to meet his father's expectations. The 1930s public stigmatization and coded literary criticisms that centered on his sexual impotence also made him think that he did not conform to established concepts of masculinity. As we have seen in his self-portrait included in "El indigno," he said, "yo sentía el desprecio de la gente y yo me despreciaba también" because "en aquel tiempo, y sobre todo en aquel medio, era importante ser valiente; yo me sabía cobarde."[71] The adjectives "brave" and "coward" alluded to his sexual potency but this binary perception of men was also one of the pillars of heteronormativity in Argentine culture.[72]

Borges's behavior around the question of male homosexuality did not go unnoticed by Estela Canto:

> Borges, que veía con diversión y hasta simpatía la homosexualidad femenina, nunca hacía alusión a la masculina, ni siquiera para denigrarla. La ignoraba en sus amigos o la ponía a un lado cuando tropezaba con ella en la literatura.[73]

His silences appear more like suppression than lack of interest and suggest that it was a question that destabilized and worried, even scared him. This is also what is suggested by a comment on the sexuality of the French poet Paul Verlaine: "Verlaine se acostaba con cualquier prostituta, para defenderse de la homosexualidad."[74] That Borges did not consider the possibility of bisexuality, given the historical and cultural context, was not exceptional. Neither was the fact that he believed that heterosexual sex was a way of redirecting

---

and for which he did most of the work. However, he never wrote literature with them: he did it with Bioy, the only person with whom he seems to have had a real authorial partnership.

69 Borges, *OC* [1974], IV, 388.
70 Bioy, *Borges*, 1441.
71 Borges, *OC* [1974], I, 1030–31.
72 Melo, *Historia de la literatura gay*, 16.
73 Canto, *A contraluz*, 170.
74 Bioy, *Borges*, 890.

homosexual desire; however, it is revealing that he thought that it could be a way of "defending" oneself from homosexuality, which clearly appeared to him as much of a threat as heterosexual sex is in his poem "El amenazado."

Borges's dialogues with Bioy Casares provide ample evidence of his homophobia. They also show that in the company of his closest friend he was not as reticent about homosexuality as he seems to have been with Estela Canto. Canto said that "cuando era inevitable, [Borges] usaba la antigua designación bíblica —sodomía— que implicaba la desaprobación divina,"[75] although he also used "pederastia" and the pathologizing terms "perversión" and "anormalidad."[76] In his published work, the clearest of his homophobic expressions appears in "Nuestras imposibilidades," which reveals, according to Daniel Balderston, both his "homosexual panic" and his fascination with homosexual sex,[77] (and in chapter 4 we will come back to this essay and Borges's controversial expression).

However, his narrative and poetry do not present clear cut and unambiguous examples of homosexual attraction and relationships. Blas Matamoro, who looked at this question, concluded that "homosexualismo como tal, perfilado y nítido, creo que no lo hay en Borges."[78] The fact that in his short stories there are close male-male relationships, but which cannot be conclusively categorized as homosexual,[79] has posed interesting interpretive challenges. Perhaps the most well known is "La intrusa," which not coincidentally has attracted most of the commentaries exploring the question of homosexuality in his literature, which we will revisit in chapter 9.

75  Canto, *A contraluz*, 171.
76  Borges, *OC* [1974], II, 284; Borges, *CS*, 187.
77  Balderston, "Dialéctica," 67, 72.
78  Matamoros, "Yo y el otro," 224.
79  Leone, "An Inventory," 175.

CHAPTER 2

# Biography in Literature and the Reading of Desire and Sex in Borges

Following the exploration of Borges's personality and sexuality, I consider here whether it is possible and logical to attempt a biographical reading of his works, while also proposing ways of reading desire and sex in the literature of a reticent writer like him.

## Life in Literature

Speaking about his own literature, Borges said, "I've never created a character. It's always me, subtly disguised ... I'm always myself, the same self in different times or places, but always, irreparably, incurably, myself,"[1] which suggests that his personal circumstances could be brought to bear on the reading of some of his work. He also pointed out that "all that is personal to me, all that my friends good-naturedly tolerate in me—my likes and dislikes, my hobbies, my habits—are to be found in my verse,"[2] thus similarly insinuating that his poetry could be read in a biographical key.

One of Borges's earliest declarations of literary principles was, precisely, that "toda literatura es autobiográfica, finalmente" and that "toda poesía es plena confesión de un yo, de un carácter."[3] Sometimes readers may have difficulties in accepting this premise or seeing this principle operating in literature, he acknowledged, because of the rhetorical challenges faced by the author or the context in which the biographical material has been placed: "A veces la sustancia autobiográfica, la personal, está desaparecida por los accidentes que la encarnan," yet the author's life experience, Borges thought, is the deeper substratum that ultimately shapes literature: "es como corazón que late en la hondura."[4]

Borges's explications of his own texts showed that this principle often guided his literary creation. Take "Junio, 1968." The poem tells about the

---

1 Cortínez and Sobejano, "Borges discusses," 57.
2 Borges, *Selected Poems*, xv–xvi.
3 Borges, *TME*, 143, 148.
4 Borges, *TME*, 146.

silent happiness that a blind man feels when placing his beloved books on the shelves of his bookcase, and, although the character in the poem is unnamed, it is easy to recognize the author in it. Indeed, Borges said that the "poem is altogether autobiographical" and explained that "the whole point of the poem is that strange happiness I felt, although I was blind, of going back [in June of 1968, after a long trip] to my own books and putting them on the shelves."[5]

So there is no question that Borges's poetry and literature can (and sometimes should) be read as biographical, addressing his sexuality and love life. Dr Kohan Miller remembered that Borges "como toda persona que tiene una disminución de su potencia sexual [vivía] acosado por el problema de la sexualidad";[6] it should not surprise us, then, that this overwhelming condition would find expression in the literature of the author who, as we have seen, said "all that is personal to me ... my likes and dislikes ... my habits—are to be found in my verse." In reality, at times Borges could be unusually transparent about the fact that the production of his literature (and others' as well) was intimately linked to his troubled sexuality:

> la impotencia [sexual] de [Nicolas] Boileau, de [Jonathan] Swift, de [Immanuel] Kant, de [John] Ruskin y de George Moore fue un melancólico instrumento para la buena ejecución de su obra; lo mismo cabe afirmar de la perversión [...]
>
> Por eso yo hablé en un poema del antiguo alimento de los héroes: la humillación, la desdicha, la discordia. Esas cosas nos fueron dadas para que las transmutemos, para que hagamos de la miserable circunstancia de nuestra vida, cosas eternas o que aspiren a serlo.[7]

Thus, as for Boileau and others, his "desdicha" (a word that alluded to the emotional pain caused by the dissonance between his desire and his impotence) and his "humillación" (the impossibility of consummating sex and his failure with women) became the point of departure for his reflections on desire and sex or for the re-creation of erotic experiences both as a reader and as an author. Actually, according to Borges, sexuality more generally could be at the origin of literature: for instance, "perversión" (homosexuality) too had motivated other authors to write (as was the case, he thought, of Shakespeare and his sonnets).

And, if sexual impotence was at the origin of literature, it could also be, of course, a point of departure for its interpretation. As we have seen in the introduction, Borges thought that "detrás" Poe's, Swift's, Carlyle's, and Almafuerte's oeuvres there was a "neurosis," and therefore, he argued, "interpretar su obra en función de esa anomalía ... es legítimo."[8] As I have

---

5 Borges, *BOW*, 83, 78.
6 Goldaracena, "Las inhibiciones del joven Borges."
7 Borges, *OC* [1974], II, 284–85. Borges refers here to his poem "Mateo, XXV, 30."
8 Borges, *TR2*, 263; on Carlyle's and Poe's sexual impotence, see McLaren, *Impotence*, 102 and 121; on Almafuerte's, see Borges, *TR2*, 195.

explained before, this proposition was a response to (Hidalgo's) personal attacks and to critical readings (such as Anderson Imbert's) that in the 1930s had assumed that there was a direct and proportional relationship between sexual potency and literary creation. Here, then, Borges inverted the old stereotype: sexual impotence could actually lead to literary creation and, therefore, it could be enlisted in the interpretation of certain (indeed, great) authors, including himself: the fact that the essay presented a self-portrait of sorts (more on this later) suggests that it was also a subtle and indirect attempt by Borges to explain his own case.

In his explications, Borges often speaks about the "transmutación," the "magnificación,"[9] and the "transformation" of the experience. That is, his proposition on the biographical origins of literature does not mean that texts are a direct imitation of life, but something different that is primarily made from the circumstances of the author. Therefore, like any other, a biographical reading creates interpretive challenges that leave us with uncertainties regarding the author's experience and the ever-elusive authorial intention. For instance, not everything that we find in "Junio, 1968" reflects Borges's experience in those circumstances. Although in the poem we read, "En la tarde de oro / o en una serenidad cuyo símbolo / podría ser la tarde de oro," Borges clarifies that "I do not know whether the evening was golden, because I couldn't see it. I'm hinting at the blindness ... For all I knew, it could have been dismal weather."[10] That is, even an apparently autobiographical piece is woven with details that are not of the same order as the personal experience of the author, and whose presence in the text is due to its expressive demands and aspirations.

In addition, there are texts where the experience of the author is masked or substantially transformed ("It's always me, subtly disguised") and, therefore, the autobiographical matter is far from evident. Speaking about what motivated him to write "Junio, 1968," Borges said that the same experience was also at the origin of "El guardián de los libros" (1968), a poem that in many respects is very different from the former. In this case Borges situated the facts in medieval China and created a blind man who survived the barbarian invasions and was left in charge of books that preserved the memory of the vanished culture. The poem is a dramatic monologue told in the voice of the main character who, in spite of being illiterate, guarded the volumes with devotion. It is illuminating to listen to Borges's explanation of the origins of this poem:

> The thought came to me that something else might be tried, based on that same experience. But when I tried it for a second time, I said, "I'll be more inventive and forget all about myself; I'll write some kind of fairy story or a

---

9 "La lírica es la complaciente magnificación de venturas o desventuras amorosas," Borges, *OC* [1974], I, 749.
10 Borges, *BOW*, 78–79; the poem in Spanish in *OC* [1974], I, 998.

parable" ... I finally ended up writing a sham Chinese poem. You can see it is Chinese because of the many details. But, in fact, the poem is a kind of transformation. It is the same experience as "June, 1968," transmogrified. Maybe to the casual reader the two poems are not the same. But I know they are the same.[11]

Borges operated, then, a "transformation" or "transmogrification" of his experience, which required forgetting about himself (as a character) and adding "Chinese" details. The result is "a sham Chinese poem"; however, Borges assures us that "it is the same experience as 'June, 1968.'" As he said in "Profesión de fe literaria," decades before he tried this variation of "Junio, 1968," "a veces la sustancia autobiográfica, la personal, está desaparecida por los accidentes que la encarnan."[12] Yet, below this imaginative veneer of Chinese erudition, we can still recognize Borges: the blindness, the love of books, the awareness of what they represent, the pleasure of keeping them close by on the shelves.

But it is also true that the transmutation adds new interpretive uncertainties. The change of place and time somehow blurs the author's figure (which was one of his intentions: "I'll ... forget all about myself") and it also implies a definite loss of historical context: we do not know any longer that the experience that motivated the poem occurred in "Junio, 1968," as we learn from the title of the other poem.

How can the personal experience of the author and the emotions it caused in him be disentangled from the fictional circumstances created by the transmutation and by the rhetorical demands of the poem? How can the biographical component in texts like this be read when, as is more often the case, we do not have the author's testimony (or explication)? If a "sham Chinese poem" is based on a personal experience, we should be prepared for an uncomfortable latitude in the biographical interpretation of Borges's literature.

The unavoidable uncertainty of interpretation, however, does not mean we should dispense with argument and the evidence that must sustain its persuasive ability. What may seem difficult or impossible to explain still deserves to be subjected to investigative criticism so its uncertainties can at least be narrowed down, as Poe implied in the literary puzzle displayed as an epigraph in "The Murders in the Rue Morgue."[13]

---

11  Borges, *BOW*, 83. For their publication, Borges decided to place the two poems side by side so they could be read together, Borges, *OC* [1974], I, 998–99.
12  Borges, *TME*, 146.
13  Poe, *Poetry*, 397.

## Desire and Sex in Borges's Texts

As I said, the point of departure for my investigation is the, in my opinion, unjustified perception of the absence of desire and sex in Borges's literature and his lack of will to talk about it. In this section I hope to make a first approximation to some of the factors that may explain this questionable reading of his work and offer alternative approaches to it.

To begin with, there is a widespread assumption about the erotic in Borges's work that can easily be proven wrong. It is the perception that few of his short stories and poems are specifically devoted to exploring desire and sex, a puzzling idea when, without any attempt at thoroughness, we can think of "La noche de los dones," "La secta del Fénix," "La intrusa," "Ulrica," "Casa Elena," "Paréntesis pasional," "El Paseo de Julio," "El amenazado," and other titles. In addition, there are other texts, such as the poems "Arrabal en que pesa el campo," "Villa Urquiza,"[14] "La espera," or "Endimión en Latmos," that perhaps are not as well known as the ones I just mentioned but that also reflect Borges's interest in sex, as I expect to show in other sections of this book. Therefore, once this list is put together, one wonders how many stories and poems on desire and sex Borges was supposed to write to be recognized as an author who spoke about these topics?

There are three other questions, however, that we have to consider more carefully if we want to comprehend how desire and sex shaped Borges's literature and to see them in his texts: first, the nature of the eroticism that we find in them; second, the form of its expression; third, and related to the previous one, the location of eroticism in his work.

## The Nature of His Eroticism

For centuries, when men expressed their eroticism in literature they rarely appeared incapable or inadequate, and sex was generally stimulating and enjoyable.[15] Yet, Borges is very different. In his work we often see allusions to the impossibility of establishing mature emotional and sexual relationships with women, sex is usually casual, and prostitution is the main milieu in which it takes place. Not surprisingly, then, sex may appear as terrifying, impersonal, and dirty, and it elicits guilt and bitterness. Thus, the sex act or sex more generally can appear as "trabazón carnal," "el vertiginoso instante del coito," "aquel desorden perplejo de sensaciones inconexas y atroces," "confusa voracidad de los viejos," "la cosa horrible," "la falacia del coito,"

---

[14] I do not refer here to the "Villa Urquiza" included in *Fervor de Buenos Aires* (1923), but the one published in the review *Alfar*, in 1926 and reprinted in Borges, *TR1*, 248. On this poem, see chapter 6.

[15] The analysis of the erotic genre in the following paragraphs is based on Pauvert, *Anthologie*, vol.5, 681–96; Goujon, *Anthologie*, 11–25; Lehman, *The Best*, XV–XXV.

and "la paternidad [es] abominable."[16] In some respects sex in Borges's work is similar to the well-known and disappointing experience of "the typist" and "the young man carbuncular" in T. S. Eliot's *The Waste Land*.[17]

So, it is hard (if not impossible) to claim that eroticism in Borges's literature can "quicken desire,"[18] as many other pieces in the genre seek and manage to do. This is especially true at the beginning of the twenty-first century, when so much explicit sex seems to saturate Western public culture, and it might even be possible to argue that pornography has disappeared as a concept.[19] Yet, although readers may expect literature on desire and sex to be sexually stimulating, it does not have to be a law of the genre. Pierre Louys, who probably produced more erotica than any other modern writer, said that "les exigences de la chair" are at the center of the creative process, "soit pour les aimer, soit pour les maudire."[20] With a similar understanding of desire and sex in literature, Jean Paul Goujon reserved a section in his *Anthologie de la poésie erotique française* for erotic nightmares. In his justification of it, which were it not limited to French poetry we would think was tailored for Borges, he explains that "Si Éros emporte au septième ciel bien des mortels, il n' en est pas moins vrai qu'il en plonge d'autres dans la terreur ou le plus noir désespoir" and highlights that the poems selected evoke "ce qui, pour le poète, constitue un vrai cauchemar ... la femme elle-même ... Tout, en elle, distille une sorte de peur essentielle."[21] So it is a limited understanding of sexuality and eroticism in literature that has blinded critics with respect to this side of Borges's texts. Granted, desire and sex in Borges are often not pleasant or titillating (the tone is rather nightmarish), but he did write about them much more than critics have dared to admit (the number of ways in which he referred to coitus and that I quoted above, in themselves suggest how willing Borges was to write about it).

The Form of the Expression

Let us now look at the second question: the form of the expression is an important factor that at the beginning of the twenty-first century certainly conspires against the reading of desire and sex in Borges. To understand this question, first we have to remember that Borges was, literally, a nineteenth-century man (born in 1899) who discovered literature and developed his literary sensibility in a Victorian library (his father's) that held, for example, erotic poetry by Dante Gabriel Rossetti but not (as far as I know) Walter's

16  Borges, *TR1*, 113; Borges, *OC* [1974], I, 327, 364, 438, 566; IV, 266.
17  The comparison is suggested by Lehman, *The Best*, XVI.
18  Lehman, *The Best*, XIX.
19  Pauvert, *Anthologie*, vol. 5, 692.
20  Quoted in Pauvert, *Anthologie*, vol. 5, 686.
21  Goujon, *Anthologie*, 807.

famous pornographic memoir *My Private Life*. Therefore, to sense and perceive his expressions of desire and sex, it is also necessary to consider Borges's ideas and expectations regarding erotic literature and how he read the genre. For instance, he did not quite like D. H. Lawrence's *Lady Chatterley's Lover* (1928) because the author expressed "el amor físico" "a veces, de un modo explícito" (to which he objected), "a veces con extraordinaria delicadeza"[22] (which he approved). More revealing about his thoughts on the genre is what he said about poetry:

> los mejores versos eróticos son los de San Juan de la Cruz, de la *noche escura del alma*: "En una noche escura / con ansias en amores inflamada, / ¡oh dichosa ventura!" Si se leen como poesía mística no pierden valor. La mejor poesía erótica no es obscena. Uno de los mejores ejemplos es la delicadeza y la sabiduría poética de Rossetti ... los versos más explícitos de Whitman no son los mejores. ¿Por qué Whitman vuelve a decir groseramente lo que ya dijo con acierto?[23]

What was, then, Borges's sensibility scale regarding erotic literature? On the one hand, we have that "lo explícito" is a quality that defines what is "grosero" and "obsceno" or even (we suspect) pornographic. On the other hand, what constitutes "la mejor poesía erótica" is its "delicadeza" or, we can infer, the degree of allusive distance reached by the handling of metaphors and other rhetorical resources. One of the qualities that such erotic literature can have, we see, is that its indeterminacy expands its meanings and multiplies possible readings. The paradigmatic case is San Juan de la Cruz, whose poems have for centuries been read as both erotic *and* mystic.[24] Generally, this criterion ruled Borges's taste, as both an author and a reader. But, as in any rule, we find exceptions (or contradictions). Borges, a very discriminating reader, was also capable, as we will see in other chapters, of enjoying texts where desire and sex were very explicit and which he nevertheless considered great pieces of erotic literature.

So, it is really exceptional to find in Borges explicit language that could create the perception of obscenity. His texts on desire and sex are modest, reticent, and self-restrained. For the author who said that "toda literatura es autobiográfica," one of the challenges of the genre was to find the right balance between what is personal (and sexual) and what can actually be said publicly (or confessed). In "Profesión de fe literaria," he wondered "¿Cómo alcanzar esa *patética* iluminación sobre nuestras vidas? ¿cómo entrometer en

---

22 Borges, *OCC*, 852.
23 Bioy, *Borges*, 1157–58. Emphasis in the original.
24 Borges also used this argument of the literary productivity of metaphorical language to justify censorship: "Cuando hay censura la literatura es más viril, más sutil, más decantada," Bioy, *Borges*, 802. Bioy commented that "Esta es la interpretación de la censura como estilo, como calzado que nos aprieta, nos incomoda, nos obliga a marchar derechos, a ser más correctos y más vigorosos," Bioy, *Borges*, 802–3.

pechos ajenos *nuestra vergonzosa verdad?*"[25] Explicitness limits the author to saying very little about himself, while ambiguity allows him to smuggle more substantive, disguised preoccupations into the conversation. Thus, very often in Borges's texts, allusive imagery and oblique references do not immediately allow an erotic reading and may easily puzzle readers into other interpretations. Estela Canto, one of the contemporaries who commented on Borges insightfully, observed that "en vez de mencionar, él prefería aludir" and, consequently, she explained, "todos sus escritos ... abundan en insinuaciones, en cosas nombradas a medias, en nombres cambiados."[26]

In addition, if we want to locate desire and sex in Borges, we have to become aware that, among other things, he rarely used those two words. Instead, his erotic language, like most of his literature, was made up of "palabras habituales" that softened the poignancy of confession and somehow worked toward the gradual, cumulative, and not always easily noticeable deflection of meaning. To read and capture eroticism in Borges, we have to sensitize ourselves to words such as "esperanza" (which he preferred instead of desire), "desesperación" (sexual urge), "ternura" (sex and women), or "urgente" (sexy and sexual urge). Then we will be better prepared to capture the meanings of "la notoria esperanza de las niñas," "el remordimiento y la vergüenza de la / insatisfecha esperanza," "la desesperación se mira en los charcos," "desesperación de ternura," "desesperada carnalidad," "desesperadamente esperanzado," "urgentes pasiones," "urgente Afrodita," "yeguas urgentes," "Urgencia de ternura, esperanza vehemente."

Similarly, we should be aware of some discreet, sometimes unexpected, but consistent use of adjectives. One of them, "admirable," usually suggests a positive sexual charge: the *Arabian Nights* is a book of "admirable lascivia," Baldomero Fernández Moreno was an "admirable poeta erótico," Dante Gabriel Rossetti's erotic "Nuptial Sleep" was one of his "sonetos más admirables."[27] On the contrary, "minucioso," in Borges's usage, alludes to an extreme and disgusting awareness of his (or a character's) body, including sex: Emma Zunz's sexual initiation is a "minuciosa deshonra," Dahlmann "minuciosamente ... odió ... sus necesidades corporales," and during insomnia the poet is overwhelmed by "los rumbos minuciosos ... de las caries dentales."[28] These examples, of course, do not cover the wide range of Borges's vocabulary on the subject, but they do help us to remain alert to his not-so-explicit erotic language that is composed of current words ("palabras habituales").

When Borges did not achieve the reticence and ambiguity that he sought in his texts, he felt that his literature was not quite realized, as revealed by his hesitation over "El amenazado," which contains, perhaps, his most explicit

25 Borges, *TME*, 148. My emphasis.
26 Canto, *A contraluz*, 18.
27 Borges, *OC* [1974], 406; Sorrentino, *Siete conversaciones*, 237; Borges, *BP*, 266.
28 Borges, *OC* [1974], 567, 526, 859.

erotic line ("me duele una mujer en todo el cuerpo"). Although the poem made it into the final edition of the *Obras completas*, in 1977 Borges did drop it from his *Obra poética: 1923–1976* because, he said,

> me pareció demasiado íntimo, demasiado inmediato y lo borré .... La poesía necesita algo fabuloso, algo ambiguo, y le faltaba a ese poema. Era una especie de interjección que no podía permitirme en público.[29]

Borges's reaction to his own poem suggests, in a weird way, the difficulties his erotic literature has created for readers. While he thought about suppressing "El amenazado" because of its uncharacteristic, unborgesian explicitness, the poem was the only one by him that I have found representing his work in an anthology of erotic poetry (an inclusion that in itself is exceptional because Borges never appears in such anthologies).[30]

## The Location of Desire and Sex

At the beginning of this section I listed texts where Borges specifically explored or re-created the experience of desire and sex, such as "La secta del Fénix," "Ulrica," and "Casa Elena." However, these texts are not the only places where Borges spoke about sexuality and eroticism, and we should not limit our exploration to them. In addition to those "specialized" texts, very frequently Borges describes sexual matters in short flashes, notes, fragments, or passages that pop up in unexpected corners of texts whose topic is not obviously related to desire and sex. Because they seem out of context, sometimes even unwarranted, and they are fragmentary, they may go unnoticed by readers. But if we pay attention we will see that this occurs with noticeable frequency and that, although brief, these moments also tell us about how Borges wrote on the subject.

Sometimes these apparently unwarranted moments of sexuality are random eruptions of Borges's latent desire onto the surface of his writing; but, in other instances, their disposition in his work suggests that they have been organized following the furtive logic that, Borges himself proposed, had guided authors in the execution of books where love and eroticism were fundamental motivations, such as the *Divina comedia* and Burton's translation of the *Nights*. With respect to the former, Borges thought that "Dante edificó el ... libro ... para intercalar algunos encuentros con la irrecuperable Beatriz ... alguna vez enumeró en una epístola sesenta nombres de mujer para deslizar entre ellos, secreto, el nombre de Beatriz. Pienso que en la *Comedia* repitió ese melancólico juego."[31] Similarly, Borges seems to have also believed that the same furtive logic explained Burton's decision to publish a new edition of the *Nights*. Concurring with one of the earliest accusations

---

29 Woscoboinik, *El secreto* [1988], 199.
30 The poem has been anthologized by Provencio, *Antología*, 412.
31 Borges, *OC* [1974], II, 373.

against the English explorer, Borges thought that Burton's project reflected not so much his interest in offering a new translation as his intention to use the annotation of the erotic tales as an excuse to publish his investigations on human sexuality when other venues, such as anthropological journals, had been effectively closed to him: "A los cincuenta años, el hombre ha acumulado ternuras, ironías, obscenidades y copiosas anécdotas; Burton las descargó en sus notas."[32] Borges's thoughts on Dante and Burton reflect an awareness of the ways two of his admired authors had smuggled and camouflaged personal and erotic material into their works, strategies that could be mirrored in his own writings.

The short and unexpected eruptions of the erotic appear in the main text or in footnotes of short stories, critical essays, philosophical explorations, and in biographical sketches of other authors (which actually turn them into self-portraits). The intrusion of sex and desire in, say, a "metaphysical fantasy" implies a mixing of the erotic and philosophy; that is, a blending of genres that he practiced in his most famous texts and which became one of his literary trademarks. In the next few pages I want to show some of them so that we can see how desire and sex were woven into other types of discourse.

While sketching out Evaristo Carriego's personality, Borges decided to give the reader an insight into the erotic sensibility of his subject. Right after telling us that Carriego liked Victor Hugo's and Alexandre Dumas's epic novels (set in Napoleonic times), he finds a way to connect them to (his) sex:

> [Carriego] también solía publicar [contar a los amigos] en su conversación esas preferencias guerreras. La muerte erótica del caudillo Ramírez, desmontado a lanzazos del caballo y decapitado por defender a su [amante] Delfina, y la de Juan Moreira, que pasó de los ardientes juegos del lupanar, a las bayonetas policiales y los balazos, eran muy contadas por él.[33]

The passage reveals Borges's preoccupation with the supposed relationship between sexual potency and courage (physical prowess).[34] This was a widespread philosophical and medical assumption about sexuality in the late nineteenth and early twentieth centuries that he himself modestly articulated in his 1932 prologue to *Discusión* ("vida [sex] y muerte [courage] le han faltado a mi vida").[35] In addition, Carriego's oral performance of *Juan Moreira* is clearly at the origin of Borges's own retelling of Gutiérrez's novel in "La noche de los dones," one of the texts where Borges talked about his own sexual initiation and that also echoes his view of the relationship between

---

32 Borges, *OC* [1974], I, 405.
33 Borges, *OC* [1974], I, 116.
34 In the first edition of *Discusión* (1932), Borges also explored "Esa inmediata sucesión de dos intensidades del cuerpo –el coito y la batalla-," telling a story about one of his nineteenth-century ancestors (General Soler) and citing Gongora's romance "Servía en Orán al Rey," 40–41.
35 Borges, *OC* [1974], I, 177.

sex and courage. Thus the reappearance, much later, of this brief passage of *Evaristo Carriego* (1930) in the form of a short story also indicates that these flashes are not always isolated outbursts of desire but that they reflect persistent concerns and interests of the author.

Let us look at another example, in this case a footnote. Borges, the convinced reader of the Idealist philosopher Arthur Schopenhauer, rejected individuation and accepted the metaphysical proposition that the individual "I" was a delusion and that what really counted was the species. In Borges we find many modulations of this concept, such as his statement about "la primacía de la especie y la casi perfecta nulidad de los individuos," that "el individuo es de algún modo la especie," "cualquier hombre es todos los hombres," or that "lo que hace un hombre es como si lo hicieran todos los hombres," all examples where it is clear that there is no need to resort to sexual imagery to evoke or to illustrate the concept.[36] Yet, in the short story "Tlön, Uqbar, Orbis Tertius," the author inserts a footnote where we suddenly find the following formulation:

> Todos los hombres, en el vertiginoso instante del coito, son el mismo hombre. Todos los hombres que repiten una línea de Shakespeare, *son* William Shakespeare.[37]

The comparison of this articulation of the concept with the others I quoted makes us guess whether the reference to coitus was necessary and think that the example of Shakespeare would probably have sufficed. But the footnote suggests the will to somehow bring sex (his own) into the text: the characterization of coitus here speaks of the nightmarish experience that we also find in his other references to the sex act, such as "minuto incoherente," "aquel desorden perplejo de sensaciones inconexas y atroces," or "mera confusión o felicidad."

"Tlön" is one of the famous "metaphysical fantasies" where Borges blended fiction and philosophy, a mixing of genres that, as we can see, included the passing erotic sign of a footnote. On other occasions the erotic will be blended with equal dexterity but more substantially into texts whose apparent purposes were not to talk about desire and sex, such as in the "Historia de la eternidad" (1936). For reasons of exposition I will consider this important aspect of Borges's literature in chapter 5, where we will see how in this metaphysical essay he integrated the erotic into the exploration of time and eternity and where the reading of Burton's *Nights* shows up in a footnote on Platonic ideas and desire.

Borges, then, spoke of his desire and sex in unexpected places: brief passages, footnotes, and metaphysical speculations. Now let's look at the last of the discreet locations of the erotic that I want to show: very compact

---

36 Borges, *OC* [1974], I, 356; 718; 494; 493.
37 Borges, *OC* [1974], I, 438.

portraits of other writers that turn into mini self-portraits. In effect, the image that Borges had of himself and his personality traits reappears in his telling of other authors' lives. Time and time again, in essays, reviews, notes, and brief biographies, he chooses to tell about their (and his) obsessions, timidity, and sexual troubles. These discreet and indirect self-portraits reflect his belief that these conditions did hold some explanatory power in regard to their literature and his hope that readers will take into account his similar circumstances when they approach his own work. But these self-portraits also suggest that Borges may have thought that their troubles did not prevent those authors from achieving literary glory and, thus he transformed the telling of their lives into self-addressed and reassuring messages of consolation and hope. Reading Borges, we learn that "Melville tenía, como Coleridge, el hábito de la desesperación"[38]; De Quincey "era muy tímido"; in Arthur Machen's "solitaria niñez ... [ha] influído ... la caótica biblioteca de su padre .... [donde] releyó las espléndidas confesiones de otro solitario, De Quincey"; Edward Gibbon "mismo ha confesado que su timidez lo incapacitó para los debates y que el éxito de su pluma desalentó los esfuerzos de su voz"[39]; Andre Gide was "Tímido y reservado" and in *Les nouritures terrestres* "exalta los deseos de la carne pero no su plena satisfacción."[40] On Lewis Carroll and *Alice in Wonderland,* Borges said that "la soledad de Alicia entre sus monstruos refleja la del célibe ... La soledad del hombre que no se atrevió nunca al amor"; of Emily Dickinson, that "No hay, que yo sepa, una vida más apasionada y más solitaria que la de esa mujer. Prefirió soñar el amor y acaso imaginarlo y temerlo."[41]

But no portrait mirrors Borges's own so neatly as that of Edgar Allen Poe. In the essay on the American writer that I have partially analyzed earlier Borges also said:

> La neurosis de Poe le habría servido para renovar el cuento fantástico... Poe se creía poeta, sólo poeta, pero las circunstancias lo llevaron a escribir cuentos, y esos cuentos a cuya escritura se resignó y que debió encarar como tareas ocasionales son su inmortalidad ... sin la neurosis, el alcohol, la pobreza, la soledad irreparable, no existiría la obra de Poe.[42]

As I explained before, the most important aspect of the essay is the proposition that the production and the reading of Poe's literature (like his own and others') was intimately linked to his troubled personality and sexual impotence: without his "neurosis" and his "soledad irreparable," we would

---

38 Borges, *OC* [1974], IV, 470.
39 Borges, *OC* [1974], IV, 502, 379, 69.
40 Borges, *OC* [1974], IV, 463.
41 Borges, *OC* [1974], IV, 102-3; Borges, *CS*, 264; see also Borges on "Sherlock Holmes": "Es casto. Nada sabe del amor. No ha querido. / Ese hombre tan viril ha renunciado al arte / de amar," *OC* [1974], II, 474.
42 Borges, *TR2*, 263-65.

not have his literature. This was a fundamental donnée of Borges's reading, which explains why he opened the text by stating this interpretive key. But the self-portrait goes beyond the similarity of the sexual condition. In the passage quoted here Poe's trajectory, with suspicious precision, parallels Borges's (and not the other way around, I am tempted to say). He says that Poe had initially aspired to be only a poet but that eventually "se resignó" to write short stories "como tareas ocasionales," which gave him "su inmortalidad." This actually was Borges's own personal history: his poetic crisis of the 1930s and his journalistic job in *Multicolor* also imposed on him the writing of short stories that, eventually, granted him the recognition that he had sought but never achieved with his poetry. In the same vein, Poe's troubled sexuality had led to a literary project comparable in form and significance to his own. Borges says that "la neurosis de Poe le habría servido para renovar el cuento fantástico," which closely anticipates the transformative role that he would assign to his own short stories a quarter of century later, in the epilogue of his *Obras completas* (1974) that he wrote in the third person: "[before the publication of his short stories] la prosa narrativa argentina no rebasaba ... el alegato ... Borges, bajo la tutela de sus lecturas septentrionales, la elevó a lo fantástico."[43] Borges's essay on Poe, then, gives us a self-portrait with sexuality and literature intertwined. More generally, it confirms that the telling of other writers' lives by Borges constitutes a discreet genre where we should also look for fragments of his insistent conversation on desire and sex.

I have reviewed, then, three questions that may help us read Borges's expressions of eroticism: the type of desire and sex that we may expect to find in his literature, the forms of their expression, and their multiple locations throughout his writings. What I have tried to show is "the figure" of Borges's erotic discourse "in the Persian carpet" of his oeuvre, and if we stop to look at it, we will see that he spoke about sex more often than we previously thought. Thus, I propose, we should approach his literature as an enigma to be deciphered or, more precisely, we should read it as he read Shakespeare's sonnets. For Borges, they were confessional poems, and because of that, he thought, "la obra es intrincada y oscura." The sonnets, he said, "son confidencias que nunca acabaremos de descifrar."[44] Then, we should not expect Borges's expression of desire and sex to be always self-revelatory and we may need to look at his texts as riddles to be solved.[45]

---

43 Borges, *OC* [1974], I, 1144.
44 Borges, *CS*, 186, 187.
45 On riddling in poetry and how to read them, see Fuller, *Who Is Ozymandias?*

CHAPTER 3

# Borges's Erotic Library
## The Poetry Shelf[1]

In "El otro," an older Borges recalls the texts he held in his bookcase in Geneva, including one "escondido detrás de los demás, un libro en rústica sobre las costumbres sexuales de los pueblos balkánicos"; and immediately afterward, he alluded to his traumatic sexual initiation: "No he olvidado tampoco un atardecer en un primer piso de la plaza Dubourg,"[2] which hinted at a meaningful relationship between his readings and his sexuality. Psychoanalyst Kohan Miller said that one of the ways Borges tried to cope with his overwhelming sexual troubles was, of course, reading: "Borges se detenía en todas las vidrieras de las librerías para ver si había un libro sobre sexualidad. Era un tema sobre el que quería leer, lo quería dominar, quería saber."[3] Dr Kohan Miller had also discovered Borges's erotic sensibility in his responses to literature and women: "a pesar de su problema, sentía placer orgástico [sic] al escuchar ciertas voces femeninas al teléfono, o *cuando leía ciertas frases o versos que indudablemente lo excitaban*. Su sensibilidad resonaba a nivel genital."[4] That is, Borges could be aroused by literature, and the reading of poetry could become an erotic interlude. A woman who experienced that sensibility was Estela Canto. She remembered that in one of their romantic encounters, Borges "se excitaba con las crípticas palabras de un poema leído y releído en la adolescencia" and, against the generalized (and wrong) idea of Borges's "frialdad sexual," she underscored that *"la literatura siempre tuvo temperatura para él."*[5]

So, Borges could be sexually stimulated by literature. Therefore, in a man who often defined himself more as a reader than as an author and who said

---

[1] I presented an incipient version of this and the following chapter at the "Jornadas Internacionales *Borges lector*" held in the Biblioteca Nacional (Buenos Aires), August, 2011. See De la Fuente, "Lecturas eróticas."
[2] Borges, *OC* [1974], II, 12.
[3] Goldaracena, "Las inhibiciones del joven Borges."
[4] Woscoboinik, *El secreto* [1991], 260. Emphasis added.
[5] Canto, *A contraluz*, 280–81. Emphasis added.

"Pocas cosas me han ocurrido y muchas he leído,"[6] the exploration of the pages that he read (and reread) is a fundamental step in locating desire and sex in his own life and texts.

Among texts that explore desire and sex, there is a continuum that begins with literature on "love," passes through "erotica," and ends in "pornography." The borders among categories are usually blurry and slippery, and it is not always easy to decide with certainty where a text fits. Whether a poem or a novel belongs in, say, erotica or pornography, has usually depended on at least two factors: the historical context and the sensibility of the individual reading them. This is a fundamental question if we want to understand Borges as a reader of erotic literature, and why he is still largely perceived as an asexual writer.

The first step, then, is to place Borges's readings in a historical context. Borges famously said that "la biblioteca de mi padre ha sido el hecho capital de mi vida,"[7] which implies that a great deal (if not most) of his favorite readings in any field (not just erotica) were written in the nineteenth century or even in earlier times; he himself has underscored this in his literature: "No en vano fui engendrado en 1899. Mis hábitos regresan a aquel siglo y al anterior."[8] His father's "biblioteca de ilimitados libros ingleses,"[9] where he discovered literature, and which partly shaped his sensibility, was made up primarily of Victorian authors. The fact that Borges had, in many respects, a transformative impact on the culture of the second half of the twentieth century often prevents critics from seeing how "old" and canonical his literary origins were (this has somewhat distorted the extraordinary fact that his radically innovative literature fed off a really "old" one).

Then we have to consider the question of readers' sensibilities, of both Borges and whoever has this book in her hands at the beginning of the twenty-first century. Borges was a modest and reticent man who, as we have seen, considered that "la mejor poesía erótica no es obscena." Yet, decorum is not the same as absence of sex or lack of interest in it but one more intriguing way to get to it: "Combien des jeux très lascivement agréables," noticed Montaigne, "naissent de la manière honnête et pudique de parler des actes de l'amour!"[10] Certainly, decorous literature (or artistic expression) cannot have the same effect on today's readers that it had on Borges. But we need to remember that "l'érotisme est une science individuelle,"[11] and that, therefore, the genre is to a large extent a creation of the subjectivity of the reader (potentially, any text can be experienced as an erotic reading). It is, then, in Borges's own sensibility (not ours) that we have to look for "his" erotic

6 Borges, *OC* [1974], I, 854.
7 Borges, *OC* [1974], II, 202.
8 Borges, *OC* [1974], II, 121.
9 Borges, *OC* [1974], I, 101.
10 Montaigne, *Essais*, II, XV, 748.
11 The insight is the French poet Robert Desnos's, quoted in Goujon, *Anthologie*, 15.

readings. This is one of the problems that Estela Canto herself perceived was behind the extended (and wrong) opinion about Borges's "frialdad sexual": she realized that "los profanos" did not understand that Borges could be aroused, for instance, by the "cryptical words" of a poem.[12]

To better comprehend Borges's reading experience and to understand how he could even be sexually excited by what we would consider very tame poetry, we have to keep in mind that for him literature was both an intellectual game *and* an emotional life experience. Talking about Lugones (and himself) he said that

> para Leopoldo Lugones, la lectura de un texto y el descubrimiento de un escritor no fueron experiencias menos íntimas y esenciales que las desventuras o los dones de una pasión. ¿Qué razón puede haber para no admitir que un literato sea sensible a la literatura?[13]

As we will see numerous times in this chapter, Borges was, indeed, "sensible a la literatura" and, like Don Quijote, he lived through the (erotic) imagination of the authors that he read. The readings became for Borges an experience as "intimate" as "los dones de una pasión" ("the gifts of a love affair").

What did Borges read? His erotic readings covered a fairly wide range of genres and approaches to sexuality and its expression, including philosophy, religion, poetry, narrative fiction, and ethnographic texts (though he was not interested in psychology).[14] Few of the readings qualified, depending on the historical context, as underground erotica or pornography, and it is clear that Borges was careful to downplay or simply hide his familiarity with them (as he did hide his book on the Balkans). However, most of his readings were part of the above-ground erotic literature written by canonized authors to whom he referred openly, and which do not need to be brought bombastically to the surface for the purpose of sensationalism.

In this and the following two chapters, I will attempt to sample Borges's erotic library: first we will look at his poetry shelf, then at his Orientalist erotica, and finally, in chapter 5, we will examine a couple of his volumes on philosophy and sex. The vastness of Borges's readings (even in the erotic genre) inevitably meant choices needed to be made about which authors or texts to include: I tried to find a balance between, on the one hand, the quality of the evidence available and the relevance of the author read; and, on the other, how these factors enhance our appreciation of Borges's sensibility as a reader of erotica and, ultimately, our understanding of his reflections and expressions of desire and sex.

12  Canto, *A contraluz*, 281.
13  Borges, *CS*, 200.
14  Woscoboinik, *El secreto* [1991], 260. According to Kohan Miller, Borges was not interested in reading psychology, which must be understood as either pyschoanalysis or as a clinical discipline; however, he did know psychologists such as William James, whose work intersected with philosophy.

In assessing the erotic literature he read, it is reasonable to conclude that the majority (if not all) of the authors who explored desire and sex *and* who interested Borges were men. To some extent the almost complete absence of women from his repertoire simply reflects that erotic literature published by women in the literary traditions that Borges knew did not become a generalized phenomenon until the second half of the twentieth century, by which time Borges's formative period had long passed (easily verified by looking at specialized anthologies).[15] Yet, the absence of erotica written by women also reflects a personal preference.[16] This can be inferred, for example, from the fact that while Borges considered Dante Gabriel Rossetti to be one of the most important erotic poets, he never read his sister Christina, who also wrote intense poetry on desire and sex. The only explicit reference to a woman's erotic literature that I have found in his writings are the 1921 hostile comments on the erotic poetry of the Argentine Alfonsina Storni. The young Borges said that Storni "se lamenta de que motejen de eróticas sus composiciones. Yo las encuentro cursilitas más bien. Son una cosa pueril ... [con] palabras baratamente románticas [y] cuyo accidental erotismo [es] vergonzante."[17] Although Borges's exclusion of women to some extent reflects the historical realities of an art at the time still dominated by men, his obliteration of voices such as Storni's was not historically inevitable: some men did open to women who wrote erotic poetry. Just across the Río de la Plata, a few years earlier, Delmira Agustini had published *Los cálices vacíos* (1913) with the endorsement of Rubén Darío and the approval of several others (apparently Borges did not read Agustini either). Perhaps the only exception in his negation of women's erotica was Emily Dickinson. It is clear that Borges liked some of her poetry on love and desire but I have not found enough evidence to allow an understanding of how, or whether, she influenced him.[18]

Similarly, after exploring many of Borges's readings, one has the impression that, with the exception of Paul Verlaine, all of the men whose erotic literature interested Borges were heterosexual.[19] Although Walt Whitman

---

15  Pauvert, *Anthologie*; Goujon, *Anthologie*; Provencio, *Antología*.
16  There were very few women authors among his readings in general: in a collection of 494 books on a wide variety of topics owned by Borges for example, only four were written by women and none of them was a major writer. Three of the books are by academics and one, published in 1970, is by a today unknown poet (the book actually seems to have been the author's gift to the already famous Borges); see Borges, *BLL*.
17  Borges, *TR1*, 137. I have found no evidence of Borges using words like "pueril" or "vergonzante" to refer to the erotica written by men.
18  Borges, *ILN*, 31–32; Borges, *CS*, 264–65; I found Borges quoting only three poems by Dickinson; # 1773, for example, he read in a context of a farewell between lovers, Bioy, *Borges*, 1064. However, when in 1962 Bioy and Borges read her poems together, Borges told his friend "casi no la conozco," Bioy, *Borges*, 854.
19  Shakespeare would, perhaps, be among the exceptions. However, it is not clear that Shakespeare's poetry really influenced Borges. He read it as erotic poetry but he rarely quoted or recited the sonnets (beyond some expected prologues). The plays

was a major influence on his poetry, he did not like and clearly rejected Whitman's erotica. As we have seen, when he praised Rossetti's poetry he also compared it to that of the American: "los versos más explícitos de Whitman no son los mejores. ¿Por qué Whitman vuelve a decir groseramente lo que ya dijo con acierto?"[20] This was more than a technical disagreement, and the evidence suggests that his judgement was influenced by the fact that Whitman wrote about gay love. Estela Canto observed that Borges never spoke about male homosexuality and that "la ponía a un lado cuando tropezaba con ella en la literatura."[21] That is, he avoided and suppressed it. This is also the behavior that his selection and translation of the American's poetry reveals. As Balderston has already shown, Borges subjected *Leaves of Grass* to a homophobic reading and translation, thus skipping almost all of the homoerotic poems and disassociating the author from homoeroticism in the only such piece that he selected.[22]

Oscar Wilde is also missing from this group of readings, although the reason for it seems to be somewhat different from the reason for Whitman's absence. Apart from his early essay on "The Ballad of Reading Gaol" (1926) and some other sporadic references or allusions to specific poems such as "The Harlot's House," it seems that Borges was not seriously interested in Wilde's poetry or, more generally, in what Wilde could say about sexuality or the expression of eroticism.[23] For Borges the high value of Wilde's personality and literature was somewhere else. In the essay titled "Sobre Oscar Wilde" (1946), Borges said that the Irish writer "fue un hombre del siglo XVIII, que alguna vez condescendió a los juegos del simbolismo. Como Gibbon, como Johnson, como Voltaire fue un ingenioso que tenía razón además."[24] In the tradition of his countryman Jonathan Swift and the others mentioned, Wilde was, primarily, a satirist and epigrammatist who was a master in the cultivation of irony (in literary and social criticism). Wilde may have condescended to "los juegos del simbolismo"—that is, given the historical context in which he lived, his poetry may have explored the sensual topics of late nineteenth-

> might be a different matter. Yet, it is interesting to note that the surviving records of his classes on English literature at the University of Buenos Aires show that he did not include Shakespeare in his syllabus. The Bard's status in Borges's library, I suspect, is still to be determined.

20 Bioy, *Borges*, 1158.
21 Canto, *A contraluz*, 170.
22 The poem is "When I Heard at the Close of the Day," in Balderston, "Dialectica," 64–66; see also Pérez Marcilla, "El canto," 88–91. The same pattern has been observed in his translation of Virginia Woolf's *Orlando* (done at the request of Victoria Ocampo and for Editorial Sur), in which he blurred and erased the gender ambiguity and homosexuality present in the novel, see Leone, "La novela," 232–33.
23 In the essay on "La balada," Borges compares Wilde to "los magistrales nombres de Swinburne, de Rossetti y hasta ... Tennyson" to his disadvantage: "... los tres lo aventajaron fácilmente en intensidad," Borges, *TME*, 131.
24 Borges, *OC* [1974], I, 692.

century Symbolists and Decadents—but those literary games, Borges thought, did not really interest him nor allow him to show his true genius.

The exploration of Borges's erotic shelves has at least two effects on our view of his personal library: on the one hand rambling through these shelves makes it possible to discover authors who have not been read in relation to Borges's literature, such as the Victorian poets Charles Algernon Swinburne and Dante Gabriel Rossetti, the Argentines Marcelo Del Mazo and Baldomero Fernández Moreno, and the Tunisian Sheikh Nefzaoui. On the other hand, such an exploration allows us to read in a new light narratives like the *Arabian Nights* or an author such as the German philosopher Arthur Schopenhauer who specialists have studied before but without considering the layer of erotic appeal that they had for Borges.

Yet, inevitably, my selection of authors has implied exclusions motivated by different factors. For example, I did not specifically consider Dante because he has been sufficiently studied in relation to Borges's love life.[25] I also left out San Juan de la Cruz, who wrote "la más encendida obra de la lengua castellana,"[26] but this time the reason was the lack of sufficient evidence that would make possible an innovative exploration of Borges as a reader.

I tried to establish a dialogue between the readings and Borges's own life and texts with two purposes in mind. First, and most obviously, because it helps explain and understand Borges's own literature. Second, because it means the realization of an important aspect of Borges's conception of literature: the multiplication and expansion of the literary experience of his readers. In his prologues, epilogues, and endnotes, Borges consistently mentions literary sources or authors, tying them more or less directly to some of his own texts. These commentaries seek to place his own writings within a certain genre or literary tradition, unobtrusively giving the key to the reader as to how he wants his texts to be approached. As an example, when in a prologue Borges says "*En el* Poema conjetural *se advertirá la influencia de los monólogos dramáticos de Robert Browning*,"[27] he is inviting us to actually read the poem along and in dialogue with Browning's dramatic monologues or, more generally, with the best Victorian expressions of that genre. In other words, with the comments on his own work Borges generously brings us into his library and, thus, seeks to multiply our literary experience, endlessly offering more and more of other authors' texts. Carlos Gamerro has commented on Borges's "rara capacidad [para] *contagiarnos* sus lecturas,"[28] and, alluding to his *Biblioteca personal* (1988), the mass market multivolume collection that sampled Borges's readings, Gamerro said that "his personal

---

25 Rodríguez Monegal, *Literary Biography*; Canto, *A contraluz*; Balderston, "*Beatriz Viterbo*"; Williamson, *A Life*; Núñez-Faraco, "Love Sickness."
26 Borges, *OC* [1974], IV, 476.
27 Borges, *OC* [1974], I, 858.
28 Gamerro, "Borges lector," 12. Emphasis in the original.

library" now belongs to all of us.²⁹ The reading of what Borges read, then, is one of the aspirations of this and the following two chapters.

"Ordenar bibliotecas es ejercer, / de un modo silencioso y modesto, / el arte de la crítica,"³⁰ said Borges. So, how to place the readings on his erotic shelves? The material presents specific challenges not easy to solve, so for the exposition of the readings I abstained from a strict analytical criterion and adopted one that followed genres, literary traditions, and disciplines. In this chapter, then, we will read Argentine, French, and British poets. Born out of expository constraints, this organization has some benefits, though: it preserves something of the experience of a Hedonic reader (as Borges defined himself) who roams through his private bookcase, his fingers sensing, one by one, books organized by genre, language (or literary tradition), and discipline.

### Argentine Erotic Poetry

Borges was an attentive and enthusiastic reader of the erotic poetry written in Argentina by the generation of poets that preceded his in the early twentieth century, a corpus that today remains virtually forgotten by scholars and the wider public alike.

One of the practitioners of the genre was the Modernist poet Leopoldo Lugones (1874–1938), the most prominent intellectual figure of Argentina at that time. In books such as *Los crepúsculos del jardín* (1905) and *Lunario sentimental* (1909), Lugones's poetry created artificially rarefied ambiances and dense experiences resorting to a characteristic Modernist backdrop of "crepúsculos" and "lunas," "jardines" and "parques," "estanques" and "cisnes." Borges was an ambitious but critical reader of Lugones, including his erotic poetry. However, although Borges's agonistic relationship with the Modernist poet has been probed,³¹ his reading of Lugones's erotic poetry has received no attention. Bioy Casares's diary, though, invites us to explore this question. In one of their conversations, the two friends discussed, for example, "Delectación morosa," a sonnet in the erotic sequence titled "Los doce gozos," included in *Los crepúsculos del jardín*.³² The poem, which re-created or imagined a sexual encounter at dusk, did not entirely convince them. For instance, Bioy derisively said that Lugones appeared in it as a sexually powerful "macho cabrío." But they also discussed these verses:

---

29 Gamerro, "Borges lector," 12. Balderston has recently also proposed this line of inquiry: "uno de los grandes privilegios de estudiar a Borges es entender la manera en que establece nexos entre sus lecturas e invita a una exploración del mundo de textos que menciona," *Innumerables relaciones*, 11.
30 Borges, "Junio, 1968," *OC* [1974], I, 998.
31 Cajero Vázquez, "Para la lectura"; *Palimsestos*; Dobry, *Una profecía*.
32 Bioy, *Borges*, 82; Lugones, *Obras poéticas*, 117–24.

> Tus rodillas exangües sobre el plinto
>
> Manifestaban la delicia inerte,
> Y a nuestros pies un río de jacinto
> Corría sin rumor hacia la muerte.[33]

In spite of his disapproval of the overall image of the poet suggested by the sonnet, Bioy recognized that the lines "rodillas exangües" that "manifestaban la delicia inerte" were "very good" ("está muy bien"), which Borges also approved: "*Manifestaban* es perfecto."[34] Overall, Borges liked "Delectación morosa": he eventually anthologized it and occasionally he even used its title as a synonym for sexual intercourse or erotic experiences more generally.[35]

But beyond Borges's familiarity with Lugones's work and the revelation of some of his tastes in matters of erotic poetry, Bioy's 1953 recording of their close reading of "Delectación morosa" offers the possibility of illuminating Borges's creative process in a more specific way. During their conversation, Borges asked Bioy: "¿Vos creés que tenía razón [Néstor] Ibarra? ¿Que el *río de jacinto* es el semen?"[36] Lugones's allusion in the last two lines created some hesitation in Borges's understanding of the poem, but, it is clear, they also interested him. He had already discussed the verses with another friend and now he interrogated Bioy, who, more confident, also offered an emphatic judgement: ¿"Qué otra cosa puede ser? La verdad es que no pudo decirlo mejor." His friends' comments on Lugones's poem must have contributed to Borges's decision when, two decades later, he too used the image of the "river" to allude to orgasm and ejaculation in "El congreso" ("oh el amor que fluye en la sombra como un río secreto"), "La noche de los dones" ("el gran río de esa noche"), and "Endimión en Latmos" ("Oh ríos del amor y de la noche").[37] Texts are written "one word at a time," says Francine Prose, and criticism often needs to operate at this level. Here, then, our close reading of the two friends' close reading of "Delectación morosa" allows us a glimpse, at least for an instant, at the creative process of Borges's expressions of desire and sex.

However, as is well known, Borges's opinions both of Lugones as a figure in the history of Argentine literature and of his poetry were ambivalent and over the years went through several ups and downs. Although capable of appreciating Lugones's poetry, Borges possessed a different sensibility, the origin of a disagreement that, in spite of his posthumous recognition and rehabilitation of Lugones, he never hid. In the prologue to a Lugones anthology that he prepared in the last years of his life, Borges pointed out both the virtues and

---

33 Lugones, *Obras poéticas*, 121.
34 Bioy, *Borges*, 82. Italics in the original.
35 Lugones, *Antología poética*, 21; see Borges, *OC* [1974], I, 405 and chapter 4 of this book.
36 Bioy, *Borges*, 82. Italics in the original. Néstor Ibarra was a personal friend of both Bioy Casares and Borges and a translator of Borges's works into French.
37 Borges, *OC* [1974], II, 29, 44, 175.

the limitations of the poems he had chosen. He explained that "Insensible al ambiente de las palabras, a su contexto emocional, Lugones las prodigaba sólo atento a su definición. Alternaba así las fealdades y las bellezas."[38] To illustrate his point, he selected "Oceánida," another sonnet in the sequence mentioned earlier. In this poem, Lugones imagined again the sex act and resorted to the image of the sea as a metaphor for desire ("hinchóse en una ola el mar sereno") and the sexual impulse that it unleashes. Borges said that "Conviven así en [el] mismo soneto" the ugliness of

> El mar, lleno de urgencias masculinas,
> Bramaba alrededor de tu cintura

And the beauty of

> Esa luz de las tardes mortecinas
> Que en el agua pacífica perdura.[39]

The calm and (intimate) rest in the interlude that separates one wave from the next appealed to Borges more than the image of the ocean's powerful movements. Borges also discussed this poem with Bioy Casares, and their conversation revolved around the same questions. But while in the prologue we read a technical and nuanced criticism (he often liked or disliked specific verses rather than entire poems), in his friend's diary we find the record of a more emotional and general reaction against the poem. In addition to the two "ugly" lines referenced in the prologue, Borges also disapproved of the last two lines of the sonnet:

> Y al penetrar entre tus muslos finos,
> La onda se aguzó como una daga.[40]

He said to his friend:

> es una locura: comparar el mar con un coito. Lo de las *urgencias masculinas* es un absurdo. Desde luego, hay que agradecerle al poeta que haya puesto como última palabra *daga*. En ese tren de vulgaridad podría haber escrito: *la onda se aguzó mismo que un pene.*

Bioy concurred: "Sí, es admirable que se haya resignado a escribir *daga*. *Daga* ahí significa *pene*."[41]

For Borges there was no sense of proportion in the comparison between the intimacy of the sex act and the vastness of the ocean, in spite of the fact that the movement and the energy of the sea had invited Lugones to think otherwise. As a result, Borges felt, the poet offered the reader more a metaphor than a believable insight. He criticized again the choice of

---

38 Borges, *CS*, 224.
39 Borges, *CS*, 224.
40 Bioy, *Borges*, 392.
41 Ibidem. Emphasis in the original.

"urgencias masculinas," which was, as we have seen, one of those instances in which Lugones showed himself "insensible al ambiente de las palabras." To understand this disagreement, it is also helpful to look at Borges's own poetry. For example, in "Villa Urquiza" (an erotic sonnet from the 1920s), he alludes to desire as "urgencia de ternura," which, I think, is evidence of Lugones's well-known influence on Borges's early poetry.[42] However, in the imitation we can also see the difference: with the noun "ternura" his desire includes the search for the woman's sentiment, while Lugones's adjective "masculinas" speaks more of the man's physiological needs than of an amorous relationship.[43] Borges also perceived in Lugones an inclination to ostentation not only in the display of his rhetoric and verbal artifices but also in the persona that his poems insinuated (Bioy agreed: he said that Lugones saw himself as a sexually powerful "macho cabrío"). In his poetry, Borges thought, Lugones was often more interested in surprising or even scandalizing than in presenting a new gaze or reality. The problem with the phallic allusion, then, was not so much that it was denominative and direct (as we will see, Borges liked some very explicit poems), but that the metaphor allowed the reader to see a rhetorically and sexually vain poet. Therefore, in this sonnet, some of Lugones's choices resulted, for Borges, in "vulgarity."

However, if the too Modernist sonnets in "Los doce gozos" created hesitations and provoked rejections in Borges, the older poet did win his approval with a later poem that Borges read biographically and that he considered one of Lugones's best. In the prologue to the 1982 anthology mentioned above, he says that Lugones was a "public" poet who "rara vez nos confía su intimidad."[44] But "Alma venturosa" (1922) was different:

> Al promediar la tarde de aquel día,
> Cuando iba mi habitual adiós a darte
> Fue una vaga congoja de dejarte
> Lo que me hizo saber que te quería.

"El poeta," says Borges in his comment on the stanza, "elude la hora romántica del ocaso, nos da a entender que se veían todos los días, y una

---

42  Cajero Vázquez, "Para la lectura"; on "Villa Urquiza," see chapter 6.
43  But this critique of Lugones, which Borges articulated later in life, may have been more than a settling of scores with the master: it may also have been aimed against his own early poetry that he endlessly rewrote and, even, suppressed. This seems to be the case also with his rejection of the sea as an erotic metaphor, which he himself had used in 1919 in "Himno del mar," a poem in which intensely sexualized imagery (but not the form) exhibits points of contact with Lugones ("Mar con ritmos amplios como las olas jadeantes," "besa los pechos dorados de vírgenes playas que aguardan sedientas," Borges, *TR1*, 24–26). Borges never included it in a book, and in his "Autobiographical Essay," he said of the poem that "Today [1970], I hardly think of the sea, or even of myself, as hungering for stars," 31.
44  Borges, *CS*, 222.

vaga congoja, no una gran pena, le revela que está enamorado."[45] That is, he approves that Lugones places the amorous encounter not in the too Modernist and erotically suggestive dusk (as was the case, for example, of "Delectación morosa") but in the more serene afternoon, which corresponds well with the sentimental moderation of "vaga congoja." The stanza re-creates not an ideal or exceptional moment but a daily affectionate occurrence, whose commonality lends a sense of credibility to the scene.

But more than anything, I think, what in this poem captured Borges's will and convinced him was the form of the revelation: the poet does not want to be separated from the woman, he wants to stay with her, and the vague sadness that he experiences at that moment reveals to him that he is in love. This is the way Borges felt in some of his own romantic relationships. In the early 1960s, as he was starting to see a woman, Bioy Casares wrote: "Dice que está enamorado; un síntoma: basta que se la nombren [cuando ella está ausente] para sentirse desdichado … le gustaría quedarse con ella."[46] The identity between Borges's sentiments and the poetry of Lugones is clear: the absence of (or the separation from) the woman causes a revelation ("un síntoma"), and he realizes that he would like to stay with her ("le gustaría quedarse con ella"). Life and literature shaped each other: Borges felt what he read, but he also accepted Lugones's poem because that is how he felt. And thus, in "Alma venturosa" the match between Lugones's and Borges's sensibilities rendered the former credible and convinced the reader of the confessional nature of the poem. It was this infrequent encounter between the sensibilities of the two poets, I think, that explains why Borges, who generally resisted Lugones's poems, considered these verses "quizá [su] mejor estrofa."[47]

★_★_★

Borges reserved a special place in his erotic library for Marcelo del Mazo (1879–1968). In 1930 Borges already considered him to be an "escritor olvidado con injusticia," and today del Mazo is unknown even among specialists. Del Mazo was a cousin of Macedonio Fernández and shared with Borges's father the friendship of Evaristo Carriego (he was "el amigo más real de Carriego"[48]). Del Mazo published only one book in two installments: the first series, *Los vencidos (La medalla)*, in 1906, and the second series, *Los vencidos (El amor en la calle)*, in 1910. Borges read and liked the latter. The

---

45  Borges, *CS*, 223.
46  Bioy, *Borges*, 1027.
47  Borges, *OC* [1974], II, 215.
48  Borges, OC [1974], I, 116–17; Del Mazo was also a friend of the thug Nicolás Paredes (whom Borges met and wrote a poem about), Bioy, *Borges*, 598. Del Mazo helped publish Carriego's poetry after his death and was one of Borges's informants for his biography of the Palermo neighborhood's poet, Borges, *OC* [1974], I, 103.

short stories and the poems of the book, he said, were "eslabonados por el nexo común de la crispatura trágica y la motivación erótica."[49] Indeed, Del Mazo's stories and poems are not sensual celebrations of sex but explorations of the sordid anxiety of unfulfilled desire among Porteños and of the painful destruction that its satisfaction often unleashes. Del Mazo was another literary inheritance that Borges received from his father, but while in Macedonio he found a kindred metaphysician, and Carriego discovered the *arrabal* for him, with *Los vencidos* he was able to see the "realidad violenta" and "admirablemente mezquina" of sex in Buenos Aires.[50]

In spite of Del Mazo's meager output and literary marginality, Borges loyally treasured his erotic poems and throughout the years included them in anthologies.[51] For the 1921 review essay "La lírica argentina contemporánea," the young Borges chose "Incontaminado," in which a married man resists and resents the sexual advances of his barely covered sister-in-law:

> ¿Por qué te aproximas mostrando tu cálido cuerpo
> apenas oculto por veste de leve tejido?
> ¿Por qué has envidiado el lecho que ocupa tu hermana
> si sabes que de ella por ley y por coito yo soy el marido?
> ...........................
> ¿Por qué me interrumpes la plácida luz de mis horas
> con invitaciones de fresas prohibidas o goces bestiales?[52]

The poem offers a disturbing scene of incestuous desire ("por ley y por coito yo soy el marido," "fresas prohibidas") and sexual competition between kin ("has envidiado el lecho que ocupa tu hermana"). Although the forbidden lust threatens the life of the family, the virtue of the "Incontaminado" object of desire deflects the base passion of his sister-in-law and, thus, annuls its destructive force ("la gota de sangre de Cristo que tengo, me salva," says the epigraph by Almafuerte[53]). Among the erotic poems of *Los vencidos*, this is the only one that touches on the question of incest; that is, it intersects with experiences that we know mattered for Borges and that his own literature shows that he too was interested in understanding. Borges resented that his father cheated on his mother and he asked himself "por qué elegía a las parientas y a las amigas de madre"[54] to do it with (his father was not "Incontaminado"). In addition, the poem re-creates a virtual "incest of the second type" that reminds us of Borges's (then recent) life in Geneva, where

---

49 Borges, *TR1*, 134.
50 Borges, *TR1*, 134.
51 Borges et al., *Antología poética*, 63–65; Borges and Bullrich, *El compadrito*, 152–54; he also included Del Mazo in *ET*.
52 Del Mazo, *Los vencidos*, 133; also in Borges, *TR1*, 133–34.
53 Del Mazo, *Los vencidos*, 133.
54 Bioy, *Borges*, 1421.

he shared a sexual partner with his father (or suspected he did) and, at the same time, anticipates his own literary exploration of sexual competition between siblings in "La intrusa."

★_★_★

Baldomero Fernández Moreno (1886–1950), whom Borges also read with interest, was one of the best-known and more widely taught poets in twentieth-century Argentina. The main subject of his poetry was the modern city, and he is still primarily recognized as the first to have truly exploited the poetical possibilities of Buenos Aires.[55] His poems looked at discreet realities and daily occurrences that the previous literature had largely not considered worthy of art. They spoke about characters and landscapes in "lacónicos versos" written with "palabras traslúcidas,"[56] one of the qualities that, according to Borges, defined the daily and plain "sencillez" of his poetry.

Fernández Moreno was part of the reaction against the rhetorical excesses of the Modernist school, and it is not a coincidence that Borges often read him in comparison with Lugones, to the detriment of the latter. For instance, speaking about Lugones's *Libro de los paisajes* (1917), Borges said that its poems had some "toques realistas" or a sort of "realismo fragmentario ... perdidos entre ornamentos retóricos y vagas efusiones líricas. No vemos los paisajes de Lugones como vemos, por ejemplo, los de Fernández Moreno."[57] While in Lugones's poems, ostentatious words and rhetorical devices rose as barriers between the reader and the experience that the poet wanted to convey, Fernández Moreno's poetry offered a neat and persuasive vision of the world around us. Thus, the directness of the vision and the realism of the images were two other fundamental characteristics that Borges liked in the "sencillista" poet.

In the prologue to the *Antología poética argentina* (1941) that he prepared with Bioy Casares and Silvina Ocampo, Borges defined Fernández Moreno as a "poeta mayor"[58] in the Argentine tradition (along with a few others such as Lugones or Ezequiel Martínez Estrada) and to support his judgement he published more poems by Fernández Moreno than by the average poet included in the volume. With his anthology and comments, Borges himself helped build the long-lasting critical consensus around Fernández Moreno as the "sencillista" poet of Buenos Aires, an image that still dominates (and rightly so) the reception of his work.

Yet, unlike most of his contemporaries and today's critical consensus, Borges also read Fernández Moreno as a great erotic poet, a dimension of his work that has been largely lost. In a 1973 interview, decades after Fernández Moreno's

---

55  Monteleone, "La invención" [2006].
56  Borges, *BEH*, 161.
57  Borges, *OCC*, 479.
58  Borges et al., *Antología poética*, 8.

death, Borges pointed out the incomplete critical memory that persisted around the poet: "hay otro aspecto de Fernández Moreno que no ha sido debidamente valorado, y es que fue un admirable poeta erótico, y esto suele olvidarse."[59] This reading was not based on how frequently the poet had written on erotic matters but on the few yet, according to Borges, great poetic achievements that Fernandez Moreno's work exhibited on the subject. An evidence of Borges's interest in Fernández Moreno's erotic poetry can be found, for example, in *Destiempo*, the short-lived literary magazine that he edited with Bioy Casares in the 1930s: Fernández Moreno contributed twice to the publication and one of the pieces was an erotic sonnet.[60] But it is the selection contained in the 1941 anthology that more clearly shows the weight that erotic poetry had in Borges's critical appraisal of Fernández Moreno: although in his books the moments of eroticism were few and far between, they are over-represented in Borges's anthology (half of them are erotic poems).[61] Moreover, the 1941 volume offers a more extensive repertoire than even the specialized anthologies of erotic poetry, which usually dispatch Fernández Moreno's production with only one title ("Soneto de los amantes," also included by Borges).[62] The silhouette of the poet that appears in Borges's anthology, then, is significantly different from the image that has been preserved by the critical consensus and that appears in recent studies on the poet.[63]

Later events in Fernández Moreno's literary history also help understand (and confirm) Borges's sensibility to reading the poet. In his canonizing and widely read *Antología, 1915–1940* (also first published in 1941), Fernández Moreno himself suppressed almost all of the erotic poems that he had published in individual books since 1915, thus fundamentally contributing to the creation of today's critical consensus around his work.[64] Borges's view of his poetry, therefore, partially contradicted what the poet himself wanted to show. Moreover, in the 1940s, unknown to Borges, Fernández Moreno would write *Libro de Sara* and *Elegía de la Alondra*, two collections entirely dedicated to erotic poetry that were kept secret and that were to be published only long after his death. It was in 1998 that these numerous poems eventually came out and, indeed, they confirmed Fernández Moreno as a dedicated and notable practitioner of the genre, as Borges, the ever insightful reader, had sensed in the 1930s and 1940s.[65]

59 Sorrentino, *Siete conversaciones*, 237.
60 "Soneto," *Destiempo*, Año 1, #1 (Octubre 1936), 2.
61 It includes "Soneto de los Amantes," "Soneto de tus Vísceras," and "Revelación."
62 Provencio, *Antología*; Latino, *Antología*.
63 Monteleone, "La invención."
64 The anthology went through numerous editions, and the author never added any of his poems on desire and sex except for "Soneto de tus vísceras," arguably not as risqué as most of them.
65 Critical consensus dies hard: even though the poems are now available, critics do not even mention them in their studies.

To further understand and illustrate Borges's reading of Fernández Moreno, I would like to take a brief look at "Roja inicial," a poem virtually unknown today. In 1940 (a year before his *Antología poética argentina* was published), Borges wrote an article in *El Hogar* (a magazine with a readership of middle-class homemakers) whose purpose was both to celebrate the twenty-fifth anniversary of the publication of Fernández Moreno's *Las iniciales del misal* (1915; his first book) and to evaluate his contribution to Argentine poetry (Borges considered him a "revolucionario"). In the article, Borges praised "Roja inicial," said that it represented "con plenitud" "la carnalidad" that could be found in Fernández Moreno's poetry, and pondered whether it was a piece of "recuerdo" (of an actually lived sexual experience) or of "esperanza" (an expression of desire). Borges also acknowledged that the poem was "demasiado explícito" to be published in its totality and, thus, he decided to quote only the beginning:

> Yo te he soñado en esta larga noche,
> toda desnuda en tu esplendor moreno
> sobre el rojo damasco de mi cama.
>
> Lacios, negros, opacos, tus cabellos
> en aislados mechones, descendían
> hasta el heroico cisma de tus senos.[66]

These first six verses were all that Borges dared to (or could) show to the readers of *El Hogar* in 1940; but now we can see the rest:

> Luego el vientre fugaz, luego el triángulo
> encrespado y oculto de tu sexo,
> luego las piernas finas y nerviosas
> y los menudos pies. La luz del techo,
> en antiguos cristales prisionera,
> era en tus ojos un punto de fuego,
> un brillo de saliva entre tus dientes,
> un relámpago de oro por tu cuerpo,
> una escama de nácar en tus uñas
> y una oleada de púrpura en mi lecho!
>
> Como brazos de cruz, eran tus brazos
> para el niño Jesús de mis deseos![67]

The enthralled poet looks at a young naked woman lying on the bed of her sexual initiation ("Roja inicial," "una oleada de púrpura en mi lecho"). Written in a bare language that harmoniously corresponds with the subject, Fernández Moreno achieves a visual and direct poem that carries a powerful

---

66 Borges, *BEH*, 161.
67 Fernández Moreno, *Las inciales*, 85–86.

sense of realism ("su visión," said Borges of the poet, "es realidad de vida, hecha directamente realidad de arte"[68]). The erotic imagination manifested in this piece is reminiscent of the one that we find in poems such as John Donne's "Love's Progress" or, perhaps more relevant in this case, Charles Baudelaire's "Les promesses d'une visage." Thus, the gaze of the poet first lands on the woman's hair and then moves down through her body, palpably stops at her pubis, and then reaches further down. The light descends and outlines her naked figure against the backdrop of the dark apricot blankets. "Roja inicial" is, indeed, one of those "poesías que son la plenitud de una sola mirada,"[69] as Borges said. A gaze whose sensual displacement through the body suggests the build-up of the (quasi mystical) desire that explicitly crowns the poem.

Borges's enthusiasm for the piece adds another layer to his views on erotic poetry. As we have seen before, he essentially equated explicitness with obscenity, a criterion that fundamentally guided his rejections. Yet, "Roja inicial" is an exception to his own rule. Or simply a contradiction, whose motivations, at least in some cases, can be discerned: explicitness was a negative quality that Borges invoked to reject Whitman's homoerotic poems, but it apparently turned into a positive one in "Roja inicial," where the subject was heterosexual desire.

The partial publication of the poem also gives us a perspective on Borges's own sense of decorum and reticence as well as on the social expectations of propriety that compounded them. The article in *El Hogar* leaves no doubt that he wanted to highlight Fernández Moreno's erotic poetry, but it is also clear that he stopped the reproduction of the text right before the verses that gave form, almost texture, to the sex of the woman. It was the poetic (yet, direct) view of the pubis that, arguably, transformed an erotic poem (that sensually allowed the reader to look at the woman's breasts) into one "demasiado explícito" that could not be published in its entirety. Most likely, the suppression was not Borges's exclusive decision, and it is reasonable to think that the editor of a magazine addressed to middle-class homemakers must have had a say in it. A somewhat similar situation may explain that, in spite of finding that "Roja inicial" represented "con plenitud" "la carnalidad" of Fernández Moreno's poetry, Borges did not include it in his 1941 anthology, in which, however, the erotic compositions occupied ample space. Once again, the avoidance of the poem might not be entirely due to Borges's sense of decorum: it could be that Silvina Ocampo and Bioy Casares did not approve of it or that it was a matter of self-restraint in the context of a politically and culturally repressive right-wing regime that had arrested authors and censored poetry, plays, and films for similar or even tamer expressions of eroticism.[70]

---

68 Borges, *TR1*, 253.
69 Borges, *BH*, 160.
70 In addition to the prosecution of Barón Biza as a *pornografista* for his novel *El derecho de matar* (discussed in the introduction), it is worth mentioning that in 1935, poet

Regardless, the case of "Roja inicial" shows that Borges could like explicit expressions of eroticism and allows us to rediscover both a dimension of Borges's reading of Fernández Moreno that has been missed and the latter's largely forgotten stature as an erotic poet.

## Paul Verlaine

Borges arguably read Paul Verlaine (1844–1896) with unparalleled pleasure ("el placer que nos da Verlaine no podemos encontrarlo en otros"[71]). He admired Verlaine's "auditiva" and "musical" poetry[72] and the delicate impressions and emotions that he found in it (Verlaine preferred "el matiz al color"[73]). For Borges, Verlaine was "el ejemplo de puro poeta lírico."[74] Borges ranked him among the most important poets of all time, such as Dante, Fray Luis de León, and Víctor Hugo, and placed him above Baudelaire, Rimbaud, and Mallarmé.[75]

Among the many meaningful literary experiences that Borges the reader had, Verlaine seems to have been special. Late in life he said that "la revelación" of Verlaine's "mágica música" had been "importante ... para [su] historia personal."[76] This is also probably why Borges chose the last verse of "Art poétique" ("Et tout le reste est littérature") to close the very personal dedication of his *Obras completas* to his mother.[77] With Verlaine's poetry, Borges developed not only a personal but also an intimate relationship: the best way to approach it, he felt, was to read one poem at a time and then "quedarse con su eco, recoger su melancolía."[78]

Verlaine, as is well known, coined the idea of the "poète maudit," and his "vices," alcohol and bisexuality, transformed him into its archetype. Rubén Darío, who met Verlaine in the 1890s, said: "Raras veces ha mordido cerebro humano con más furia y ponzoña la serpiente del sexo."[79] Indeed, Verlaine's desire for women prostitutes and his passionate love for men (most famously for Arthur Rimbaud) largely defined him in the eyes of his contemporaries, while he struggled painfully with the shame and guilt that his sexuality caused him.

---

and journalist Raúl González Tuñón had been jailed because of his leftist poetry and journalistic writings and that in 1936 *Tumulto*, a book of poetry by José Portogalo, had been censored also for its alleged pornography, see Cane Carrasco, "Unity," 443, 448–53.

71 Bioy, *Borges*, 882.
72 Borges, *OC* [1974], II, 281.
73 Borges, *OC* [1974], II, 338.
74 Borges, *OC* [1974], I, 79.
75 Bioy, *Borges*, 662, 888, 1200.
76 Borges, *OC* [1974], II, 425.
77 Borges, *OC* [1974], Ibidem, I, 9.
78 Bioy, *Borges*, 887–88.
79 Darío, *Los raros*, 48.

Verlaine's entire work is traversed by an extraordinary sensuality and, not surprisingly, Borges read him also as an erotic poet. Although apparently he did not know the clandestine *Femmes* and *Hombres* (the latter on gay love), he did find Verlaine's eroticism in books such as *Poèmes saturniens* and *Romances sans paroles*. Thus, and just as an example of how those canonical works could be read in an erotic key, Bioy told Borges that in the poem "Green," the verses "sur votre jeune sein laissez rouler ma tête / toute sonore encor de vos derniers baisers" referred to "el sueño antes del coito."[80] While Bioy's reading may sound almost crude, for Borges Verlaine's eroticism could become part of his own personal and intimate experience. In 1921, after enjoying sex with two prostitutes in a Spanish brothel, Borges wrote a literary friend,

> la gloire s'est éteinte. Je me sens "tel qu'un orphelin pauvre sans sœur aînée." Vraiment j'ai aimé cette Luz [one of the prostitutes] qui me traitait en gamin et dont les gestes étaient d'une indécence ingénue.[81]

In the letter Borges quoted one verse and echoed others from "Vœu," a sonnet in *Poèmes saturniens*, in which Verlaine re-created the warm sensations of his early heterosexual experiences in brothels, and the melancholia and solitude that followed:[82]

> Ah! les oaristys! les premières maîtresses!
> L'or des cheveux, l'azur des yeux, la fleur des chairs,
> Et puis, parmi l'odeur des corps jeunes et chers,
> La spontanéité craintive des caresses!
>
> Sont-elles assez loin toutes ces allégresses
> Et toutes ces candeurs! Hélas! Toutes devers
> Les printemps des regrets ont fui les noirs hivers
> Des mes ennuis, des mes dégoûts, de mes détresses!
>
> Si que me voilà seul à présent, morne et seul,
> Morne et désespéré, plus glacé qu'un aïeul,
> Et tel qu'un orphelin pauvre sans sœur aînée.
>
> Ô la femme à l'amour câlin et réchauffant,
> Douce, pensive et brune, et jamais étonnée,
> Et qui parfois vous baise au front, comme un enfant![83]

Borges's narration of his sexual experience closely parallels the emotional insights and sentiments that we find in Verlaine's poem: in both we find the

---

80 Bioy, *Borges*, 881.
81 Borges to Maurice Abramowicz, Barcelone, March 2, 1921, *Cartas del fervor*, 146.
82 On "Vœu" as Verlaine's re-creation of his sexual initiation, see Richardson, *Verlaine*, 26–27.
83 Verlaine, *Œuvres Poétiques Complètes*, 62–63.

Edenic innocence ("gestes ... d'une indécence ingénue" / "La spontanéité ... des caresses"), the sense of loss and melancholia after sex ("la gloire s'est éteinte" / "Sont ... assez loin ... ces allégresses"), the emotional vulnerability that follows ("tel qu'un orphelin pauvre sans sœur aînée"), and the quasi motherly love that they believed they found in the prostitutes ("j'ai aimée cette Luz qui me traitait en gamin" / "Ô la femme à l'amour câlin et rechauffant ... vous baise au front, comme un enfant").

Borges lived and observed his sexual experience through Verlaine's re-creation of his own. Life through literature, again. But here I would like to point out two questions that would allow us to have a more comprehensive understanding of Borges's reading. First, the fact that he lives his brothel experience through "Vœu"—a poem that, Verlaine scholars have pointed out, re-created the poet's early sexual experiences with prostitutes—implies that Borges read rather literally and in a biographical key an author who was, however, "el ejemplo de puro poeta lírico."

Second, if it is true that he said "Pocas cosas me han ocurrido y muchas he leído,"[84] it would be wrong to assume that the identity between Verlaine's poetry and Borges's sentiments was the result of a one-way process in which the poem of the former shaped the feelings of the latter. Actually, it is better to think of it as an encounter in which Borges's own sensibilities, both literary and personal, prepared him for the poem. For example, commenting on Verlaine's evocation of the women's young and perfumed bodies ("la fleur des chairs ... l'odeur des corps jeunes"), Borges told Bioy: "Qué bien que hable del olor de los cuerpos [jóvenes] de las muchachas."[85] Borges seems to have been sensitive in this respect and to have thought that the age of bodies somehow corresponded with their odor, which apparently was a factor in his attraction to women. Or in their rejection: talking about an older woman, Borges also told his friend: "las mujeres, a esa edad ... esos pechos en desorden ... hasta feo olor tendrá."[86]

Other relevant evidence also allows us to see the type of sensibility that Borges brought into his own reading of Verlaine's poem. In "Vœu," as in Borges's letter, we find a love relationship that is both saintly and profane and that reveals a sense of unequal power between an emotionally vulnerable young man and a stronger, motherly prostitute. This type of relationship will reappear many years later in Borges's representations of the experience of venal sex: in "La noche de los dones," in which a mature and weathered prostitute carefully initiates a trembling youth ("Acercate que no te voy a hacer ningún mal"), and in "Emma Zunz," when the protagonist pretends to be a prostitute ("De uno, muy joven, temió que le inspirara alguna ternura y optó por otro").[87] Certainly the reading of "Vœu" and other similar works

---

84 Borges, *OC* [1974], I, 854.
85 Bioy, *Borges*, 886.
86 Bioy, *Borges*, 1151.
87 Borges, *OC* [1974], I, 566 and II, 43.

must have contributed to the formulation of this insight in Borges's narratives. Yet, and as we will see in chapter 7, in other moments of his literature and life not necessarily linked to venal sex, Borges established and re-created this type of asymmetrical relationships with women, a kind of emotional tie whose ubiquity and persistence suggest that it was a trait of his personality. As Julio Woscoboinik pointed out: "Borges fue siempre un niño-grande, un grande-niño. Las relaciones que estableció con las distintas mujeres que figuraron en su vida, tienen las características propias de las filiales, con los matices típicos del hijo tierno, arbitrario, caprichoso, seductor y exigente."[88]

British Erotic Poetry

The Victorian Dante Gabriel Rossetti (1828–1882), a founder of the Pre-Raphaelite Brotherhood, was one of Borges's references in erotic literature and a poet that he read with true passion. To start, I want to quote a passage of *A contraluz*, in which Estela Canto remembered one of the walks that she took with Borges around Buenos Aires, in the mid-1940s:

> [Borges] me apretaba entre sus brazos, yo podía sentir su virilidad, pero nunca fue más allá de unos cuantos besos.
> Estaba exaltado; citaba poemas en inglés ... recuerdo en especial los versos de un poema inglés que me recitaba ... acerca de un hombre "who thought, as his own mother kissed his eyes / Of what her kiss was when his father woed [sic]" ...Versos muy extraños, por cierto. Y los repetía como formulando una pregunta.[89]

The "strange" verses of an apparently unknown poet that Borges recited when he was aroused actually came from the sonnet "Inclusiveness," by Rossetti. Rossetti was an important figure for Borges, which has generally been overlooked by studies of his life and work. He considered the English writer "uno de los grandes poetas del mundo."[90] But for him, Rossetti was, more than anything, an erotic poet: "El tema esencial de toda su poesía es el acto sexual; cuando no trata del acto sexual, no escribe con fuerza; el acto sexual es *su* tema," he told Bioy Casares.[91] As we have seen, Rossetti also set a standard for erotic poetry and guided Borges's expectations for the genre: "La mejor poesía erótica no es obscena. Uno de los mejores ejemplos es la delicadeza y la sabiduría poética de Rossetti."[92] Borges's taste for Rossetti's eroticism certainly responded to the sensibilities of a certain historical period, as he himself warned his students at the University of Buenos Aires: "ahora [en 1966 los sonetos de Rossetti] no nos parecen demasiado eróticos, como

---

88 Woscoboinik, *El secreto* [1988], 47.
89 Canto, *A contraluz*, 95–96.
90 Borges, *BP*, 259.
91 Bioy, *Borges*, 389, emphasis in the original.
92 Bioy, *Borges*, 1157–58.

pudieron parecer en la época Victoriana."[93] Yet, as Borges well knew, in his own time Rossetti's erotic poetry had been very controversial and got him involved in one of the most notorious literary exchanges in Victorian England.[94]

The sonnet "Inclusiveness" that Borges recited to Estela Canto is one of the best-known pieces in the one-hundred-and-one-sonnet sequence *The House of Life* (1870), the most ambitious of Rossetti's poetic enterprises and one that meant his recognition as the master of the genre in late Victorian times. Specifically, Borges quoted these four lines:

> What man has bent o'er his son's sleep, to brood
> How that face shall watch his when cold it lies?—
> Or thought, as his own mother kissed his eyes,
> Of what her kiss was when his father wooed?[95]

In the sonnet Rossetti explores the passing of time, taking the spiritual life of the household (inhabited by people as well as by souls) as the landscape of his investigation. Thus, the rooms and the furniture have seen different generations and many individual experiences and, in turn, for each of them a corner or a table meant something different. In the same vein, in the four lines quoted above, Rossetti articulates the turnover of generations in the inversion of the position of the father's and son's faces and in the differing meanings that the same expressions of love might have for parents and children.[96] In addition, the last two lines also express, within the domain of the household, the theme of the relationship between "sacred love" or "spiritual beauty" on the one hand, and "profane love" or "body's beauty" (and eroticism), on the other, a key component of Rossetti's poetry and art. In "Inclusiveness" the poet interrogates the two sides of the love of the mother: the kiss that for the new generation is the realization of "sacred love" but that for the previous one was part of "profane love."

93 Borges, *BP*, 266.
94 The Scottish critic Robert Buchanan, Borges said, "se había escandalizado ante la franqueza, digamos, de ciertos poemas de Rossetti" (Borges, *BP*, 266) and in 1871, in a pseudonymous review titled "The Fleshly School of Poetry," he attacked Rossetti for his erotic poetry and accused him of "[extolling] fleshliness as the distinct and supreme end of poetic and pictorial art" (to which the latter responded with a legendary essay titled "The Stealthy School of Criticism"), Rossetti, *Collected Poetry*, 335.
95 Rossetti, *Collected Poetry*, 155. "Inclusiveness" is sonnet 63 of the 101 comprised in the sequence.
96 In this respect it is interesting to note that William Rossetti, the brother of the poet and editor of his works, called attention to the limitations of "Inclusiveness" as a title and said that the words "many-sidedness" or "divergent identities" might be more apt to convey what Dante Gabriel meant by the sonnet, quoted in Holmes, *Dante Gabriel Rossetti*, 15. Borges also found the title insufficient: "a sonnet that labors under the not-too-beautiful title 'Inclusiveness,'" Borges, *CV*, 12.

The poem appears in Borges's classes, conferences, and testimonies of his life with a frequency rarely paralleled by other pieces of poetry. The ubiquity of Rossetti's lines, particularly of the last two, tells of Borges's noticeable preoccupation with his parents' sex and the related question of incest. Indeed his own explicit reflection on the verses indicates the nature of his interest in them: he said that "psychology has made us more sensitive to [the] lines 'Or thought, as his own mother kissed his eyes, / Of what her kiss was when his father wooed?'"[97] It is certainly from this perspective that we may study their presence in his life and literature.

These lines, for instance, seem to have been the point of departure for the interrogation of the sex life of parents in "Emma Zunz." A look at the ways Borges translated them into Spanish makes it easier to see it:

*O pensó cuando su propia madre* le besaba los ojos / lo que habrá sido su beso *cuando su padre la cortejaba*.[98]

In this translation, done in class for his students at the University of Buenos Aires, Borges preferred to be literal and to maintain the rather muted Victorian eroticism of Rossetti's original ("wooed" her / "la cortejaba"). But in his conversation with Bioy Casares, we find a slightly different rendition, in which sex is more explicit:

se pregunta también *si el hijo*, cuando la madre lo besa, *piensa en los besos que ella dio (o recibió) al concebirlo*.[99]

And Borges thus articulates the thoughts of the narrator (not of Emma) when the character has sex for the first time:

*Pensó (no pudo no pensar)* que su padre le había hecho a su madre la cosa horrible que a ella ahora le hacían. *Lo pensó* ....[100]

The formulation is certainly reminiscent of "Inclusiveness" and, equally significant, there is a similar questioning gaze on the parents' sex life from the standpoint of the offspring, which parallels Borges's mode when he recited it to Estela Canto ("Los repetía como formulando una pregunta"). Along with other authors, such as Schopenhauer, then, Rossetti was one of the readings to which Borges resorted to think about his parents' "horrible" sex life.

However, although Rossetti's verses include the father, what triggers the son's interrogation is the kiss that he receives from his mother, which makes him aware of her sex life and erotic appeal. In Borges's work, we find discreet and oblique speculative allusions about the sexiness and eroticism of mothers (and his mother), which allow the establishment of another

---

97 Borges, *CV*, 13. Here Borges does not refer to his own knowledge or reading of psychology but to the sensibility of readers in the second half of the twentieth century.
98 Borges, *BP*, 268. Emphasis added.
99 Bioy, *Borges*, 1128. Emphasis added.
100 Borges, *OC* [1974], I, 566. Emphasis added.

continuum between his insistent interest in Rossetti's lines and his own texts. In "La señora mayor," the narrator asks himself, "Quién sabe qué tumulto de pasiones, ahora perdidas y que ardieron, hubo en esa vieja mujer, que había sido agraciada," and in "El amenazado," probably his best-known erotic poem, he invokes "el joven amor de mi madre" as one of the talismans against the threat of love and sex with women.[101] Borges's thoughts regarding the sex life of mothers also include reflections on incest: in "La secta del Fénix" he says that the sexual act "se transmite de generación en generación, pero el uso no quiere que las madres lo enseñen a los hijos,"[102] a formulation that suggests that Borges may have considered that this sexual taboo was as arbitrary as other social norms. He also wrote about this question in "El incesto," a text situated in Ancient times, in which a man dreams that he has sex with his mother.[103] How to interpret this presence of mothers' eroticism in Borges? We can hypothesize that in the same way that impotence seemed to have provoked in him a fear of homosexuality, perhaps it was his unusual emotional closeness with Leonor that fed his oblique reflections on the sexuality of mothers and on incest.

Finally, to fully grasp the presence of Rossetti's lines in Borges's life and literature, we should not forget that they also had an undeniable erotic appeal for him: in his romantic encounters with Estela Canto, while he was aroused, he insistently recited the verses to her.

As we have seen, Borges said that Rossetti achieved his best poetry when he wrote about the sex act, which in part explains why we find echoes of "Inclusiveness" in the scene where Emma has sex. Borges also relied on Rossetti's poetry to write a passage about sexual intercourse in the short story "El congreso" (1971). But in this case he resorted to "Nuptial Sleep," a piece that was at the center of the attacks against Rossetti's erotic poetry (the author had to drop it from his work, and it was restored only long after his death) and that, according to Borges, was "uno de [sus] sonetos más admirables."[104]

"Nuptial Sleep" is the middle sonnet in a series of three that in themselves form a smaller sequence within *The House of Life*.[105] "The Kiss," in which

---

101 Borges, *OC* [1974], I, 1050; 1107.
102 Borges, *OC* [1974], I, 523.
103 Borges, *LDS*, 57.
104 Borges, *BP*, 266. "At length their long kiss severed, with sweet smart: / And as the last slow sudden drops are shed / From sparkling eaves when all the storm has fled, / So singly flagged the pulses of each heart. / Their bosoms sundered, with the opening start / Of married flowers to either side outspread / From the knit stem; yet still their mouths, burnt red, / Fawned on each other where they lay apart. // Sleep sank them lower than the tide of dreams, / And their dreams watched them sink and slid away. / Slowly their souls swam up again, through gleams / Of watered light and dull drowned waifs of day; / Till from some wonder of new woods and streams / He woke, and wondered more: for there she lay," Rossetti, *Collected Poetry*, 130.
105 Rossetti, *Collected Poetry*, 129–31, sonnets 6, 7, and 8.

the author presents a moment of intense desire and foreplay, is followed by "Nuptial Sleep" or the consummation of the marriage, and concludes with "Supreme Surrender," when the lover proudly reflects on the finally conquered woman. In "The Kiss" the poet says, "I was ... a man / When breast to breast we clung" but in "Nuptial Sleep," after the climax, their bodies slowly begin to separate, they fall asleep, and dream ("Sleep sank them lower than the tide of dreams, / And their dreams watched them sink and slid away"), until dawn, when "He woke, and wondered more: for there she lay." In one of his classes at the University of Buenos Aires in 1966 Borges offered this commentary on the sonnet:

> Rossetti con una hermosa metáfora, dice: "Sleep sank them lower than the tide of dreams," *"El sueño los hundió más abajo de la marea de los sueños."* Pasa la noche y luego *el alba los despierta* ... están debajo del sueño ... "El se despertó y se maravilló aún más porque ahí estaba ella." Es decir, el hecho de despertarse, de volver de un mundo fantástico, de volver a una realidad y *ver que en esa realidad estaba ella*, la mujer que él había querido y reverenciado durante tanto tiempo, y *verla dormida a su lado*, en sus brazos, era más maravilloso que el sueño.[106]

In "El congreso" Borges echoes some of Rossetti's lines to write about a night of love and sex between the protagonist and a long-desired woman:[107]

> Oh noches, oh compartida y tibia tiniebla, *oh el amor que fluye en la sombra como un río secreto*, oh aquel momento de la dicha en que cada uno es los dos, oh la inocencia y el candor de la dicha, oh *la unión en la que nos perdíamos para perdernos luego en el sueño*, oh las primeras claridades del día y yo contemplándola.[108]

In his erotic scene Borges sought to maintain a similar moment ("el alba los despierta," "verla dormida a su lado" / "las primeras claridades del día y yo contemplándola"); but more interesting, he tried to transport Rossetti's "hermosa metáfora": in "Nuptial Sleep" we read "Sleep *sank* them lower than the tide of dreams, / and their dreams watched them *sink*, and slid away," while in "El congreso" Borges seeks to create the same effect of the double layer of descent by repeating the verb twice, as Rossetti did: "la unión en la que nos *perdíamos* para *perdernos* luego en el sueño."[109] The reading of

---

106 Borges, *BP*, 267–68. Emphasis added.
107 Right before the passage the main character says that "Ser de cepa italiana ... en Londres ... para muchos es un atributo romántico," a hint about the author and the tone that Borges had in mind for writing the scene, Borges, *OC* [1974], II, 28; Borges said "a Dante Rossetti lo han llamado, siguiendo el título de un poema de Browning, 'The Italian in England,'" indeed a glamorous portrait of an Italian Romantic revolutionary, Borges, *BP*, 261.
108 Borges, *OC* [1974], II, 29. Emphasis added.
109 Emphasis added.

"Nuptial Sleep" lets us see how Borges's own expressions of desire and sex were partly indebted to the "delicadeza" of Rosetti's erotic poetry.

Yet, the passage also marks a difference from the English poet that allows us to observe the discriminating Borges parting ways with his admired Rossetti and choosing, instead, the company of the, for him, usually less convincing Latin American Modernists. To represent orgasm and the man's semen, Rossetti comes up with a metaphor of rain "drops" ("And as the last slow sudden drops are shed / From sparkling eaves when all the storm has fled"). However, Borges prefers the "stream"[110] of a "river": "oh el amor que fluye en la sombra como un río secreto," a choice that he makes again in "La noche de los dones" ("el gran río de esa noche") and, later, in "Endimión en Latmos" ("Oh ríos del amor y de la noche"[111]). This is the metaphor that we find in Rubén Darío's "Propósito primaveral" ("canta el agua bajo el boscaje obscuro")[112] and in the verses of Lugones's "Delectación morosa" that, if we recall, created some hesitation in Borges and that Bioy approved ("un río de jacinto corría sin rumor hacia la muerte").[113]

Finally, a comment on another aspect of Borges's familiarity with Rossetti's erotic poetry: its reading proved for Borges to be extremely productive, in ways that transcended its erotic appeal or the writing of his own moments of desire and sex. Borges also knew Rossetti's "Jenny," a dramatic monologue titled after the name of a fictional prostitute and in which the English author explores social attitudes toward sex and prostitution in Victorian London. Like "Nuptial Sleep," "Jenny" was one of the pieces targeted in the attacks against Rossetti's erotic poetry. The poem looks at sex and prostitution from the standpoint of men, specifically from the perspective of a poet who is Jenny's customer and who, while he is with her in the bedroom, silently broods on poignant ethical and emotional questions. But more important, in this piece Rossetti introduced an innovative technique for dramatic monologues: the poem is a fascinating exploration of the internal workings of the mind of the man, a highly formalized stream-of-consciousness poem (avant English Modernism). It is in Rossetti's "Jenny" (and not only in Robert Browning's dramatic monologues) that we have to look for the origins of Francisco Narciso de Laprida's perspective in Borges's famous "Poema conjetural."[114]

★_★_★

Borges also liked the poetry of Charles Algernon Swinburne (1837–1909), another member of the Pre-Raphaelite Brotherhood and a personal friend

---

110  We do find a "stream" in Rossetti's sonnet, but to represent (and rhyme with) dreams.
111  Borges, *OC* [1974], II, 44, 175.
112  Darío, *Poesía*, 294. Emphasis added.
113  In Borges, besides, the qualities ("obscuro / sombra"; "sin rumor / secreto") that the two Modernist poets gave the stream coalesce.
114  On Rossetti's influence on "Poema conjetural," see De la Fuente, "Conjectures."

of Dante Gabriel Rossetti. For Borges, Swinburne was the enchanting poet whose "músicas verbales"[115] had renewed English poetry[116] and the ideologically persuasive atheist and republican who rejected Christianity and denounced despotic regimes (in poems such as "On the Russian Persecution of the Jews," to which Borges's "Judería" is indebted). The Victorian poet was a reading that he had found in his father's library and a literary taste that he had inherited from him: "es la voz, que aún escucho, de mi padre, / conmemorando música de Swinburne."[117]

But for Borges, Swinburne was *also* "el gran poeta erótico."[118] Actually, Swinburne's literary notoriety was largely due to his erotic poetry, which, like Rossetti's, was very controversial. When the first series of *Poems and Ballads* (1866) came out, the Press attacked them as "indecent" and "blasphemous."[119] One of his critics wondered if Swinburne was "the libidinous laureate of a pack of satyrs,"[120] which suggests that the attacks might have been fed by a biographical reading of his poetry. In effect, Swinburne was part of a coterie of elite Englishmen who wrote public erotic literature and clandestine pornography, who collected erotica, and who were interested in studying sexuality. Two of his friends in this small circle were the eventually famous collector of erotica H. S. Ashbee (also thought to have authored the pseudonymous pornographic memoir *My Private Life*) and Sir Richard Francis Burton, translator of the *Nights* (more about him in the next chapter). The interest of these men in sexuality and its expression was motivated, at least partially, by their own guilt-ridden sex lives. Swinburne himself was attracted to flagellation, a not uncommon but morally condemned sexual practice in nineteenth-century England. Not coincidentally, the (then clandestine) writings by the Marquis de Sade, discreetly made available to him by a friend in the above-mentioned group, were, he said, among his most influential readings.[121]

The English author's sexuality was a fundamental fact in the production of his literature. Gay poet and critic Luis Cernuda, for example, considered that "La sensualidad de Swinburne [lo hizo] pues 'diferente' de los demás hombres, con todas las consecuencias humanas y artísticas de dicho sentimiento de 'diferencia.'"[122] Indeed, Swinburne's erotic poetry was, in

---

115 Borges, *CS*, 32.
116 Borges, *OCC*, 844.
117 Poem "Yesterdays," Borges, *OC* [1974], II, 312.
118 Borges, *OCC*, 844.
119 His answer was that whether they were "moral or immoral" was "a matter of infinite indifference" to him, Swinburne, *Poems and Ballads*, 404.
120 Quoted in Bate, "Libidinous," 15.
121 In reference to his "Atalanta in Calydon," Swinburne said that Sade was "the poet, thinker, and man of the world from whom the theology of my poem is derived," Swinburne, *Poems and Ballads*, 381.
122 Cernuda, *Obra completa*, vol. 2, 429.

some respects, a modulation of his personal experience and, more generally, a reflection on sexuality. In "Ave Atque Vale," an elegy to Baudelaire that Borges thought was beautiful ("bella"), we find a reading of the French poet that is also Swinburne's mirror image and, thus, an indirect revelation about the role of his conflicted sexuality in the origin of his own poetry:

> Thou sawest, in thine old singing season, brother,
> Secrets and sorrow unbeheld of us:
> Fierce loves, and lovely leaf-buds poisonous,
> Bare to thy subtler eye, but for none other
> Blowing by night in some unbreathed-in clime;
> The hidden harvest of luxurious time,
> Sin without shape, and pleasure without speech.[123]

The "difference" pointed out by Cernuda carried, as we can see, guilt ("sin") and shame ("hidden," "without speech") with it. And rebellion too: Ezra Pound said that "The passion not merely for political, but also for personal, liberty [was] the bedrock of Swinburne's writing."[124] Not surprisingly, then, his erotic poetry often re-created and explored marginalized sexualities. For example, among the Swinburne's works that Borges praised we find poems on intersex figures ("Hermaphroditus"), lesbianism ("Anactoria"), flagellation and sadomasochism ("Dolores"), and unusual forms of desire and erotic stimulation, perhaps agalmatophilia ("Aholibah").[125]

Ezra Pound also said that Swinburne's "biography is perfectly well written in his work," a reading with which Cernuda concurred in more precise terms: "esa mezcla de dolor y placer en una misma sensación" that we find in his poetry "nos revela un rasgo profundo y característico de su sensualidad."[126] Indeed, in his poems his tormented preference for flagellation resurfaces in the varied formulations of painful desire, and its frequency transforms it into a sort of trademark of Swinburne's poetry, as Cernuda implied. In "Anactoria," an intense poem of lesbian love, we read that "Pain animates the dust of dead desire" or "I feel thy blood against my blood: my pain/ Pains thee,"[127] which tells of Sappho's emotional suffering. But it is in "Dolores," a poem that Swinburne himself said was "autobiographical" and in which he interrogated his sadomasochism,[128] where he more amply formulates the association between desire and pain (this time physical as well as emotional).

---

123  Vv.23–29, Swinburne, *Poems and Ballads*, 160–61.
124  Pound, *Literary Essays*, 294.
125  Borges, *BES*, 148.
126  Pound, *Literary Essays*, 292; Cernuda, *Obra completa*, vol. 2, 428.
127  V.180 and vv.11–12, Swinburne, *Poems and Ballads*, 52, 47.
128  Swinburne said that it "expressed the passion with which he had sought relief, in the madness of the fleshly Venus, from his ruined dreams of the heavenly," Swinburne, *Poems and Ballads*, 354.

In the poem, a sarcastic yet desperate prayer to "Notre-Dame des Sept Douleurs," the speaker asks the "Lady of Torture":

> Could you hurt me, sweet lips, though I hurt you?
> ............................................................
> There are sins it may be to discover,
> There are deeds it may be to delight.
> What new work wilt thou find for thy lover,
> What new passions for daytime or night?
> ............................................................
> What tortures undreamt of, unheard of,
> Unwritten, unknown?
> Ah beautiful passionate body
> That never has ached with a heart![129]

Borges pointed out that this poem, along with "Anactoria," was among Swinburne's "obras literalmente espléndidas,"[130] a reading of the Victorian poet that invites us to guess at the origins of what is, perhaps, the best-known expression of Borges's eroticism: in the last line of "El amenazado" he speaks about the bodily symptoms of his excruciating anxiety and the emotional pain caused by his desire: "Me *duele* una mujer en todo *el cuerpo*," which carries echoes of verses such as "Ah beautiful passionate *body* / That never has *ached* with a heart."[131]

Swinburne's treatment of controversial sexualities (including his own) was neither direct nor confessional but allegorical and (almost) as allusive as Victorian society demanded. While in his republican poetry he aimed directly at current figures and situations ("The White Czar," "To Victor Hugo"), he framed his erotic poetry in remote historical times and largely resorted to religious or mythical figures of classical Greece and biblical lands, as can easily be appreciated in the titles of his compositions. He did not talk directly, but indirectly through those characters and often in the form of dramatic monologues. This is what Borges partially meant when he referred to "la afición arcaica de Swinburne":[132] it was not only a matter-of-fact recognition of his Pre-Raphaelism and philhellenism but it also alluded to his oblique erotic poetry, an indirect procedure that Borges adopted to talk about his sexuality, for example, in his dramatic monologue "Endimión en Latmos" (1976), included in *Historia de la noche* (1977). It is helpful to look at this poem because it is a good example of Swinburne's influence and, in particular, of how Borges actually realized the indirect procedure.

The poem is based on the classical myth of Endymion, a beautiful shepherd, and Diana, the goddess of hunters and a determined and brave

---

129 Vv.73–76, 79–82, Swinburne, *Poems and Ballads*, 124–25.
130 Borges, *BES*, 148.
131 Emphasis added.
132 Borges, *OC* [1974], I, 412.

huntress herself (she was also the moon or known as Selena in Greece). Zeus offered Endymion a favor, and he chose to sleep forever and, thus, to remain "ageless and deathless."[133] The young man laid down on Mount Latmus, and Diana, who was looking from above, fell in love with Endymion and came down from the sky to make love to him. The myth has been variously alluded to and re-created throughout the centuries. In modern literature, one of the best-known pieces is John Keats's narrative poem "Endymion," which Borges was familiar with.[134] Painters and sculptors, perhaps even more than writers (particularly since the Renaissance), evoked the myth and often did so in ways that suggested the erotic possibilities of a story in which a woman descended on a young man and made love to him.

As in any other dramatic monologue, in Borges's poem the story is told by a persona or speaker, in this case by an old Endymion who, unlike the one in the myth, is awakened and has aged ("Mi cuerpo, que los años han gastado").[135] The speaker remembers or he thinks he remembers the blissful sexual experience with Diana in his youth ("Me pregunto ... / Si ... / Fue verdadero o no fue más que un sueño / ... el recuerdo / De ayer y un sueño son la misma cosa"), while now, in old age, he is alone, and in his solitary walks he feels that he has lost all appeal for the moon, although he still looks for her ("Mi soledad ... pero siempre busco ... la indiferente luna").

The poem includes a distantly allusive but still sensual re-creation of the sex act:

> Oh las puras mejillas que se buscan,
> Oh ríos del amor y de la noche,
> Oh el beso humano y la tensión del arco.

The lines reveal some consistent choices in Borges's erotic writing. "La tension del arco" that alludes to the state of the body immediately before the climax is a rewriting of earlier and more explicit (or younger) verses in the sensual "Himno al mar" (1919): "Y mi cuerpo tendido como un arco / lucha contra tus musculos."[136] Similarly, "Oh ríos del amor y de la noche," the allusion to climax and orgasm, closely follows previous versions in "El congreso" and "La noche de los dones" ("Oh el amor que fluye en la sombra como un río secreto," "el gran río de esa noche").[137]

---

133 Apollodorus, *The Library*, book I, chapter VII, 6; *Oxford Classical Dictionary*, 384.
134 Borges, *CV*, 115; Oscar Wilde also wrote a homoerotic poem titled "Endymion," in which the poet expresses his sorrow for the loss of his lover, the shepherd, who now is with the moon. Borges must have known this poem but I have found no evidence of how he read it, Wilde, *Complete Works*, 750–51.
135 Borges, *OC* [1974], II, 175.
136 Borges, *TR1*, 25.
137 As I showed before, the metaphor is indebted to Lugones, Borges's main precursor in the poetization of the moon in Argentina, a tradition within which we may also place "Endimión."

The fact that Borges wrote about the same myth that Keats famously revisited in his poetry may tempt us to think that there was an obvious and direct influence of the latter on the former, but this was only partially the case. Borges's 36-verse dramatic monologue does somehow engage Keats's very long narrative poem and it seems to converge with the latter's "A thing of beauty is a joy for ever": indeed, Borges's old Endymion has kept in his memory and treasures the beautiful sexual encounter with the moon that occurred in his youth. However, the agreement with Keats's assertion is only partial, because in Borges this reminiscence cannot be a substitute for the love that he still desires.

In addition, it is necessary to understand that Borges approached the figure of Keats and the myth of Endymion filtered by the influence of the Pre-Raphaelites. Keats had been an important source of inspiration for their poetry and painting, and among the artists who re-created the myth was George Frederic Watts, who also painted "The Minotaur," a work that, Borges said, inspired his "La casa de Asterión."[138] Swinburne too explored the myth in a sonnet titled "Love and Sleep" that recounts an erotic dream in which a woman leans over the poet's bed and makes love to him.[139] That is, the theme was as much the Pre-Raphaelite's as it was Keats's, and Borges's will to revisit and engage (even if tangentially) Keats's poetry is in itself a gesture that echoes the project of the Victorian brotherhood. Moreover, Borges's depiction of the arrival of the woman is reminiscent of Swinburne's sonnet ("Diana, la diosa ... / Me veía dormir ... / Y lentamente descendió a mis brazos" // "Lying asleep ... I saw my love lean over my sad bed"[140]).

But most important of all, the combining of the form of the dramatic monologue and a classical theme to speak about controversial sexualities (including the author's own) was a distinct Swinburne practice. In the case of "Endimión en Latmos," though, Borges's realization of the "manera indirecta" of speaking goes beyond the text of the poem itself: he adds two more pieces and thus builds a three-text puzzle of meaning and explication that the reader, now turned into a "detective of poetry," is expected to put together and in which the dramatic monologue of the classical theme is only the first piece.[141] To fully comprehend "Endimión," it is necessary to reach the following page where the reader will find a second text, a very brief prose piece titled "Un escolio" that is apparently unrelated to the previous composition. Its title derives from the Latin "scollium" and means an explanatory

---

138 Borges, *OC* [1974], I, 629.
139 Although Swinburne does not name the woman, he alludes to the myth, "And all her body *pasture* to mine eyes" suggests the imagery of a shepherd; "hair smelling of the south" is an English allusion to the Greek and Latin, that is, Mediterranean, myths; my emphasis.
140 Vv.1–2, Swinburne, *Poems and Ballads*, 219.
141 The expression is John Fuller's *Who is Ozymandias?*, 34, whose overall approach to reading poetry has been very helpful, particularly in the case of this poem.

note that has been added to a main text to aid in its comprehension, in this case the poem that precedes it, "Endimión en Latmos." However, at first glance "Un escolio" seems to be about something else. In this second text Borges relates the story of Odysseus's return, Penelope, and the test of the rooted bed, but concludes with what is the true "escolio":

> Homero no ignoraba que las cosas deben decirse de manera indirecta. Tampoco lo ignoraban sus griegos, cuyo lenguaje natural era el mito. La fábula del tálamo que es un árbol es una suerte de metáfora.[142]

Borges's explication of Homer's *Odyssey* is, more than anything, an "explanatory note" that seeks to help read the poem on the previous page as an autobiographical text and, thus, it also explicates Borges's use of myth in his "manera indirecta" of speaking. And, yet, this is not the last piece in the puzzle of meaning and explication that the reader is expected to solve. There is a third text: in the "Epílogo" of *Historia de la noche* Borges says that "para eludir la controversia [in the texts included in this book] "he elegido ejemplos pretéritos";[143] that is, to talk about "controversial" (personal) matters, he resorted to myths and figures of the past (Swinburne's "afición arcaica").

This "manera indirecta" of speaking both engages the reader in a rather uncertain puzzle solving and, simultaneously, works toward the softening of the biographical components of the poem. For example, as far as I know, the three pieces are not usually considered together; in particular, readers miss the relationship between the first two texts and, therefore, a key part of the explication.[144] The reading of "Endimión en Latmos" alone may also pose problems because even curious and capable readers may think of it as just another version of the classical myth. That is, for example, what an experienced poet who interviewed Borges seems to have thought; however, Borges clarified that he "[had] never attempted myth" and then explained what had been his main intention when he wrote the poem:

> I wrote a poem of Endymion because I wanted to say that Endymion is a matter of fact and not myth, since every man who has been loved has been loved by a goddess. I have been Endymion. All of us have been Endymion who have been loved by the moon, who have felt unworthy of it, and who have sought to thank it. That was the meaning of the poem. I wasn't playing around with myth.[145]

The poem, then, is not so much about Endymion as it is about Borges's love experience. That, he said, was the "meaning of the poem." It is an autobiographical poem rooted in his sexual biography. Myths, as ideas and

---

142 Borges, *OC* [1974], II, 176.
143 Borges, *OC* [1974], II, 202.
144 J. P. Bernes thought that the first two texts could be related but did not explain how, Borges, *OC* [2010], II, 1376.
145 Borges, *Borges at Eighty*, 69.

archetypes, comprised the experience of all individuals and, thus, in speaking about the myth, he also spoke about himself. The use of myth in this indirect procedure, as Borges once explained, is not "puramente ornamental" but "significativo de situaciones individuales."[146]

As we have seen, in "Profesión de fe literaria" Borges said that in some texts "la sustancia autobiográfica, la personal, está desaparecida por los accidentes que la encarnan." How to find, then, "the autobiographical substance" that the poetic writing of the myth has both helped and required to camouflage? We can think of at least two forms of trying to read his biography into the poem: one is what it may reveal about Borges's love, sex life, and relationships with women in general; the other, more problematic, is what it may say about some specific events or relationships in his life. With regard to the latter, we could speculate that it refers to a rare positive experience of sexual intercourse in his youth and, for example, it could lend credibility to one of the versions of his sexual initiation, which, as we have seen in the first chapter, said that it was "una experiencia irresistible." From what is known, then, it would have been one of the few times that he was able to consummate sex, which would help explain, in spite of the loss that memory always implies, the nostalgic happiness that the recollection brought the speaker of the poem. I propose this form of biographical reading as a possibility but I am not convinced that it is the best way to find Borges's life in the poem.

I think we are on firmer ground when we look for what the poem may reveal about Borges's emotional and sexual biography more generally. For instance, during the foreplay and right before the consummation of sex, the speaker says, "yo aspiré la fragancia de la luna": it is clear that the author believed it was important to allude to the enchanting smell of her body. We may think this is a possibility in any text of erotic literature as, for example, we have read in Verlaine's "Vœu"; yet, as I have suggested in that case, Borges approved of the French poet's insight on the experience of sex because it was in tune with his own sensibility regarding the smell of women's bodies. Therefore, this verse would not just show Borges's familiarity with the conventions of a genre but could also be a manifestation of his sensuality.

Similarly, in spite of the bliss of that early experience of sexual intercourse, there are lines that suggest the guilt and fear that women and sex provoked in the author ("Profanaban," "Yo quería no ver el rostro bello"); in the same vein, the speaker says that now, in old age, "Una zozobra / Da horror a mi vigilia," which hints at, once again, the fear of sex and the impotence that it caused in the author.

These are a few examples of what the poem could reflect of his emotional and sexual biography. But more important is what it reveals about the type of relationships that he tended to establish with women. In his explanation of the autobiographical nature of the poem Borges said that "every man who

---

146 Borges, *OCC*, 468.

has been loved has been loved by a goddess" and that he "felt unworthy of it," which corresponds very well with the asymmetrical relationships that Borges established with women that he thought were emotionally stronger and morally more courageous than him (I address this question in chapter 7). I pointed out before Borges's low self-esteem when it came to interpersonal relationships, and Estela Canto said that for him "la mujer [era] un ídolo inalcanzable, al cual no se atrevía a aspirar."[147] In the same vein, we saw the vulnerable, mother-child position he took regarding prostitutes in a Spanish brothel, which, for example, corresponds with Woscoboinik's general assessment in this respect. It is in relation to this biographical donnée, I propose, that we have to consider Borges's choice of the topic. In classical mythology Diana, the goddess of hunters, is frequently represented as an arms-bearing huntress herself, and in the particular case of her story with Endymion, she is often portrayed as an assertive woman standing above the sleeping and vulnerable young shepherd. Similarly, in the myth, love and sex are dictated by Diana: it is the goddess who decides to make love to the young man and it is she who leans over him and, as many artistic representations suggest, could end up on top. The emotional asymmetry and vulnerability of the words "Diana, la diosa ... / Me veía dormir ... Y lentamente descendió a mis brazos" recalls other situations of sex in Borges's literature. In the same way that Diana decides to make love to Endymion, in "La noche de los dones" it is the prostitute who decides to sexually initiate the youth ("acércate que no te voy a hacer ningún mal"[148]). And sex in "Ulrica" reveals the same type of asymmetry. As the protagonist says, "El milagro [or the goddess] tiene derecho a imponer condiciones" because "el ofrecido amor es un don,"[149] a gift that depends on the woman. The relationship between Endymion and Diana in the myth, then, does comprise Borges's relationship with women and corresponds with other moments of his autobiographical literature. Thus, instead of trying to pin the poem down to a specific event or relationship, a more general interrogation will allow us to glimpse the author's biography through the indirect procedure.

Borges's "indirect way," then, was a form of speaking about his sexuality for which Swinburne provided, perhaps, the best model. But beyond the technical inspiration that he found in the author of *Poems and Ballads*, Borges also looked at Swinburne's troubled sexuality and his devotion to literature as a kindred destiny. This can be observed in his portrait of the Victorian poet, which, as the latter had done with Baudelaire, was a mirror image of Borges's own. In his note on the commemoration of Swinburne's centennial, Borges agreed with Swinburne's biographers that "Vida y muerte le han faltado a esa vida," yet he urged them to also look at "su opulencia intelectual,"[150] which

---

147 Canto, *A contraluz*, 81.
148 Borges, *OC* [1974], II, 43.
149 Borges, *OC* [1974], II, 18.
150 Borges, *BES*, 148.

paralleled Borges's self-perception to the point of self-plagiarism: "Vida y muerte le han faltado a mi vida. De esa indigencia, mi laborioso amor por estas minucias," literature.[151]

Swinburne's poetry was not only a reading but a life experience for Borges: he felt "en [su] boca el ... goce físico de su métrica,"[152] and Swinburne's poems triggered early recollection of Borges's father reciting them. More telling, Swinburne's poetry heated up Borges's romantic relationships. A student who had fallen in love with Professor Borges asked him in their amorous encounters: "No me hable. Recite versos. Recite versos de Swinburne."[153]

★_★_★

Now let's return to Estela Canto and her romantic walks with Borges in the Buenos Aires of the 1940s. In her recollection, in addition to Rossetti's "Inclusiveness," Borges

> También citaba los misteriosos versos de un poema de Wordsworth sobre Leda y el Cisne "Did she put on his knowledge with his power?"[154]

The verse that Borges also quoted to Estela Canto when he was aroused belonged to the sonnet "Leda and the Swan" (1923) by William B. Yeats (1865–1938), and not by Wordsworth. In the sonnet the Irish poet (another admirer of Swinburne) revisited a classic erotic theme in Western tradition, the rape of Leda by Zeus, whose sexual union resulted in offsprings, among them Helen of Troy: "A sudden blow ... / Above the staggering girl, her thighs caressed," "How can those terrified vague fingers push / The feathered glory from her loosening thighs? / And how can body, laid in that white rush, / But feel the strange heart beating where it lies? / A shudder in the loins engenders there / The broken wall ... / Did she put on his knowledge with his power ...?"[155] However mythologized, the poem is a pretty explicit re-creation of the sex act that also brutally reveals the power relations at play in a rape.

It should not surprise us that Borges brought Yeats to his romantic encounters, since it is clear that he liked Yeats's erotic poetry.[156] But there was

---

151 Borges, *OC* [1974], I, 177.
152 Borges, *BES*, 148.
153 Bioy, *Borges*, 968.
154 Canto, *A contraluz*, 96.
155 Yeats, *Collected Works*, 218.
156 In the section dedicated to Yeats in his *Historia de la literatura inglesa* Borges says "Elegimos, al azar, unos versos llenos de belleza y hondura. Un grupo de mujeres espléndidas desciende lentamente por una escalera. Alguien pregunta para qué han sido creadas. Recibe la respuesta: *For desecration and the lover's night* (para la profanación, para la noche del amante)," Borges, *OCC*, 855. This is the only work that Borges quotes to represent Yeats's literature. In the same vein, it helps to remember that the epigraph of his short story "Biografía de Tadeo Isidoro Cruz (1828–1874)"

something else: Yeats himself had gone through a traumatic sexual decline that late in life ended in impotence, an experience about which he reflected in poems that Borges knew well.[157]

Including "Leda and the Swan." The end of the sonnet depends on the connotative rhetorical question that Borges quoted to Estela Canto: "Did she put on his knowledge with his power ...?" which opens several possibilities: did Leda (and any woman) acquire through sex some of the knowledge that Zeus (or, generally, men) possessed? Or, I believe more significant for our case, in addition to the sexual power that she felt, did she also understand or recognize the enormous knowledge of God (or the man)? Or was it that she only felt his sexual power? If so, is knowledge truly powerless in sex? In another poem in which Yeats alluded to his sexual decline (and that Borges also read), the Irish poet considered the relation between knowledge and sexual power, suggesting that there was a proportionally inverted relationship between them: to more knowledge corresponded less sexual power (and vice versa): "Bodily decrepitude is wisdom; young / We loved each other and were ignorant."[158] The idea of an inverted relation between knowledge and sexual power, which Yeats seems to affirm in the verses just quoted but that, more inconclusively, he interrogates in the penultimate verse of "Leda and the Swan," had been extensively proposed in the nineteenth century as an explanation for male sexual impotence. It was called "neurasthenia" and it affected middle-class, over-educated men or "brain" workers, while it spared working-class, "muscle" workers. In other words, sexual impotence could be the consequence of too much intellectual development.[159]

Although Yeats's poem clearly helped Borges interrogate his own situation, he also encountered this explanation in a trusted author of his. In the *World as Will and Representation*, in the chapter on "The Metaphysics of Sexual Love," Schopenhauer said about the relationship between sexual power and knowledge (and about his own disappointing emotional and sexual life):

> [Women] are won mainly by a man's strength, and the courage connected with it; for these promise the production of strong children ... Intellectual merits, on the other hand, do not exercise any direct and instinctive power over her ... in fact, extraordinary mental power, or even genius, as something abnormal, might have an unfavourable effect. Hence we often

---

("I am looking for the face I had / Before the world was made") comes from the 11-poem sequence titled "A Woman Young and Old," about women and the role sex plays in different moments of their lives, Yeats, *Collected Works*, 275–82.

157 On Yeats's sexual decline and his poetry, see Wyndham, "Versemaking and Lovemaking."

158 Borges, *CV*, 82–83. Yeats also suggested it in "The Last Confession": the woman says that she only loved the men that loved her bodily, Yeats, *Collected Works*, 280.

159 McLaren, *Impotence*, 115–16.

see an ugly, stupid, and coarse fellow get the better of a cultured, clever, and amiable man when dealing with women.[160]

The contradictory relation between knowledge and sexual power (and emotional realization) interrogated by Yeats and affirmed by Schopenhauer contributed, in some measure, to Borges self-perception.[161]

"Leda and the Swan" was one of the readings that helped Borges think and imagine an explanation and a justification for his impotence. In addition, the episode with Canto shows that he made a very vivid and "practical" use of it: the poem allowed him to allude to his own situation, to bring it into their conversation, and to test her reaction to it without risking an open confession. However, Yeats's poem and Borges's maneuver with it proved too "indirect" for her: "Muchos, muchos años después, yo iba a tener vislumbres de lo que él estaba tratando de expresar con esos versos."[162]

But the presence of the poem in their amorous encounter can also be partly explained by its sensuality, which arguably contributed to the arousal of Borges that Canto remembered. Actually, Yeats's sonnet kept a long-lasting erotic appeal for him. In November 1985, a few months before his death, Estela visited her octogenarian friend, and they read once more the penultimate verse of "Leda and the Swan"; and, again, she said "volví a notar su excitación sexual al repetir los versos: 'Did she put on his knowledge with his power?'"[163]

---

160 Schopenhauer, *WWR*, II, 544.
161 As in the prologue to *Discusión* (1932) already quoted, in Borges, *OC* [1974], I, 177.
162 Canto, *A contraluz*, 96.
163 Canto, *A contraluz*, 280.

CHAPTER 4

# Sir Richard Burton's Orientalist Erotica

## *The Thousand Nights and a Night* and *The Perfumed Garden*

Borges, let us not forget, was born at the height of the age of imperialism, when European colonial possessions covered most of the world. Empires were the realization of European economic and military power, and white men derived from these empires many business and career opportunities. And some other benefits too: colonies also became a sort of global sexual slums in which European men lived their sexuality in ways that, confined by legal, social, and moral norms, they could not at home.[1] The sexual possession of distant lands was in itself a manifestation of the power relations that made empires possible. Several realities and motivations were at work in this phenomenon: in some cases, it was the necessity of the young colonial officials and soldiers who spent long periods of times away from European women and in contact with the native populations; in others, it was simply sexual tourism, as can be glimpsed in the Orientalist travelogues and private correspondence of European men, such as Flaubert.[2] There was a whole Orientalist ideology that justified this domination: the ideology explained not only that European culture was superior (hence the legitimacy of the "civilizing" mission that empires took upon themselves) but also that white men were sexually more powerful than their effeminate Eastern counterparts, which "explained" why native women "welcomed" European men. Sexual imperialism was another facet of European superiority.[3]

But within the imperialist experience and the ideology that justified it, there was a marginal trend and view that, while sharing the racism and social Darwinism of mainstream Orientalism, also differed significantly from it. Some of the colonial officials and/or sexual tourists were also interested in the sexual mores of Eastern peoples and, thus, not only engaged in sex but

---

1 Hyam, *Empire and Sexuality*, see especially chapters 3, 4, and 6. See also Bernstein, *The East*, 33–34.
2 Flaubert to Louis Bouilhet, on the Nile, March, 13, 1850, Flaubert, *Correspondence*, 118–30; also, Bernstein, *The East*, chapter 2.
3 Bernstein, *The East*, 35.

also undertook comparative research of sexualities.⁴ What animated them was both a very critical view of repressive European morality and the Christian religion that sustained it (à la Swinburne) and the belief that the East had not yet been corrupted and weakened by higher degrees of civilization as the Metropolitan societies had. Thus, the East for them was also a repository of less civilized, wiser, and healthier sexualities. The colonized societies also possessed knowledge and wisdom that could be imported to ameliorate the miserable sex life of Victorian Europe. Therefore, in addition to their observations and research, these "participant observers" also searched for and eventually translated into European languages ancient Eastern medical books or sex manuals. But they also looked for and translated erotic poetry and fiction that presented insights into sexual customs and behaviors; that is, titillating literature was also part of the ethnographic and "scientific" information they were interested in.⁵

The "biblioteca de ilimitados libros ingleses" where Borges discovered literature was put together during those times and by a man (his father) who himself was interested in erotic literature and who had an inclination to reflect on matters of sexuality.⁶ It is not a surprise, then, that the book collection that was "el hecho capital" in Georgie's life contained Orientalist erotica and that he became an armchair sexual tourist who enjoyed exploring the distant lands and mores that European translations brought near him. Borges's readings ranged from Chinese classics, such as *El sueño del aposento rojo* ("una desesperada carnalidad rige toda la obra") and *The Golden Lotus* (the German translation "es de una franqueza que no excluye la obscenidad"),⁷ to really rare pieces of Afghan poetry such as "Les tresses noires," which Borges judged "el más desolado y urgente de todos los poemas eróticos."⁸ But the most relevant of the Orientalist erotica that he read were Sir Richard Francis Burton's famous translations of *The Book of the Thousand Nights and a Night* (1885) and the Arab sex manual *The Perfumed Garden of the Cheikh Nefzaoui*, which will be the object of our study in this chapter. As I mentioned before, although criticism of Borges has often addressed the presence of the *Nights* in his literature, as

---

4 Mary S. Lovell, "Introduction" in Nefzaoui, *The Perfumed Garden*, vii–xx; Gibson, *Erotomaniac*, chapter 2; "Burton did for the Kamasutra what Max Muller did for the Rig Veda during this same period," Wendy Doniger, "Introduction," in Vatsyayana, *Kamasutra*, LV; Rice, *Captain*, 51–53 and chapter 29.
5 Gibson, *Erotomaniac*, chapter 2; Rice, *Captain*, 51–53.
6 Jorge Guillermo Borges translated into Spanish Edward FitzGerald's *Rubáiyát of Omar Khayyám* and wrote a version of "El cantar de los cantares"; similarly, his annotations in *La senda* show his interest in questions of sexuality; see also Sarah Roger's "Apuntes sobre Jorge Guillermo Borges," in *La senda*, 89–107.
7 Borges, *BES*, 211; Borges, *OC* [1974], IV, 329.
8 Borges, *OC* [1974], IV, 331. Borges read the poem in Adolphe Thalasso's *Anthologie de l'amour asiatique* (42–50), whose influence on "Los traductores" is noticeable in the editor's discussion of how to translate erotic literature, 9–26.

far as I know, it has not interrogated Burton's translation (or any other) as erotica, which in itself is another evidence of the assumptions about Borges as an asexual writer.[9] *The Perfumed Garden* has not been read in relation to Borges either and, as I expect to show, its study should add to our understanding of how Borges saw Richard Burton's translations and publishing endeavors.

Burton's *Nights*

Let us consider first Borges's "Los traductores de las *1001 Noches*" (1936), an essay that at first glance might have little to say about Borges's sexuality and its expression.[10] The piece has received a lot of attention as a key moment in Borges's reflections on the art of translation, in which he argues that the translator is, essentially, a rewriter.[11] However, although the essay certainly invites this kind of reading, commentators seem to have overlooked what, paradoxically, is very visible: one of the most significant questions that Borges addresses is how to translate or rewrite or, better, simply write, erotic literature.[12] And so, through the essay Borges examines the way different translators dealt with the erotic material contained in the *Arabian Nights*: Weil's omissions are "equidistantes de la hipocresía y del impudor"; Littman is not deterred by "las obscenidades más inefables," Galland's modesty is inspired by "el decoro, no la moral," and Mardrus has a "Destino paradójico [...]. Se le adjudica la virtud *moral* de ser el traductor más veraz de las *1001 Noches*, libro de admirable lascivia, antes escamoteada a los compradores por la buena educación de Galland o los remilgos puritanos de Lane."[13]

Borges's favorite translation was Richard Burton's.[14] Borges said that

9 See, as examples, Borges, *OC* [2009], I, 809, note 234; Borges, *OC* [2010], I, 1531; Fishburn, "Traces"; Kennedy, "Missing pages"; Waisman, *Borges and Translation*, 66–70. Similarly, A. S. Byatt, "Introduction," *Nights*, XVI, and Robert Irwin, in his wonderful *The Arabian Nights: A Companion*, 282–87, see Borges's reading of the Eastern classic from the narrative standpoint, but they largely miss the angle proposed here. Rodríguez Monegal, *Literary Biography*, 72, does mention the erotic nature of the work but does not see this aspect of Borges's reading. However, Suzanne Jill Levine has recently suspected that Borges was interested in the *Nights* as erotica, "Borges on Translation," 52.

10 Borges published the sections on Mardrus's French translation and Burton's on February 3, 1934 and on March 10, 1934, respectively, in *Revista Multicolor de los Sábados*. It was later included in *Historia de la eternidad* (Buenos Aires, 1936).

11 e.g. Waisman, *Borges and Translation*.

12 Waisman, *Borges and Translation*; the other, very significant, question that concerned Borges and which has received the attention of students of Borges's theory of translation is the one of how to maintain and re-create the "local color" in the target language, see Willson, *La Constelación*.

13 All quotations from "Los traductores" in Borges, *OC* [1974], I, 397–413.

14 Eventually Borges would prefer Galland's, "la más grata de todas," *OC* [1974], IV, 504; see also Bioy, *Borges*, 490, 828.

as a publisher by subscriptions, Burton faced the challenge of first getting subscribers and then keeping them interested in a book that others (particularly Lane) had already translated and annotated, and in stories whose magic could look too naïve to Victorian gentlemen. So Burton's contribution was to add and to annotate the erotica that was missing from the previous translations, which secured the loyalty of the buyers. Not surprisingly, then, Borges places Burton's translation not only within the English literary tradition but also, and more specifically, within the tradition of erotic literature. In a well-known passage of his essay, he says:

> [la version] de Burton ... solo se [deja] concebir *después de una literatura* ... presupone un rico proceso anterior. En algún modo, el casi inagotable proceso inglés está adumbrado en Burton—la dura obscenidad de John Donne, el gigantesco vocabulario de Shakespeare y de Cyril Tourneur, la afición arcaica de Swinburne.[15]

The passage is often quoted as Borges's lucid insight about the relation between a translation and the history of the target language, but that is not my point here. What I want to highlight is that the choice of authors within English literature who, according to Borges, would explain Burton's work reflects Borges's awareness of a tradition of erotic literature. The reference to John Donne is pretty explicit, but the other three are not so obvious. In the case of Swinburne, we can make sense of his invocation here only after understanding how much Borges's knew and liked his erotic poetry with classical themes. In addition, what perhaps has prevented critics from fully grasping the meaning of the passage are the (not fully canonical) references to Shakespeare and Cyril Tourneur. With respect to the former, it suffices to remember, as the editor of a thick glossary of the Bard's sexual language tells us, that since "the seventeenth century, his authorial identity was very much bound up with the use of sexual language and treatment of erotic themes."[16] And Tourneur too, according to Borges, excelled in the expression of eroticism: the Elizabethan's line that he quoted most frequently was "for the poor benefit of a bewildering minute," an allusion to (troubling) sexual intercourse that he translated as "el pobre beneficio de un minuto incoherente."[17]

Burton belonged to a small circle of elite British men, among whom several were attracted to socially stigmatized and guilt-ridden forms of sex (predominantly flagellation). Preoccupations with their own sex life had also awakened in them a genuine interest in investigating and reflecting about sexuality and in disseminating their critical views of Victorian norms and the Christian morality that justified them. Some members of the circle wrote erotic literature (clandestine and not), others thoroughly collected erotica,

---

15 Borges, *OC* [1974], I, 412.
16 Williams, *Shakespeare's Sexual Language*, 1.
17 Mastronardi, *Borges*, 73; Borges, *BLL*, 335.

and some took advantage of their class and imperialistic entitlements to embark on sexual tourism and record their observations (the East was their preferred destination). Among the members of the group was Swinburne, who developed a relationship of complicity with Burton (the poet called the explorer "my tempter and favourite audience"[18]) and in his poetry praised Burton's translation of the *Nights* (with it, "All that glorious Orient glows"[19]).

Burton was professionally a diplomat and an explorer, but his interests turned him into a researcher who gathered anthropological information across cultures with the purpose of reflecting comparatively on social norms and human sexuality. In the 1870s he cofounded the Anthropological Society of London and created the journal *Anthropologia* with the intent of opening a venue to discuss and publish investigations on the subject. However, the explicit findings eventually became too much for Victorian "respectability" and "propriety," and the publication was shut down.[20] Like Swinburne and Rossetti, Burton was a controversial figure and for similar reasons. That is, in Victorian England, Borges's favorite writers may have been professionally and socially "in," but their erotic literature was not.

In the preface to *Nights*, Burton placed his translation within the wider project of his anthropological investigations and his comparative research on human sexuality. One of the purposes of his annotation of the monumental collection of stories was to educate the Victorians (including women) not only about the customs of the East but about their own sexuality.[21] The lack of education on the subject, he explained in the preface, had had devastating effects on the life of "civilized" British society: "the consequences of ignorance [were] peculiarly cruel" and knowledge about sexual matters was usually acquired "at the price of the bitterest experience."[22] Both the stories of *Nights* and his own notes, he thought, could help educate readers on the theory and practice of social and sexual relations. Moreover, the publication of the *Nights* (1885–1886) was part of a larger research and educational project that led Burton to translate and disseminate in the West three Eastern love and sex manuals: Kalyana Malla's *Ananga Ranga: The Hindu Art of Love* (1885), *The Perfumed Garden of the Cheikh Nefzaoui: A Manual of Arabian Erotology (XVI Century)* (1886) and, most famously, the classical Hindu erotic textbook *The Kama Sutra of Vatsyayana* (1883).

Borges's interest in Burton's life and work (and in the *Nights* as part of it) not only was fed by his curiosity in Oriental cultures, narratives techniques, or the case it presented for reflections on translation but also was clearly motivated by his desire to know materials that Burton considered primarily scientific and that in the next century Westerners would often consider simply

18 Gibson, *Erotomaniac*, XIII.
19 Wright, *The Life*, vol. 2, 127.
20 Burton, "Preface," *Arabian Nights*, xxxii.
21 *Nights*, Suppl. VII, 437–39.
22 *Arabian Nights*, xxxii–iii.

erotic or outright pornographic. This is the reading of Burton's work that emerges from "El Signo," a short story by H. Bustos Domecq. The story tells about two men who run a semi-underground publishing house that provided "obras científicas" and "postales" (erotic or pornographic postcards) to the bookstores located in the "Paseo de Julio y la Ribera [La Boca]," two districts in Buenos Aires notorious for their brothels. But one of the men ended up in jail and charged as "pornografista" for selling books decorated with naked women and whose titles were, among others, "*El Jardín perfumado*" and "*Kama-Sutra y/o Ananga-Ranga.*"[23] Borges knew the first title very well and, perhaps, the last two also.[24]

Recovering Borges's Erotica

The recovery of Borges's erotic reading of the *Nights* fundamentally depends on "Los traductores"; yet, it is also important to understand the limitations of the essay if we want to grasp his experience of Burton's edition. A critical interrogation of "Los traductores" allows us to see that some of the most problematic erotica that Borges undeniably encountered in the book did not make it into the essay. Therefore, if we want to approximate his reading, we have to go beyond Borges's own text and engage in investigative criticism; that is, we must also read closely his literary sources, as I hope will be clear in the next few pages.

As an example of the limitations of "Los traductores" to explain Borges's reading, I propose looking at the comparison that he made between Galland's and Burton's translations. In the essay he says:

> Las reservas de Galland son mundanas; las inspira el decoro, no la moral. Copio unas líneas de la tercer página de sus *Noches: il alla droit à appartement de cette princesse, qui, ne s'attendant pas à le revoir avait reçu dans son lit un des derniers officiers de sa maison*. Burton concreta a ese nebuloso "*officier*": *un negro cocinero, rancio de grasa de cocina y de hollín*. Ambos, diversamente, deforman: el original es menos ceremonioso que Galland y menos grasiento que Burton.[25]

The brief passage compared by Borges comes from the liminal story involving King Shahryar and Shahrazad that frames the rest of the multivolume work and is the first scene of female infidelity of the many that the reader will encounter in the monumental collection of tales. Here, as he consistently does throughout his translation, Burton "concreta"; that is, he is explicit and

---

23 Borges, *OCC*, 134–42.
24 The comment that Clement Egerton in his translation of *The Golden Lotus* resorts to "el remoto latín para velar las precisiones físicas" (Borges, *BES*, 211) seems to echo Burton's methodological clarifications in his prologue to the *Ananga Ranga*: "to dress it up in Latin," Kalyana, xiii.
25 Italics in the original.

provides details that Galland usually does not, and thus, Borges's comparison somehow captures the different intent and tone of the translators.

However, if we read Borges's comparison carefully, it is possible to sense a slight dissonance between his assessment of the translations and the passage of the *Nights* quoted to illustrate it. Because, is there really anything "decorous" in not showing a "cocinero rancio de grasa"? Could such a figure scandalize Galland to the extent that he had to cover it with his "decoro" when, after all, he had decided to show the princess in bed with one of the lowest ranked officials of the palace? Or, conversely, is there anything daring or undecorous (let alone sexual) in Burton's decision to show a dirty cook? If we do not limit ourselves to Borges's essay and do actually read the French and English translations of the story we may agree with Borges's general assessment of the two translations but we can also clearly see that with *his choice of passages to illustrate it,* he hid as much as he revealed about their differences, which was, ultimately, a way for Borges to partially bowdlerize his own erotic reading.

Let us see. Borges said that what largely defined Burton's translation was his annotation of the erotica of the tales; yet, for his comparative analysis he selected a passage that the explorer did not annotate; that is, Borges's choice seems to disregard his own appreciation of Burton's contribution. In addition, there is another intriguing decision in Borges's comparison, this time pertaining to the French text. In the passage quoted above, Borges says that Galland's reservations are inspired by "el decoro," a point that the French translator very explicitly made not in the scene compared by Borges but in another passage that occurs barely two pages later, a second scene of female infidelity and that also involves a black slave. In the French translation of that second scene of marital betrayal, we read that

> La sultane ... frappa des mains ... et aussitôt un autre noir ... courut a elle avec beaucoup d'empressment.
> 
> *La pudeur ne permet pas de raconter tout ce qui se passa* entre ces femmes et ces noirs, et *c'est un détail qu'il n'est pas besoin de faire.* Il suffit de dire que ....[26]

So, it is clear that Borges stopped at this scene and that he lifted from it his insight on the principle that guided Galland's translation ("la pudeur ..."). But why did he decide to remove Galland's explanation from its original context? Why not choose the second scene of infidelity for the comparison, if it was here, after all, that Galland had made the choice of not telling the details? In addition, why not comment on this second scene that, contrary to the first one, the English explorer did annotate? The answer, I propose, is not in the French version but in Burton's. The English translates the same passage thus:

---

26 *Les Mille*, I, 27. Emphasis added.

[the Queen called her lover, a slave], a big slobbering blackamoor with rolling eyes which showed the whites, a truly hideous sight.[27]

Burton's version is rather explicit about the arousal ("slobbering") and the sexual enjoyment of the slave ("rolling eyes which showed the whites").[28] In other words, this passage carries stronger sexual overtones than the view of a "cocinero, rancio de grasa," and its use could have been more problematic. But this was not the most important of the factors that, I understand, induced Borges to illustrate his assessment with a different scene. There is another reason. It is this second scene of female infidelity involving a black man that the Englishman commented upon with a long and detailed footnote:

> Debauched women prefer negroes on account of the size of their parts. I measured one man in Somali-land who, when quiescent, numbered nearly six inches ... Moreover, these imposing parts do not increase proportionally during erection; consequently, the "deed of kind" takes a much longer time and adds greatly to the woman's enjoyment ... Upon the subject of Imsák = retention of semen and "prolongation of pleasure," I shall find it necessary to say more.[29]

In the note, the British explorer offers an "explanation"[30] of male sexual potency and consequent female sexual preferences, a question that concerned Borges directly and personally.

But my purpose here is to consider what the passage and the note reveal about Borges's comparison of Galland's and Burton's versions. All seems to indicate that Borges did notice this passage in Burton's translation and its corresponding footnote. This is the first of all the erotic notes that the Englishman will offer in his 17 volumes; that is, this is a very visible moment in his annotation. In addition, in "Los traductores" Borges shows that he read very closely the Englishman's rendition of the first tale and his notes: "Burton reescribe íntegramente—*con adición de* pormenores circunstanciales y *rasgos fisiológicos*—la historia liminar ...,"[31] a comment that is also an allusion to the annotation quoted above because that footnote is the only moment in the whole liminal story in which Burton adds a "rasgo fisiológico." In other words, there is no question that he read the passage and the note.

So, if Borges wanted to compare the two translations and if he was inclined to do it with a passage of infidelity (as he actually did), was it not this second scene (where Galland's "decoro" actually pixeled the details on

---

27 *Nights*, I, 6.
28 A vision compounded by Burton's racist value judgement whose purpose is to introduce a sense of ugliness in the scene ("a truly hideous sight").
29 *Nights*, I, 6.
30 It was "scientific" for the 1870s, however racist and fallaciously unscientific we now know it was.
31 Emphasis added.

which Burton's annotation, instead, zoomed in) that more fairly represented the gazes and intents of the translators? Would it not have been truer to Borges's own evaluation of the two versions to comment on the second scene instead of the first? But doing it was out of the question for a couple of reasons: given the standards of propriety of the time and the right-wing and culturally repressive climate of Argentina in the 1930s, the passage was not fit for a literary discussion, either in a journalistic piece or even in a book;[32] nor, given his reticence and well-known troubles, would Borges have dared to acknowledge in public the reading of a passage on male sexual potency. Thus, in his comparison of the two texts, by moving Galland's explanation of the rationale that guided his translation ("la pudeur") from the second to the first scene of infidelity, Borges himself performed a "Gallandesque" decorous maneuver and avoided (and suppressed) problematic erotic material. But the suppression did not mean that he did not read it or that he was not interested in it. It only shows that he could not and did not want to share his erotica with readers.[33]

Let me now address a related but somewhat different issue that may also create some difficulties in the recovering of Borges's erotic reading. I refer to some of our assumptions about how and what he read. As is well known, from volume 4 of Burton's *Nights*, Borges gathered "The Ruined Man Who Became Rich Again through a Dream," the story that he translated and published as "Historia de los dos que soñaron" (1935). The fact that an author, famous for his "fantasías metafísicas" and known for his interest in dreams and nightmares, selected this story may inadvertently induce us *to equate that particular choice with the whole of Borges's experience of the "Nights."*

Yet, as we have seen in the previous chapter, Borges was also sincerely interested in literary re-creations of the sex act. So we need to consider the possibility that in a book of "admirable lascivia" (as he qualified the *Nights*) he would also look for and indeed found such types of erotica. For example, in volume 4 that he knew so well, and merely pages away from the tale that

---

32 On the political and culturally repressive right-wing climate of Argentina in the 1930s, see the introduction and note 70 in chapter 3.

33 Maneuvers such as this, then, contributed to unsex his experience of the *Nights*. Borges also consistently bowdlerized his reading of Burton's translation by other means. Many years later, in his "Autobiographical Essay" (1987; written in 1970), he said that his family owned Burton's *Arabian Nights* but that since the book was "filled with what was then considered obscenity, was forbidden, and I had to read it in hiding up on the roof. But at the time, I was so carried away with the magic that I took no notice whatever of the objectionable parts, reading the tales unaware of any other significance" ("Auto," 25), an unconvincing disclaimer that sounded too Victorian: in her *Biography of Captain Sir Richard Burton* (1893), Lady Isabel Burton had similarly explained the paradox of how she had prepared her expurgated, six-volume version of the *Nights* without reading the most controversial material: "Richard forbade me to read them till he blotted out with ink the worst words," quoted in Brodie, *The Devil*, 310.

he translated, we find "Ali Shar and Zumurrud," a love story between a slave woman and her master that culminates in the following scene of sexual intercourse:

> she lay down on her back and taking his hand, set it to her parts, and he found these same parts softer than silk; white, plumply-rounded, protuberant, resembling for heat the hot room of the bath or the heart of a lover whom love-longing hath wasted ... and lust gat hold on him, and his yard rose and stood upright to the utmost of its height ... he kissed her and embraced her and threw himself upon her as the lion upon the lamb. Then he sheathed his steel rod in her scabbard and ceased not to play the porter at her door and the preacher in her pulpit and the priest at her prayer-niche, whilst she with him ceased not from inclination and prostration and rising up and sitting down ... with passionate movements and wrigglings and claspings of his member*....[34]

Some modern readers may actually be turned off by the highly figurative language and the mannerisms of Burton's translation. Yet, in the first decades of the twentieth century, men of Victorian sensibilities must have found the eroticism of passages like this sensually persuasive, as apparently was the case for Borges. Burton also annotated the scene with the purpose of both explaining a specific practice described in it and informing the West about a superior Eastern sexual technique. In reference to the "claspings of his member" that Zumurrud performed on Ali Shar, he introduced the following note:

> *Arab "Fi zaman-hi," alluding to a peculiarity highly prized by Egyptians; the use of the constrictor vaginae muscles, the sphincter for which Abyssinian women are famous. The "Kabbázah" (= holder), as she is called, can sit astraddle upon a man and can provoke the venereal orgasm, not by wriggling and moving but by tightening and loosing the male member with the muscles of her privities, milking it as it were. Consequently, the *casse-noissette* costs treble the money of other concubines (Ananga-Ranga, p. 127).[35]

As I said, for Borges, the *Nights* was a book of "admirable lascivia," a quality that, if glimpsed through his own texts, it is never fully revealed to the reader. To recover part of his experience, and particularly the one related to the most problematic erotica, we need to go beyond his own writings and follow him, in the guise of literary detectives, through the pages of the *Nights*.

---

34 *Nights*, IV, 227.
35 Ibidem.

## Borges, Reader of Footnotes

Fundamental to a clear appreciation of what Burton's *Nights* meant for Borges is an understanding of how familiar he was with its footnotes and how he read them. In his essay, Borges said that the interest of the footnotes "está en relación inversa de su necesidad"; that is, they did not always help clarify the tales nor was it necessary to read the latter to make sense of the former or to justify their reading. In effect, the enormous body of footnotes forms in itself a substantial text, loosely related to the tales, that can be read in parallel and independently from the stories. Actually, that was what Borges did with volume 6 to illustrate to the reader the richness of Burton's annotation: without even mentioning the stories that they explained, he provided a cursory inventory of the three hundred notes that the volume contains so the reader could appreciate the Englishman's contribution. Moreover, he also roams through Burton's annotation guided by the two very long and detailed indexes of the "anthropological" notes that allow the reader to jump thematically from one to another. That is, collectively the footnotes themselves can be read as another work that would probably occupy more than one volume (the two indexes alone comprise 130 pages!).[36] The notes cover many subjects, from principles of translation (which included criticisms of other translators of the *Nights*) and religious beliefs, to social customs and Eastern erotica. In terms of the latter, in his notes Burton addressed a really wide range of questions, including female circumcision, male homosexuality, erotic dreams, dildos, adultery, sexual positions and techniques, lesbianism, types and uses of condoms, impotence, pederasty, the psychological dimensions of sex. That is, Burton's annotation constituted, in itself, an "Orientalist" sex manual.

And if we approach Borges's "Los traductores" without too many preconceptions about what he read in the *Nights* and how he did it, we find sufficient evidence that indicates that he was interested in Burton's erotic annotations. A first and simple step to identifying his reading of the notes is to pay attention to what he said about them. In a few cases he was pretty explicit and said, for example, that in the *Nights* the English "abundó en notas explicativas [sobre] la erótica [islámica]." Yet, more often Borges refers to the English explorer and the material that he added in a more indirect language that, while not completely obliterating the sexual connotations, does camouflage them to some extent. For example, Borges said that Burton "tenía la pasión [por conocer] las innumerables maneras de ser un hombre, que conocen los hombres" or that "las muy poco variadas variaciones del amor físico" occupied a large proportion of the explorer's commentary. Revealing also of his reading of Burton's annotation is the fact that to talk about it Borges resorted to the allusive language that he and other poets, like Lugones, used

---

36 *Nights*, X, and *Nights, Suppl.*, VII. [The Burton edition of *Nights* comprise 17 volumes, numbered 1–10 and seven more (subtitled the "Supplemental Nights") numbered 1–7.]

in their erotic poetry. Thus, to refer to Burton's vast personal knowledge in sexual matters, Borges said that, throughout his life, the British diplomat had accumulated "ternuras" (experiences of sexual intercourse or women with whom he had had them), a term that Borges distinctly used in poems such as "Villa Urquiza" or "Cercanías."[37] Similarly, he spoke of Burton's notes on erotica as "delectaciones morosas," which is the title of a poem by Lugones that re-created the sex act and that Borges enjoyed revisiting in his conversations with Bioy Casares (and that he eventually anthologized).[38]

I propose, then, to look at some of the notes that Borges mentioned and others that he seems to have alluded to or that he might have possibly checked, which will allow us to re-create at least part of his experience of reading the erotica that Burton included in the *Nights*. As an example, Borges points to a note "graciosamente titulada en el índice [of anthropological notes in volume 10] *capotes mélancoliques*." The note is, in fact, about the history of condoms, the materials employed to make them, the state of the industry in the 1880s, the main reason to use prophylactics ("venereal infections"), and how uncomfortable and ineffective they were according to the ironic French and English slang that named them:

> The bag ... was ... a "Cundum" (so called from the inventor, Colonel Cundum ...) or ... "a check upon child" ... [That is] the dried gut of a sheep worn by a man in the act of coition to prevent venereal infection ... Others term them "cuirasses against pleasure" and "cobweb against infections" ... The articles are now [1880s] of two kinds mostly of baudruche (sheep's gut) and a few of caoutchuc. They are made almost exclusively in the faubourgs of Paris ... The Cundum was unknown to the ancients of Europe although syphilis was not: even prehistoric skeletons show traces of its ravages.[39]

Borges probably read the note with serious interest: he had become an adult when syphilis still had devastating effects on men and women and, apparently, he was especially apprehensive about it. But perhaps for him this note was also one of Burton's "eruditas obscenidades," as Borges sometimes qualified the traveler's knowledge; regardless, it is clear that he had fun with it and enjoyed the humor of the British commentator that in the index obliquely referred to prophylactics not as "condoms" but as "capotes mélancoliques," a name that reflects Burton's (unacknowledged) use of Alfred Delvau's clandestine French *Dictionnaire Erótique Moderne* (1864), where he found some satirical verses that he quoted in the note:

> Les capotes mélancoliques
> Qui pendent chez les gros Millan

---

37 See chapter 6 and "Cercanías" in *Fervor de Buenos Aires* (1923).
38 See chapter 3.
39 *Nights*, VII, 190–91.

> S'enflent d'elles mêmes, lubriques,
> Et déchargent en se gonflant.[40]

Borges's humorous reading of the note and these verses would eventually reappear in H. Bustos Domecq's short story "El signo" (1946), where, as I have said before, one of the protagonists was arrested as a "pornografista" for publishing (real Burton's) titles such as *El jardín perfumado* and the *Kama Sutra* and (Burton-originated but) inexistent erotic books such as *Las capotas melancólicas*.[41]

When Borges praised Burton's *Nights*, he celebrated, among other qualities, "la gloriosa hibridación del inglés" that the explorer's version exhibited, which entailed the use of foreign words such as "*castrato*," "*langue fourrée*," etc. This evaluation of Burton's work has contributed to the reading of Borges's essay as a piece essentially concerned with questions of language and translation. There are certainly ample and justified reasons for this type of approach, but critics have also missed a significant dimension of what Borges's comment meant: the vocabulary that he lists is not just the one used in the translations of the stories but is also the terminology that Burton used in his own notes to talk about sexuality. And as such, they are fragments and pieces of evidence that allow us to go upstream back to the notes that interested him and that he obviously read. One of them was on castrated men and their sexuality:

> There are many ways of making the castrato: in some ... only the penis is removed, in others the testes ...; but in all cases the animal passion remains; for in man ... the *fons veneris* is the brain .... almost all these neutrals have wives with whom they practice the manifold *plaisirs de la petite oie* (masturbation, tribadism, irrumation, tête-bêche, feuille-de-rose, etc.), till they induce the venereal orgasm.[42]

The vastness that Burton's sexual knowledge both exhibited and hinted at in notes like this could not, it is clear, but arouse the curiosity of Borges. But independently of it, the note offered a perspective on alternative practices for men whose sexual potency was diminished, whatever the origin of the condition. More important, here Burton's comment presented an insight on the psychological and emotional dimensions of sex that must have resonated with Borges: "the *fons veneris* is the brain." Actually, as we will see in the next chapter, this insight overlapped with a philosophical discussion of desire, sex, and the imagination, for which Borges resorted to some tales from the *Nights*.

But the reading of this and other notes also allows us to understand the major role that French sexual slang played in Burton's "hibridación del inglés." To refer to the subject of the note, the English explorer uses the

---

40 *Nights*, VII, 190–191 and Delvau, *Dictionnaire Érotique*, I, 131–32.
41 Borges, *OCC*, 139.
42 *Nights*, V, 46.

Italian term "castrato" but when he explains the sexual practices described, he relies to a large extent on the French sexual argot ("la langue verte"),[43] a language whose use seems to go beyond a simply "pornographic" or "obscene" intent and suggests that it was the medium in which sexual knowledge was often communicated among nineteenth-century students of sexuality or collectors of erotica.[44] The presence of Delvau's clandestine dictionary in the note on condoms is, in itself, evidence of the importance that French sexual slang had in Burton's investigations and annotation of the *Nights*. In addition, the tales reveal Burton's preference in this respect, and it is possible to sense how his English echoes the French "langue verte": in the second scene of infidelity that I quoted earlier, to show the slave's sexual enjoyment, Burton said that he "[rolled the] eyes which *showed the whites*," which is a close rendition of "*montrer le blanc* des yeux" or "*faire les yeux blancs*," two expressions of French slang that served to illustrate the intensity of sexual pleasure.[45] Borges, like other intellectuals of the time, was very familiar with French sexual slang (in the 1930s he reviewed a book on the topic in *El Hogar*)[46] and was, certainly, very capable of appreciating that the "langue verte" was one of the resources employed by Burton in his "hibridación del inglés."

Another foreign term used by Burton that Borges highlighted in his essay was "langue fourrée," an expression that originated in French sexual argot. The quotation of this word by Borges takes us directly to a note on certain kinds of sexual techniques. In "The Nazarene Broker's Story" the narrator says that a woman "... put her mouth to my mouth and sucked my tongue (and I did likewise)," which led Burton to add this note alluded to by Borges:

> "Kissing with th'inner lip" as Shakespeare calls it; the French *langue fourrée*; and Sankrit "Samputa." The subject of kissing is extensive in the East. Ten different varieties are duly enumerated in the "Ananga-Ranga, or the Hindu Art of Love" (Ars Amoris Indica) translated from the Sanscrit, and annotated by A.F.F. and B.F.R. It is also connected with unguiculation, or impressing the nails, of which there are seven kinds; morsication (seven kinds); handling the hair and tappings or pattings with the fingers and palm (eight kinds).[47]

Burton wanted to educate readers about the importance of kissing in amorous relations (hence his reference to the variety of techniques) at the same time

---

43 "la petite oie" meant foreplay; to make "la tête bêche" refers to the position that allows the two lovers to simultaneously perform oral sex on each other (also known as "69"); "feuille de rose" meant anilingus.
44 In the second half of the nineteenth century, a significant proportion of underground European erotica was published in Brussels, Gibson, *Erotomaniac*, 27.
45 See "faire les yeux de carpe," Delvau, *Dictionnaire Érotique*, II, 293. Emphasis added.
46 Pierre Devaux, *La Langue Verte* (1930) in Borges, *OC* [1974], IV, 232–33.
47 *Nights*, I, 270.

that he reminded (or introduced) the Victorian West to the many uses that hair, nails, biting, or patting could have in sexual enjoyment. As a scientific justification for these practices, Burton here (as he does in many other notes) refers readers to the quasi clandestine edition of the *Ananga Ranga* that he himself had translated and published and that Borges also knew of and might have read. But the note allows us, once again, to also comprehend more fully Borges's comments on the language of Burton's work. As we have seen, in "Los traductores" he said that translations such as the explorer's could only happen "después de una literatura"; that is, when the translator could exploit all the possibilities of the language previously tried by foundational writers. Thus Burton's translation was an heir to, among others, "el gigantesco vocabulario de Shakespeare," an appreciation that, as I pointed out earlier, included the Bard's rich sexual language and of which "kissing with th'inner lip" (in this note) or "the deed of kind" (in another quoted earlier), are good examples.

To conclude with the exploration of the notes, and in order to represent more fairly the range of the notes and better approximate what may have been Borges's reading experience, I would like to highlight one footnote. It is highly probable that he checked this note, and it seems that he reelaborated on it in his own literature. At the end of the first note on sexuality that Burton included in the liminal story, and that, we have seen, Borges alluded to, the explorer said that "Upon the subject of Imsák = retention of semen and 'prolongation of pleasure,' I shall find it necessary to say more." That is, he sends the reader to another note that the index makes very easy to locate and that also deals with sexual potency and female preferences. Burton placed the note in a poem in which a Caliph expresses his desire to make a "gazelle" (a beautiful woman) enjoy sex, which gives Burton the opportunity to expand on the sexual technique anticipated in his first note on sexuality:

> We do not find in the *Nights* any allusion to that systematic *prolongatio veneris* which is so much cultivated by Moslems under the name of Imsák = retention, withholding *i.e.* the semen. Yet, Eastern books on domestic medicine consist mostly of two parts; the first of general prescriptions and the second of aphrodisiacs especially those *qui prolongent le plaisir* as did the Gaul by thinking of *sa pauvre mère*. The Ananga-Ranga ... gives a host of recipes which are used ... to hasten the paroxysm of the woman and delay the orgasm of the man ... The essence of the "retaining art" is to avoid over tension of the muscles and to pre-occupy the brain: hence in coition Hindus drink sherbet, chew betel-nut and even smoke. Europeans ignoring the science and practice, are contemptuously compared with village-cocks by Hindu women who cannot be satisfied ... with less than 20 minutes."[48]

48 *Nights*, V, 76–77.

The note represents well Burton's agenda and his comparative judgement of Westerners' and Easterners' attitudes toward sexuality, in which the latter appeared wiser, healthier, and, ultimately, more powerful, an assessment "scientifically" supported by Eastern sex manuals ("books on domestic medicine"), such as the *Ananga Ranga*. And, as with the comparison to the better-endowed African men, the desire of Indian women also proved too much for ignorant, self-centered, and sexually incapable European men. Similarly to what we have seen in other notes, here too, the technique discussed by Burton implied the recognition of the emotional and psychological dimensions of sex. To achieve mutually satisfying relationships, men may need "to pre-occupy the brain," to momentarily take their minds off the erotic stimulus, as some French did "by thinking of *sa pauvre mère*." Apparently informed by insights such as these and other readings that pointed in a similar direction (among them Montaigne, as we will see in the next chapter), Borges too seemed to have practiced the "pre-occupation" of his mind, not to prolong the sexual relationship but to escape the fear that the amorous encounter aroused in him. In a poem on the psychological effects of his "Talismanes," he engages in a long enumeration of pleasant readings and objects, a mental exercise that, however, proves useless "contra la sombra que no puedo nombrar, contra la sombra que no debo nombrar."[49] And in "El amenazado" to stave off the "sueño atroz" (love and sex), he again pre-occupies his brain with several of his mental "talismanes," which include, similarly to the French in Burton's note, "el joven amor de mi madre."[50]

## The *Nights* in "Nuestras imposibilidades"

The exploration of the notes makes clear that Burton's annotation of the *Nights* constituted in itself a sex manual and that it could be read as such, which Borges did. But Burton's commentary on the sexuality of the *Nights* was not limited to the notes and included also the very controversial "Terminal Essay,"[51] a key piece in the troubled reception of his translation. In this very long essay (approximately 240 pp.), Burton treats important literary questions (e.g. the historical origins of the *Nights* and how they became known in Europe)[52] at the same time that he explores the standing of women in Arab societies and the origins and nature of the pornography contained in the tales. As part of the latter, Burton includes a 50-page section on "Pederasty,"[53] which is actually a wider and comparative

---

49 Borges, *OC* [1974], II, 111.
50 Borges, *OC* [1974], I, 1107.
51 *Nights*, X, 63–302.
52 Borges read with a lot of interest Burton's insights on the history and translation of the collection of tales, and some of those offered in "Los traductores" are already present in the very rich essay by the English explorer.
53 *Nights*, X, 205–54.

exploration of human sexuality across times, cultures, and regions, including the Americas. In "Los traductores" Borges mentions that Burton's first literary work had been "un informe harto personal sobre los prostíbulos de Bengala," a clear reference to the anecdote that Burton tells in the opening paragraphs of the section.

This was not the first time that Borges showed he had read the famously controversial essay. In fact, the most explicit reference to homosexuality in his published work, a homophobic statement in "Nuestras imposibilidades," (1931)[54] is indebted to it. In the "Terminal Essay," the explorer cites a Brazilian author who condemned male homosexuality in his country and, in particular, its tolerance and acceptance by Brazilian society:

> A crime which in England leads to the gallows, and which is the very measure of abject depravity, passes with impunity amongst us.[55]

Burton's source stated a comparative condemnation of Brazilian tolerance toward male homosexuality in which England is said to uphold higher and desirable (and, implicitly, "civilized") standards of morality. Burton added his own anecdotal evidence in support of the Brazilian author:

> Till late years pederasty in the Brazil was looked upon as a peccadillo ... one of Her Majesty's Consuls [in Brazil] used to tell a tale of the hilarity provoked in a "fashionable" assembly by the open declaration of a young gentleman that his mulatto "patient" had suddenly turned upon him, insisting upon becoming "agent."[56]

Burton's anecdote underlined the higher moral and social standing (based on conceptions of masculinity and race) that Brazilian upper-class men accorded to the "agent" over the "patient" in homosexual relations, which was revealed by the laugh that it provoked. But the British Consul distanced himself from it, which implied a condemnation of the practice and the values that it revealed. Borges's homophobic statement in "Nuestras imposibilidades" is molded after this passage in Burton's essay:

> Añadiré otro ejemplo curioso: el de la sodomía. En todos los países de la tierra, una indivisible reprobación recae sobre los dos ejecutores del inimaginable contacto. *Abominación hicieron los dos; su sangre sobre ellos*, dice el Levítico. No así entre el malevaje de Buenos Aires, que reclama una especie de veneración para el agente activo—porque lo embromó al compañero. Entrego esa dialéctica fecal a los apologistas de la *viveza* ... que tanto infierno encubren.

Borges did not need to read Burton to know that in Argentina also the social and moral standing of the one who played an active role in a male

---

54 All quotes from the essay in Borges, *BES*, 117–20.
55 *Nights*, X, 245–46.
56 *Nights*, X, 246.

homosexual relationship was higher than his partner's. But the "Terminal Essay" showed him that the dynamics of the male homosexual relation offered an opportunity to talk about the morality of national communities and, more important, it also offered him a form to articulate it. Like the Brazilian author cited in the *Nights*, Borges also condemns homosexuality through a comparison of morality among nations, but while Burton's source only contrasts Brazil to England, Borges opposes Argentina to "todos los paises de la tierra." To support his totalizing judgement, he cites Leviticus, which the English explorer also did with similar purposes in another passage of the essay ("The ancient lawgiver ... speaks with no uncertain voice ...; their blood shall be upon them [Levit.XX 13])."[57] With the universalizing of his judgement, Borges departs from the source and ignores the case of Brazil, a decision that we will be able to understand further below. Finally, as in the anecdote told by Burton, Borges points out the humor that sanctions the value system of male homosexuality and, as did the British diplomat, he also rejects it. So Borges's familiarity with Burton's controversial "Terminal Essay" is clear and, among other things, it reveals that his erotic readings do not appear necessarily in a context of desire and sex but can be displaced and show up among other types of discourses, such as his polemical prose.

Yet, while tracing the passage back to its source allows us to understand the origin of its form, it does not quite permit us to explain why the reading of Burton appears in this political text. For that, we have to briefly reevaluate "Nuestras imposibilidades." Borges's essay was a denunciation of the right-wing military dictatorship ruling the country and of the social and cultural roots of Argentine nationalism, the ideology that enabled such a regime. Thus, Borges constructs an argument that pays attention to class, religion, and race, and, how they coalesced into national culture and identity. In the argument he underlines some insidious Argentine behaviors and the values they reflect while at the same time he compares and contrasts them with the realities of foreign nations. For instance, whenever the Argentine national soccer team loses a game against the Uruguayan team, the Press and popular opinion explain the defeat by arguing that "los once compadritos buenos de Buenos Aires fueron maltratados por los once compadritos malos de Montevideo" because, according to Borges, "el extranjero [es] un sujeto imperdonable." Similarly, the typical Argentine is disdainful of the USA, but when it comes to organized crime, he is proud of the fact that Buenos Aires is comparable to Chicago. In the same vein, the film *Hallelujah*, acclaimed in other nations, fell flat in Argentina because the audience was incapable of relating to the subject of the movie "por tratarse de negros"; that is, the topic was too foreign for the limited and racist Argentine imagination. As Borges explained, "para el argentino ejemplar todo lo infrecuente es monstruoso—y como

---

57 *Nights*, X, 228.

tal, ridículo." This narrow-mindedness was both cause and consequence of nationalism, an ideology that implied, inevitably, a comparative assessment of the nation's worth: "Esa mortal y cómoda negligencia de lo inargentino del mundo, comporta una fastuosa valoración del lugar ocupado entre las naciones por nuestra patria."

Although Borges is not explicit about it, this generalized perception of Argentina's disproportionate worth in relation to other nations also included sexual stereotyping. In his *Textos eróticos del Río de la Plata* (1923), a book banned because of its content and of whose existence Borges was aware, the German anthropologist Robert Lehmann-Nitsche explained one of the Argentine (and Uruguayan) sexual stereotypes used against Brazil:

> Los habitantes de las regiones del Plata imputan inclinaciones homosexuales a los brasileños, exactamente como los peruanos a sus vecinos norteños del Ecuador. *Brasilero* significa directamente "uranista," especialmente activo; *a la brasilera*, "coito anal." La prensa difamatoria de Buenos Aires ataca con frecuencia en forma descarada, en parte haciendo dibujos, a los poderosos vecinos del Norte. Así, por ejemplo, las iniciales del lema *Ordem e Progresso*, que aparece en la bandera nacional de Brasil, son interpretadas maliciosamente como *¡Ojete en Peligro!* Debería ponerse fin a este abuso provocativo mediante medidas gubernativas. ¡La prensa difamatoria peruana es, por lo demás, aún más terrible![58]

The homophobic stereotyping of Brazil, it is easy to guess, was fed by a racist view of its Afro-Brazilian majority. The prejudice was deeply entrenched in the sexual slang of Argentina but it was not limited to marginal groups or popular culture: the stereotype was shamelessly displayed in the print media and clearly tolerated (if not promoted) by the cultural and political elite. The prejudice was articulated in the context of national rivalries ("los poderosos vecinos del Norte") and amounted to an affirmation of Argentine (masculine and racial) superiority. Finally, the German anthropologist makes clear that this phenomenon was not limited to the Brazilian-Argentine rivalry and that it also existed between Perú and Ecuador; that is, homophobic stereotyping was part of the symbolic constructions of nations in early-twentieth-century Latin America. Borges must have known about the stereotyping of Brazil and, more generally, the uses of homophobia in the nationalistic game of negating-affirming identities. So, I would like to propose that this is one of the reasons for placing his well-known homophobic statement in a political text such as "Nuestras imposibilidades": he flipped a widespread prejudice against Brazil upside down and turned it against Argentine nationalism and its regime. And to write it, he stripped the (Brazilian) anecdote told in the *Nights* of its original national context and planted it in Argentina.

58 Lehman Nitsche, *Textos eróticos*, 312.

The attack against Argentine nationalism, then, explains both the presence of the statement in the essay and why it is here that we find the most explicit reference to homosexuality in all of his texts. Yet, neither the historical context nor the reading of Burton's *Nights* can entirely explain the choice of words: Borges speaks of the "inimaginable contacto" and debases male homosexuality, calling it "dialéctica fecal." Daniel Balderston has argued that Borges's violent language reflects his own homosexual panic and, indeed, there are numerous evidences of the doubts and fear that homosexuality raised in him.[59] In addition, the historical context alone cannot completely explain his decision to still resort to homophobia in national controversies. He could have avoided or ignored this aspect of nationalistic discourses but he did not; that is, it was a choice consistent with the repeated rejections and attacks on homosexuality that we find not so much in his published texts but, for example, in Bioy Casares's private diary.[60]

Finally, it is also important to consider the possibility of another personal motivation that is related to his fears of homosexuality and homophobia but not identical to them. "Nuestras imposibilidades" was published in the early 1930s, at a time when his sexual impotence was already known by other writers and was used against his work and to attack him personally with implications of homosexuality. In this context, such denunciation might have had more than one goal: on the one hand, this homophobic overacting in public might have also served to unequivocally erase any doubt about his sexual orientation and, on the other, with his exposure of homosexuality in Argentina, he might have wanted to remind his hypocritical colleagues that they belonged to a culture that was not so "macho" as their attacks implied.

## *The Perfumed Garden*

Borges also read *The Perfumed Garden of the Cheikh Nefzaoui*, considered by specialists as "the most famous of all pornographic manuals written in Arabic."[61] As I mentioned earlier, this book was another of Burton's translations that was part of his larger research project on human sexuality and the dissemination of Eastern sexual knowledge in the West. In "Los traductores" (1934), Borges does include "El jardín fragante de Nafzauí" among the

---

59 Balderston, "Dialectica," 72; Bioy, *Borges*, 890.
60 See chapter 9.
61 Irwin, *Arabian Nights*, 165; Nefzaoui was a fifteenth-century Tunisian Sheikh whose sex manual became known in the West in the mid-nineteenth century, when it was "discovered" in Algeria by the French. It was first translated into French and published in a limited edition by Isidore Liseux in the 1880s, which Burton translated into English. However, at the time of his death (1890), Burton was apparently preparing another translation from the Arabic original; but according to accepted accounts, following the explorer's orders, after his death his widow burned his work in progress and the Arabic original disappeared.

British explorer's works, and years later (1951) Bioy Casares recorded in his diary that Borges read it to him, apparently from a personal copy.[62] Some of the reasons why Borges (and many other men) may have been interested in reading it can be glimpsed from a statement by the author about the purposes of his work:

> The principal object of this work is to collect together all the remarkable and attractive matters concerning the coitus, so that he who is in trouble may find a consolation in it, and the man to whom erection offers difficulties may be able to look into it for a remedy against his weakness. Wise physicians have written that people whose members have lost their strength, and are afflicted with impotence, should assiduously read books treating of coition, and study carefully the different kind of lovemaking, in order to recover their former vigour ... books on the subject of generation are indispensable. In every country, large or small, both the rich and the poor have a taste for this sort of books, which may be compared to the stone of philosophy transforming common metals into gold.[63]

One of the main goals of the book was to offer "remedies" to men "afflicted with impotence"; one way of dealing with this problem was to "assiduously read books treating of coition," not only because they offered a variety of solutions but because "scientific" sex manuals also worked as erotica ("in every country ... both the rich and the poor have a taste for this sort of books") whose reading helped men get aroused and perform the sexual act ("transforming common metals into gold").

The problem of male impotence was addressed in two short chapters, one of them titled, in Burton's translation, "Undoing the Aiguillettes (impotence for a time)."[64] In it Sheikh Nefzaoui explained that "impotence arises from many causes," among them "the tying of the aiguillettes": "It happens sometimes at the encounter of man and woman that the former, though burning with desire, cannot accomplish the act of coition ... It is then said of him that his aiguillette (needle) is tied."[65] "The impossibility of performing the coitus," explained the Tunisian author, was due to several causes: "it is simply the result, may be, of an exaggerated respect for the woman, may be of a misplaced bashfulness, may be because one has observed something disagreeable, or on account of an unpleasant odour."[66] Such explanations of

---

62 Bioy cites an edition published (in English) in Paris, by Astrea, 1920.
63 Nefzaoui, *Perfumed Garden*, 138–39.
64 Which shows, once again, his familiarity with French sexual slang. It also suggests his reading of Michel de Montaigne, who famously addressed the question of impotence using this same expression in his essay "Le pouvoir de l'imagination," which nineteenth-century French authors often read looking for guidance in sexual matters.
65 Nefzaoui, *Perfumed Garden*, 187.
66 Nefzaoui, *Perfumed Garden*, 188.

sexual failure, based on the evidence, could all apply to Borges, who, like his fictional homonym in "El Zahir," could have said, "en aquel libro estaba declarado mi mal."[67]

In addition to male impotence, the *Perfumed Garden* covered a wide range of topics (as other sex manuals and Burton's annotation of the *Nights* did), including instruction on sexual positions, the many ways of naming male and female genitalia, and advice on how to prevent pregnancies and cause abortions. The information and instructions offered by Nefzaoui came, in part, in the form of long lists of prescriptions or instructions on therapies, typical of "medical" and "scientific" books. However, the explanations and advice often were offered in the form of tales, adventures, anecdotes, and poetry, making the sex manual also a highly literary text. Among the abundant passages of the *Perfumed Garden* that exhibit this quality we find some that, when read from the perspective of Borges's own literature, clearly show that his curiosity for the book was compounded by this aspect of the manual. For instance, and as I mentioned before, Bioy Casares recorded that Borges read him the book:

> Borges abre *The Perfumed Garden* y me dice: "Aquí está la versión oriental, y desprovista de gracia, de 'con paciencia y con saliva el elefante se la metió a la hormiga.'" Lee: "*Women [...] would succeed in making an elephant mount on the back of an ant, and would even succeed in making them copulate.*"[68]

The passage that Borges read is at the end of the chapter "On the Deceits and Treacheries of Women" and intends to be a summary of the many stories told in it to demonstrate women's extraordinary abilities to cheat on their husbands and to trick other men into sex. It is clear that Borges liked the humor of the passage but he also reacted to it as a translator: he tried to "acclimate" the Eastern text to the creole culture of Argentina and for that he looked to the Spanish equivalent in the local sexual slang, an approach that also guided some of his translations, such as the one of Joyce's *Ulysses*.[69]

The manual offered other literary attractions for a reader like Borges. Thus, in the same chapter mentioned above there is a short tale that instructs readers in one of the tricks that women could use to cheat on their husbands and in which the cuckolded man is told his own story[70]; that is, the tale contains a narrative within a narrative, a mise-en-abime, which suggests "la posibilidad de infinitas involuciones" or infinite repetitions. The device is similar to the theatre within the theatre in *Hamlet* or, more appropriately, to Night 602 in which Shahrazad tells Shahryar their own story. Borges commented on this device in his essay "Cuando la ficción vive en la ficción."[71] In another

67 Borges, *OC* [1974], I, 593.
68 Bioy, *Borges*, 61. Italics in the original.
69 Willson, *La constelación*, 129–32.
70 Nefzaoui, *Perfumed Garden*, 168–69.
71 Borges, *OC* [1974], IV, 434.

instance, in a tale of seduction and explicit sex, a woman communicates her desire in highly allusive verses, which requires the potential lover to consult with Abu Nouas, a famous Arab poet and philosopher. The sage explains to the man the meaning of the verses and, in turn, composes others to respond to the woman; thus, the story is also a brief lesson on the explication and writing of erotic poetry.[72]

The author of *The Perfumed Garden* also told and interpreted many dreams, most of them erotic. Borges, a famous reader and writer of dreams, was, of course, interested in them. Actually, he appropriated one and transformed it into his own literature. In the manual, the Sheikh explains that:

> Generally speaking, to see the vulva in dreams is a good sign; so it is of good augury to dream of coition, and he who sees himself in the act, and finishing with the ejaculation, will meet success in all his affairs. ...
>
> The man who dreams of cohabiting with women with whom to have sexual intercourse is forbidden by religion, as for instance his mother, sister, etc. ... must consider this as a presage that he will go to sacred places [such as the holy soil of Mecca]; and, perhaps, even journey to the holy house of God, and look upon the grave of the Prophet.[73]

The realization of the sexual act in dreams, including incestuous ones, was "of good augury" and "presaged" transcendence to the dreamer. In his *Libro de sueños* (1975), Borges included a short and pseudonymous text (signed by a non-existent Rodericus Bartius, author of *Los que son números y los que no lo son*, also a non-existent book[74]) telling of a dream supposedly experienced by Julius Caesar and titled "El incesto." In it we read:

> César informa que, antes de cruzar el Rubicón y marchar sobre Roma, soñó que cohabitaba con su madre. Como es sabido, los desaforados

---

72 Nefzaoui, *Perfumed Garden*, 140–49.
73 Nefzaoui, *Perfumed Garden*, 124–25.
74 I am aware that what I do here is to "de-attribute" a text by "Rodericus Bartius" and to attribute it to Borges himself. As far as I know Bartius's "authorship" has never been questioned before and, similarly, I am not aware that Borges has ever been proposed as the author of the brief prose. I base my conclusion on a few factors. First, I have checked the database WorldCat and no "Rodericus Bartius" seems to have ever existed (there are, however, a Gasparus and an Adrianus Bartius from the sixteenth and seventeenth centuries respectively, authors of a few texts that do not correspond with the one mentioned by Borges). Second, a search of the title of the work "cited" by Borges led to the same result: World Cat has no book titled *Los que son números y los que no lo son*. Third, other collections of texts edited by Borges, such as *El matrero*, also contain short proses "extracted" from inexistent books written by non-existent authors which were actually written by Borges (Sorrentino, "Travesuras Borgeanas," 1999). These verifications along with the textual evidence that links this prose to *The Perfumed Garden* have led me to conclude that "El incesto" is another of Borges's frequent literary hoaxes.

senadores que terminaron con César a golpes de puñal, no lograron impedir lo que estaba dispuesto por los dioses. Porque la Ciudad quedó preñada del Amo ("hijo de Rómulo y descendiente de Afrodita"), y el prodigioso retoño pronto fue el Imperio Romano.[75]

The "presage" on the historical role of Caesar in this text is a free rearrangement of the prophecies on the future of Rome that Anchises tells Aeneas in Book VI of *The Aeneid* (including the one that shows Caesar during the civil wars and right before fording the Rubicón).[76] But in Virgil's poem the prophecies have nothing to do with sex. The matrix for Borges's reworking of them is the incestuous and prophetical dream that he found in *The Perfumed Garden*, which is evidenced by the verb chosen for the sexual act, "cohabitaba," a tell-tale remnant of the source, or one of Ginzburg's "slender clues" that allows us to establish a relationship between two texts and, thus, opens another window into Borges's sexual preoccupations.

Borges's choice is in itself significant: the fact that of the numerous and varied erotic dreams described and interpreted in the manual he appropriated and reworked the only one dealing with incest speaks about one of his persistent and, although often camouflaged, still noticeable worries. This selectivity was also at work in the occasion of at least two other readings: as we have seen "Incontaminado" was the only text in Del Mazo's *Los vencidos* that treated the question of incest; and similarly, in an anthology of the Spanish Silverio Lanza that contains more than thirty texts what caught the attention of a young Borges was a story that shows Judas unknowingly having sex with his mother, the only passage of the book related to the question of incest (he thought the episode was "très fort").[77] That is, the three readings invite us to think that, when available, he dwelt on texts dealing with this thorny issue, a preoccupation also suggested by his insistence on Rossetti's "Inclusiveness." In addition, the intent of his text analyzed above is pretty explicit: it is not about Caesar or Rome, it is about "El incesto," as the title clearly states.

But what he did with the original Arab dream also deserves to be pointed out. The *Libro de sueños* is a compilation of texts by many authors in which Borges could easily have included the original. Yet, to have it published as it was would have meant to make sex more explicit and to have acknowledged his familiarity with the sex manual. Instead, his reworking had the effect of removing himself from the original reading and from the authorship of

---

75 Borges, *LDS*, 57.
76 Virgil, *The Aeneid*, Bk.VI, particularly vv.897–961; see also Bernard Knox's analysis in his "Introduction," 27–33.
77 Jorge Luis Borges to Maurice Abramovitz, Seville, January 12, 1920, *Cartas del fervor*, 72–74. The Lanza anthology read by Borges is *Páginas escogidas e inéditas. In memoriam y Epílogo por Ramón Gómez de la Serna*, Madrid, 1918; the story translated and commented by Borges is "Judas (Fotografía del natural)," 96–100.

the new text: he acclimated it to Antiquity, as Swinburne taught him to do when talking about controversial sexual matters, and referred it back to a non-existent book by a non-existent author.

CHAPTER 5

# Schopenhauer and Montaigne, Philosophy and Sex

Borges's erotic library included philosophy as well. His most important reading in this respect was the work of Arthur Schopenhauer, who had made sexuality one of the cornerstones of his metaphysics. But beyond the specific insight on desire and sex that Schopenhauer's work contained, it also showed Borges the opportunities that the discipline of philosophy presented to reflect on the subject and offered a model for writing texts that moved between metaphysics and the erotic. These philosophical reflections, I propose, became another discreet location from which Borges spoke about desire and sex, as were also the footnotes or short biographies of authors discussed earlier.

In this chapter I will consider first the presence of Schopenhauer's work in the short story "La secta del Fénix," and later I will explore the essay "Historia de la eternidad" (1936). In the case of the latter, I will begin by looking at how in his speculation about eternity and time, Borges blended erotic materials and sexual preoccupations; then, I will investigate the continuities between the reflections about time presented in the essay and some of his poems on sex; and finally, we will read a footnote in the essay in which Borges speculates about the workings of desire. Although it is clear that Schopenhauer was the most important author in this section of Borges's erotic library, this chapter will also allow us to see how he integrated other readings, such as Michel de Montaigne's *Les Essais* and, once again, Burton's *Nights*, in his philosophical explorations.

## Schopenhauer in "La secta del Fénix"

The importance of Schopenhauer (1788–1860) among Borges's readings can hardly be overstated. He considered the German philosopher "la autoridad máxima"[1] in metaphysics, and, not coincidentally, Borges frequently cites him throughout his work. Yet, for all its importance, the relationship between Schopenhauer's work and Borges's literature has rarely been discussed

---

[1] Borges, *OC* [1974], IV, 178.

systematically.[2] In addition, even those who have recognized the importance of this intellectual influence have overlooked the centrality of sex in the German's philosophy: as an example, while the editors of the critical edition of the *Obras completas* use two pages to explain the presence of Schopenhauer in Borges's work, they completely ignore the fundamental role that the former accorded to sexuality in his system.[3] However, I want to propose, this aspect of the German's metaphysics was one that consistently interested Borges and became one of the sources of his own thinking and writing on the subject. Not by chance Borges referred to him as "el apasionado y lúcido Schopenhauer,"[4] an oxymoronic summary of the philosopher's work in which the first adjective was meant to underscore the erotic content of his philosophy. My aim in this section is to look at one of the forms that Schopenhauer's reflection on sexuality takes in Borges's own literature and to propose that the German's *The World as Will and Representation* (1844; hereafter *WWR*) was a fundamental literary source for the short story "La secta del Fénix."

In 1939, in his review of Thomas Mann's biography of the thinker, Borges highlighted Mann's (and Nietzsche's) view that Schopenhauer's philosophy "lleva la marca de la edad juvenil, en la que predominan lo erótico y el sentido de la muerte."[5] As Borges's own comment suggested, Mann's reading of Schopenhauer followed a tradition whose highest point was, probably, Sigmund Freud's reflections on the centrality of sexuality in civilization (an influence that, apparently, the Viennese physician was not always ready to acknowledge).[6]

Schopenhauer himself had underscored the relevance of sexuality for his philosophy and clearly invited the reading of his work along these lines. In *WWR*, in the chapter titled "The Metaphysics of Sexual Love," he said that

> instead of wondering why a philosopher for once makes this constant theme of all the poets his own, we should be surprised that a matter that generally plays so important a part in the life of man has hitherto been almost entirely disregarded by philosophers, and lies before us as a raw and untreated material.[7]

Schopenhauer's exploration of sexuality was, by the standards of nineteenth-century philosophy, very explicit ("[to some] my view will appear too physical, too material, however metaphysical, indeed transcendent, it may

---

2 An exception and a useful contribution is Almeida's "De Borges a Schopenhauer."
3 Borges, *OC* [2009], I, 64–66. In an otherwise very helpful contribution to our understanding of Borges's reading of Schopenhauer, Almeida, however, does not address this fundamental question either.
4 Borges, *OC* [1974], I, 438.
5 Borges, *OC* [1974], IV, 410.
6 Young, *Schopenhauer*, 238–41.
7 Schopenhauer, vol. 2, 532.

be at bottom")[8] and provocative, thus proposing, for example, a reasoned explanation of "pederasty" not with the goal of delivering a "moral admonition against the vice, but of a proper understanding of the essential nature of the matter."[9]

Let us briefly recapitulate some of Schopenhauer's main ideas and the role of sexuality in them. According to his philosophy, the "Will" is the underlying reality of everything or the ultimate reality (Kant's "the thing-in-itself"); that is, nature or, simply, the world. The Will both creates and is the Will, because the Will is a self-creating entity. The main purpose of the Will is its own continuation, and therefore the Will is also the will-to-live, the impulse that makes possible the reproduction of the world. Thus, "the *will-to-live* ... is the only true description of the world's innermost nature. Everything presses and pushes toward *existence*, if possible toward *organic existence*, i.e. *life*."[10] Since the human species is one of the many species that are the phenomenological appearance of the Will, its main purpose is also to reproduce. Hence, according to Schopenhauer, the importance of desire, copulation, and the genitals; that is, the centrality of sex in the world:

> the sexual impulse is the kernel of the will-to-live, and consequently the concentration of all willing; in the text, therefore, I have called the genitals the focus of the will. Indeed, it may be said that man is concrete sexual impulse, for his origin is an act of copulation and the desire of his desires is an act of copulation, and this impulse alone perpetuates and holds together the whole of his phenomenal appearance.[11]

But for the "pessimist" Schopenhauer, suffering (in the form of desire, fear, death, etc.) is an intrinsic characteristic of this world, so the affirmation of the will-to-live through reproduction is ethically contradictory and fundamentally morally wrong, which would explain the shame and guilt associated with sex:

> With that affirmation beyond one's own body to the production of a new body, suffering, and death ... are also affirmed anew ... Here is to be seen the profound reason for the shame connected with the business of procreation.[12]

It is this shame and guilt that explains a paradox: in spite of "the important role played by the sex-relation in the world of mankind ... it is really the invisible central point of all action and conduct." This, explains Schopenhauer, is

> the piquant element and the jest of the world, that the principal

---

8 Schopenhauer, vol. 2, 533.
9 Schopenhauer, vol. 2, 566.
10 Schopenhauer, vol. 2, 350. Emphasis in the original.
11 Schopenhauer, vol. 2, 513–14.
12 Schopenhauer, vol. 1, 328.

concern for all men *is pursued secretly* and ostensibly ignored as much as possible ... arrangements [are] made to subdue it, to imprison it, or at any rate to restrict it, and, if possible *to keep it concealed*, or indeed so to master it that it appears only as an entirely subordinate and secondary concern of life.[13]

As I said, some of Borges's reflections about sex are indebted to Schopenhauer's insights. Thus, and as an example, Borges's famous "Los espejos y la paternidad son abominables, porque multiplican y afirman [la Tierra]"[14] in "El tintorero enmascarado" betrays, even in the phrasing, Schopenhauer's reflections quoted above on the pessimistic origins of the shame and guilt associated with sex.

The presence of the German philosopher is more fundamental in "La secta del Fénix" (1952). The short story, Ronald Christ pointed out, has the form of "an unstated riddle," which "leaves the reader with a puzzle." Unable to quite figure out what the story was about, Christ asked during a personal meeting with the author "if he ever revealed the answer to the riddle" and, eventually, Borges told him that "the act," "the rite," or "the Secret" told in the story was sexual intercourse.[15]

The form of the story, I propose, reflects Borges's very productive reading of the chapter "On the Affirmation of the Will-to-Live," a section of *WWR* in which Schopenhauer precisely articulates the idea of the world and humanity as a "riddle" that can only be solved with the knowledge of the concealed or secretive act of copulation. Actually, almost three decades before the publication of the story, in an essay published in the 1920s, Borges had already quoted that chapter:

> *la cópula es al mundo lo que la palabra al enigma*. A saber, el mundo ... no es sino la manifestación de la voluntad de vivir y *la concentración, el foco de esta voluntad, es el acto generativo*.[16]

which in Schopenhauer reads

> *The act of procreation is further related to the world as the solution to the riddle* ... the world ... has an inexhaustible multiplicity of forms. Yet all this is only the phenomenon of the will to live; and *the concentration, the focus of this will is the act of generation*. ... that act, as the most distinct expression of the will, is the kernel, the compendium, the quintessence of the world. Hence, we obtain through it a light as to the true nature and tendency of the world; *it is the solution to the riddle*.[17]

---

13 Schopenhauer, vol. 2, 513. Emphasis added.
14 Borges, *OC* [1974], I, 327.
15 Christ, *The Narrow Act*, 155, 190.
16 Borges, *IA*, 72. Emphasis added.
17 Schopenhauer, vol. 2, 570. Emphasis added.

In addition to the form of the story, the logic of Borges's choice for the title (the logic, not the mythical figure) also reflects his creative reading of Schopenhauer. In his comments on the myth of the Phoenix, Borges said that "el Fénix fue alegado por los teólogos para probar la resurrección de la carne" and that "los egipcios buscaron eternidad [en] el mito de un pájaro inmortal y periódico."[18] Schopenhauer, for whom not the individual but "the species alone has infinite life," articulates the nature and the workings of the will-to-live in a way that easily reminds us of the myth of the Phoenix:

> [the] willing of the animal presents itself as such an animal form maintained throughout an infinite time by the ever repeated replacement of one individual by another, and hence by the alternation of death and generation. Thus considered, death and generation appear to be the pulsation of that form (*species*) enduring through all time.[19]

Borges's debt to Schopenhauer can also be appreciated in the insights and details he used in the construction of the "riddle." Schopenhauer refers to the contradictory and paradoxical status of sex in human society. In spite of being what keeps humanity alive, people always try to conceal it and "*if they are caught in the act*, they are as alarmed *as if they had been detected in a crime.*" The sex act, he continues,

> is *the great unspeakable, the public secret which must never be distinctly mentioned* anywhere, *but is always and everywhere understood* to be the main thing as a matter of course, and is therefore always present in the minds of all. For this reason, *even the slighter allusion to it is instantly understood* .... What is *amusing* is to be found only in *the constant concealment* of the main thing.[20]

Borges's clues about "the Secret" closely follow Schopenhauer's insight:

> El Secreto es sagrado pero no deja de ser un poco *ridículo: su ejercicio es furtivo* y aún *clandestino* y los adeptos *no hablan de él.* No hay palabras decentes para nombrarlo, pero se entiende que todas las palabras lo nombran o mejor dicho, que inevitablemente *lo aluden,* y así, en el diálogo yo he dicho una cosa cualquiera y los adeptos han sonreído o se han puesto incómodos porque sintieron que yo había tocado el Secreto.[21]

(Again, decades before the writing of "La secta," in a 1920s essay, Borges had already highlighted the philosopher's insight on the language of eroticism: "Cabe rememorar aquí lo que Schopenhauer dijo de las alusiones eróticas.

---

18 Borges, *OCC*, 689, 587.
19 Schopenhauer, vol. 2, 512.
20 Schopenhauer, vol. 2, 570–71.
21 Borges, *OC* [1974], I, 523. Emphasis added.

Todos las desentrañan en seguida, pues la materia suya es vivaz en toda conciencia"[22]).

In Borges's story we also read that when the young devotees of the sect finally discovered it,

> el secreto, al principio les pareció baladí, *penoso, vulgar* y (y lo que aún es más extraño) *increíble. No se avenían a admitir* que sus padres se hubieran *rebajado* a tales manejos.[23]

The insight into the discovery of sex and the beginning of life certainly echoes a widely shared experience, particularly among earlier, pre-sexual revolution and education generations. Speaking about the story, Borges himself told Ronald Christ:

> *When I first heard about this act, when I was a boy*, I was shocked, *shocked to think that my mother, my father had performed it*. It is *an amazing discovery*, no?[24]

Having seen the relationship between Borges's story and *The World as Will and Representation*, we realize that Schopenhauer's insights on this matter also helped Borges tell about and formulate his own personal experience. In his work the German philosopher pointed out, in very similar terms, this crucial moment in the development of the individual's self-awareness:

> But see now how *the young, innocent human intellect is startled* at the enormity, *when that great secret of the world first becomes known to it!* ... and from the standpoint of pure, hence *innocent, knowledge is horrified thereat*.[25]

The close reading of what Borges read has made it possible to know that his short story about sexual intercourse is fundamentally organized around Schopenhauer's reflections on sex and, thus, has opened another perspective on how and why he read the German philosopher. On the one hand, it dates Borges back to the intellectual climate of the late nineteenth and early twentieth centuries, when Schopenhauer was read by Richard Wagner, Nietzsche, and, more importantly, Freud, for what the philosopher had to say about sex, not just metaphysics.[26] On the other hand, this angle of the German Idealist allows us to see that he also appealed to Borges's sexual self-awareness and sensibility. Schopenhauer himself famously had a miserable love and sex life, which explains in part his pessimism and the dark insights on sex that largely define his work. Some of them connected directly with Borges's own personal history, so much so that it is possible to think that Borges could read them even as "therapy." Speaking about

---

22 Borges, *Inq.*, 68.
23 Borges, *OC* [1974], I, 524. Emphasis added.
24 Christ, *The Narrow Act*, 190.
25 Schopenhauer, vol. 2, 571. Emphasis added.
26 Young, *Schopenhauer*; Dreyfus, *Wagner*.

the sentiments that sex arouses in human beings, especially in their sexual initiation, the German thinker said

> It is an action of which, on cool reflection, we think often with *repugnance*, and in an exalted mood, with *disgust* ... a peculiar *sadness* and *remorse* follows close on it; yet these are felt more *after the consummation of the act for the first time*. ...²⁷

"Repugnance," "disgust," "sadness," and "remorse" is what Schopenhauer himself must have felt, and what all the evidence suggests that Borges experienced in Geneva. Schopenhauer's work, then, must have helped Borges make sense of his suffering, and the affinity of their sensibilities surely was a factor in his interest in the philosopher's thinking more generally.

While the story undeniably speaks about sex, it is also true that it does it very obliquely. On the one hand, it has the form of a riddle (it never mentions the word "sex"), and most readers rarely figure out the first time what the story is about (as Ronald Christ's dialogue with Borges demonstrates). On the other, resorting to the religious connotations of terms such as "sect" and "rite" and with historical and mythological allusions, Borges sets the tale in some undefined Ancient time, which allows him to depersonalize his own voice. This was a strategy masterfully practiced by poets such as Swinburne and Yeats to speak about their own sex and that Borges himself adopted in a dramatic monologue such as "Endimión en Latmos." Yet however oblique and depersonalized Borges's voice is in the story, it is still possible to read his biography in the text. The narrator says that "una suerte de horror sagrado impide a algunos fieles la ejecución del simplísimo rito; los otros los desprecian, pero ellos se desprecian aún más,"²⁸ which shows that the writing of his short story about sexual intercourse is pretty explicitly related to his impotence and the social stigmatization that he had to endure because of it.

## The Eroticism of Eternity and Time

Schopenhauer's influence, as I explained before, went beyond his specific insights on the role of sexuality in civilization, and, more generally, his metaphysics seem to have also worked as a model that showed Borges that philosophy was a discipline quite apt for discussing desire and sex. This is what is revealed in "Historia de la eternidad" (1936), a philosophical essay in which Borges primarily explores the idea of eternity and time but where noticeable erotic motivations are woven into a metaphysical reflection, and although the text apparently has nothing to say on our subject, it turns out to be another discreet location from which Borges hinted at his preoccupations.

---

27 Schopenhauer, vol. 2, 569. Emphasis added.
28 Borges, *OC* [1974], I, 523.

As is well known, Borges was deeply interested in the phenomenon of time. He said that "time," the idea "del ayer, del hoy, del porvenir, del siempre y del nunca," was the only true enigma of our reality. It was, he said, "el problema capital de la metafísica."[29] It was his fascination with time that in part motivated him to write a history of the idea of "eternity." The essay is divided into four parts: in the first two, he reviews the most relevant authors and texts on the concept of eternity; in the third section, he offers a general interpretation about the origins of the idea and opposes it to the experience of time; in the fourth, and final, section, he narrates a personal mystical experience that, Borges believed, somehow approached the state called "eternity." Here I want to focus on the third section, on the origins of the idea of eternity and the opposite experience of time, where it is noticeable that desire and sex are important components of the argument.

But before we get to it, it is important to understand that the eternity that interested Borges was not the endless sequence of time without beginning or end; it was not time endlessly elapsing. Borges was thinking about another type of eternity:

> Yo había leído en los teólogos que la eternidad no es la suma del ayer, del hoy y del mañana, sino un instante, un instante infinito, en el cual se congregan todos nuestros ayeres … todo el presente y todo el incalculable porvenir o los porvenires.[30]

This idea of eternity goes back to the Pre-Socratics, such as Parmenides, and eventually was Christianized by theologians like Saint Augustine and, in particular, the schools of the Middle Ages.[31] The concept emerged from the need to explain the Creator and the origins of the world. If history starts with creation, the Creator must have existed before history, in other words, before or outside of time; or, if God created everything, he must have also created time. If before creation there was no time, what was that "before" or "outside" time like? On the other hand, the idea of God implies that he "remains" or he is "eternal," meaning he does not "change" or is not affected by time, and, therefore, he must be outside of time, he is not temporal. What is that state outside of time like? "Eternity" is a pure and permanent present, it is an infinite present, but since it is not time, it does not elapse, and it concentrates everything we live not only as present, but also as past and future. As Borges said in his explanation, "eternity is not just adding the yesterday, today and tomorrow, but an instant, an infinite instant, in which all of our yesterdays congregate … all the present and the incalculable future or futures." The "congregation" of all times implied that in eternity we would find or see all the events, people, etc. of the past, present, and future in the same instant (as was the case in "El Aleph"). It was also in this permanent state or reality

---

29 Borges, *OC* [1974], II, 36; IV, 199.
30 Ortega and Del Río Parra, *'El Aleph'*, 107.
31 Russell, *Western Philosophy*, 45–46, 144–45.

outside time that, according to Plato, the perfect and unchanging "ideas" or "archetypes" existed. (The Schoolmen referred to "eternity" with the Latin expression *Nunc-stans*, which means "a now that remains").

For us, immersed in time, this "eternity" may seem like a strange idea, literally unimaginable or incredible, and it actually is in many senses. It is a paradoxical and logically unacceptable idea because it tells us about an "infinite instant." As we can expect, the imagination that the paradox revealed was one of the qualities that attracted Borges and in different moments he called it "una de las más hermosas invenciones del hombre," "un artificio" ("a fiction") or an idea "mágica"; an idea so foreign and inaccessible to human experience that Borges suspected that it could only have been "intuited" in moments such as "la muerte," "la locura," or in a "pesadilla."[32] That is, access to eternity implied a special state of the soul. And, thus, in "Historia de la eternidad" when he asks himself how was this concept created? where did it come from? ("¿Cómo fue incoada la eternidad?"), he offers an answer infused with the language of love and eroticism, in which the experience of longing and desire is the cornerstone:

> Pienso que la nostalgia fue ese modelo. El hombre enternecido y desterrado que rememora posibilidades felices, las ve *sub specie aeternitatis*, con olvido total de que la ejecución de una de ellas excluye o posterga las otras. En la pasión, el recuerdo se inclina a lo intemporal. Congregamos las dichas de un pasado en una sola imagen; los ponientes diversamente rojos que miro cada tarde, serán en el recuerdo un solo poniente. Con la previsión [del futuro] pasa igual: las más incompatibles esperanzas pueden convivir sin estorbo. Dicho sea con otras palabras: el estilo del deseo es la eternidad.[33]

The erotic is lived as "recuerdo" of what happened or as "esperanza" of what we want to happen. This is exactly the language of eroticism that Borges used, as we saw before, when he pondered whether the image presented in Fernández Moreno's "Roja inicial" reflected the "recuerdo" or the "esperanza" of the author. In "nostalgia" or "recuerdo" we eliminate the many experiences that we have had and freeze the past in one happy, intense image, in one moment that eliminates the others and that remains the same (the image becomes an archetype that stays in "an infinite instant"). With the "esperanzas" (desire) projected toward the future, something similar happens: we fix our minds on one desired goal that we picture to ourselves in an image of a single moment; and we believe it to be possible, even when we know many other events or facts may stop or derail our march toward it. That is, like "nostalgia," desire lives outside of time or, as Borges marvelously put it, "el estilo del deseo es la eternidad."

---

32 Borges, *OC* [1974], IV, 199; I, 351; I, 354; I, 357; I, 355.
33 Borges, *OC* [1974], I, 365.

"Nostalgia," "enternecido," "felices," "pasión," "recuerdo," "dichas," "esperanzas," are all words that suggest in themselves the erotic tenor of Borges's metaphysical exploration. This becomes even more evident when he discusses the passing of time or "sucesión," the real experience that puts into question the idyllic idea of eternity and that is its opposite. Borges explored this question on numerous occasions, and before looking at how he dealt with it in "Historia de la eternidad," it will be helpful to hear another of his explanations. In a public lecture he reflected on the passing of time and pointed out the paradoxical quality of the "present," the time in which we live, and, yet, because of its fleeting quality, we cannot grasp:

> ¡Qué raro pensar que de los tres tiempos en que hemos dividido el tiempo—el pasado, el presente, el futuro—el más difícil, el más inasible, sea el presente! El presente es tan inasible como el punto ... Nosotros sentimos que estamos deslizándonos por el tiempo, es decir, podemos pensar que pasamos ... del pasado al futuro, pero no hay un momento en que podamos decirle al tiempo: "Detente ...." El presente no se detiene. No podríamos imaginar un presente puro; sería nulo.[34]

The present exists but we cannot grasp it, and although we experience it we cannot get ahold of it; that is, it is somehow as illusory and deceptive as a mirage. En "Historia de la eternidad," to illustrate the impossibility of grasping and arresting the flow of time, Borges quoted what he himself defined as "aquel terrible pasaje de Lucrecio, sobre la falacia del coito":

> Como el sediento que en el sueño quiere beber y agota formas de agua que no lo sacian y perece abrasado por la sed en el medio de un río: así Venus engaña a los amantes con simulacros, y la vista de un cuerpo no les da hartura, y nada pueden desprender o guardar, aunque las manos indecisas y mutuas recorran todo el cuerpo. Al fin, cuando en los cuerpos hay presagio de dichas y Venus está a punto de sembrar los campos de la mujer, los amantes se aprietan con ansiedad, diente amoroso contra diente; del todo en vano, ya que no alcanzan a perderse en el otro ni a ser un mismo ser.[35]

In *The Nature of Things*, in the book *On the Senses*, Lucretius speaks about the uniqueness of desire and sex among the needs of human beings: while thirst can be quenched with drinking, desire can never be satisfied with sex.[36] Yet, deceived by Venus, lovers wrongly believe it is possible, and they try to satiate desire with sexual intercourse; but when they hold each other's bodies and are about to become one, the illusion vanishes (and, thus, eventually, they will have to have sex again). This section of Lucretius's long poem is a classic of erotic literature that can be found in some of the best anthologies on the

---

34 Borges, *OC* [1974], IV, 204–5.
35 Borges, *OC* [1974], I, 364.
36 Lucretius, *The Nature*, vv.1076–120.

genre,[37] and it fits perfectly into a discernible pattern of Borges's readings: as we have seen, he was genuinely interested in re-creations of the sex act (particularly in poetry) by authors such as Lugones, Rossetti, W. B. Yeats, and Richard Burton. To illustrate the deceiving and unseizable quality of time, Borges quoted a classic of the literature of sexual love that described and explained coitus, a choice that reveals the erotic undercurrent that fed his metaphysical speculation.

Borges surrounds the passage with an almost strident negative tone. Before quoting it, he qualifies it as "terrible" and speaks of "la falacia del coito." In closing he says, "Lo cierto es que la sucesión es una intolerable miseria y que los apetitos magnánimos codician todos los minutos del tiempo …";[38] at the same time, though, he opposes the problematic qualities of the passing of time to the good ones of eternity: "Los arquetipos y la eternidad—dos palabras—prometen posesiones más firmes." Borges formulated this contrast between the "bad" passing of time and the "good" eternity more than once. In another moment, he says that "la eternidad, anhelada con amor por tantos poetas, es un artificio espléndido que nos libra, siquiera de manera fugaz, de la intolerable opresión de lo sucesivo."[39] That is, while the fiction of eternity creates an idyllic out-of-time reality where an equally perfect love was or will be possible, time or "la sucesión" is an "intolerable miseria" or "intolerable opresión." Why? "La sucesión" of time is not a fictional paradise like eternity but the too-real dimension where he experiences his troubling desire and the fear of sex: e.g. in "El amenazado" he also speaks of "el horror de vivir en lo sucesivo."[40] Time, for example, measures (and makes it impossible to ignore) his endlessly unsatisfied desire: "los apetitos magnánimos codician todos los minutos del tiempo." Thus, in Borges one of the fundamental aspects of the real experience of desire and sex is the extreme, almost excruciating awareness of the passing of time; an awareness that, in turn, is caused by the fear and anxiety that sex arouses in him.

## Montaigne, Sex, Fear, and Time

It is not a surprise, then, to find that in Borges's literature, important expressions of desire and sex are framed by specific conceptions of the psychological dimensions of time. This can be clearly seen in poems such as "La espera" and "El amenzado," which I will analyze in the next few pages. But to have a wider perspective on how they fit into Borges's work and appreciate them better, first we must first look at some of his personal experiences and *Les Essais* of Michel de Montaigne, one of the readings that helped him reflect on the subjective dimension of time.

---

37 Pauvert, *Anthologie*, I, 182–92.
38 Borges, *OC* [1974], I, 364.
39 Borges, *OC* [1974], I, 351.
40 Borges, *OC* [1974], I, 1107.

As we have seen, Borges suffered anticipatory anxiety: for instance, before one of his public speeches, because of "[el] miedo tan tremendo que tenía," his hands were shaking and he was sweating.[41] In a man so interested in the phenomenon of time, stressful experiences like this contributed both to make him more aware of it and to reflect about it. Thus, in one of his classes he explained that the objective time of the clock was different from the time measured by physical suffering or fear:

> Well, time as given by the watch is conventional, isn't it? But real time, for example, when you're having a tooth pulled, is only too real ... [it is] the time of fear, when the sands of [the] time [clock] run out[42]

Clocks cannot measure the time of fear. Or the anxiety of waiting: "cuando uno espera el tiempo pasa despacio; sin embargo, lo que uno siente es que pasa mucho tiempo."[43] For Borges, fear, physical pain, and anxious waiting expose us to a different notion of time.

Borges's anxieties also oriented some of his readings on the subjective experience of time. Perhaps the most important author in this respect was Michel de Montaigne, whose *Essais* offered the thoughts of the Stoic tradition on these matters (Stoicism was a major aspect of Borges's thinking that we will explore in more detail in chapter 7). In essays such as "Sur la physionomie" and "Que philosopher c'est apprendre à mourir," the French thinker explored the relation between subjectivity (imagination), physical suffering, death, and the experience of time. Although he was some sort of hypochondriac, Montaigne realized "que [étant] en bonne santé, j'avais eu les maladies beaucoup plus en horreur que lorsque je les ai ressenties" and that it was only "par l'imagination, [que] je grossis ces désagréments."[44] It was just his imagination that made him disproportionally fear illnesses, only to find out, when they eventually did affect him, that they were not as bad as he had anticipated. For Montaigne, "imagination" is a tricky quality. It creates present worries for things that may or may not occur, and therefore, this fearful manner of living in the future makes the passing of the present time unnecessarily painful and unbearable:

> Pendant ce temps ... Que te sert d'acueillir et de devancer ta mauvaise fortune, de perdre le présent par la crainte du futur et d'être à cette heure malhereux parce que tu dois l'être avec le temps.[45]

This perspective on present and future times also framed the fundamental question of death. According to the Stoic doctrine, the most important event

---

41 Goldaracena, "Las inhibiciones del joven Borges."
42 Borges, *BOW*, 57.
43 Bioy, *Borges*, 518.
44 Montaigne, *Essais*, I, XX, 111.
45 Montaigne, *Essais*, III, XII, 1267–68. In this passage, Montaigne quotes and paraphrases Seneca's letters to Lucilius XIII and XXIV.

in life was death, and therefore, human beings were expected to use their lives to learn how to confront death and die. It was useless to worry about it, Stoics thought, because an individual's death was determined by her fate, and therefore, it never arrived too early and always came at the right time. Worrying about the future not only did not stop death but only served to needlessly torment the individual in the present, especially because death in itself was less painful and traumatic than what our fearful imaginations led us to believe:

> La vue de la mort à venir a besoin d'une fermeté longue et difficile, par conséquent, à garder. Si vous ne savez pas mourir, ne vous en souciez pas ... [parce que] "Poena minor certam súbito perferre ruinam, / Quod timeas gravius sustinuisse diu."[46]

Do not worry about death, Montaigne says, because "it is less painful to go through a sudden and precise disgrace than to suffer for a long time the fear caused by the idea of the event."[47] In another of his formulations about the uselessness of worrying in the present about the death that will occur in the future, Montaigne also said: "Et puisque nous sommes menacés de tant de sortes de mort, n'y a-t-il pas plus de mal à les craindre toutes qu'à en supporter une?"[48] Instead of dying every time with each worry, it is preferable to relax and wait until the real death arrives; that is, it is better to die only once. (Shakespeare, also a reader of Montaigne, rewrote: "Cowards die many times before their deaths; / The valiant never taste of death but once").[49]

The torments of the present because of the feared events of the future were a problem only for the learned classes who had fed their imaginations with education and capacity to reflect. However, the uneducated, roughened up, lower classes lacked imagination and did not worry about death or other disgraces that the future reserved for them: "le manque de l'intelligence du bas peuple lui donne cette endurance des maux présents et cette profonde insouciance des sinistres événements futurs."[50]

Borges's literature was influenced by this aspect of Stoicism. For instance, in "El otro duelo," Stoic gauchos showed no fear before battles because, as the narrator explains, "la falta de imaginación los libró del miedo."[51] The presence of the doctrine is also very clear in "La espera" (1950), a short story whose main argument, as the title suggests, revolves around the relationship between present and future times and, more specifically, about the question

---

46 Montaigne, *Essais*, III, XII, 1268.
47 Montaigne, *Essais*, III, XII, 1268. The quote is Maximianus or Pseudo-Gallus, *Elegies*, I, v.277–78.
48 Montaigne, *Essais*, I, XX, 113.
49 In his prologue to Macbeth, Borges says, "Shakespeare, lector frecuente de Montaigne," *OC* [1974], IV, 134. Shakespeare's quote comes from *Julius Caesar*.
50 Montaigne, *Essais*, III, XII, 1270.
51 Borges, *OC* [1974], I, 1059.

of how to wait for or prepare for death. The protagonist is a gangster who knows that he has been sentenced to death by his former accomplices and waits for months in a room in a boarding house for the executioners to show up and pull the trigger. The man is of Italian origin, a culture that in Borges's imaginary did not possess Stoic qualities, as gauchos did.[52] Therefore, during that apparently endless wait, his anxiety makes him perceive danger where there is none, and nightmares about his execution torment him during his sleep at night. Finally, though, when the killers catch up with him, he does not resist and accepts his death with tranquility because he finally realizes that "es menos duro sobrellevar un acontecimiento espantoso que imaginarlo y aguardarlo sin fin."[53]

In Borges's literature, relationships with women and, in particular, amorous encounters are similarly framed by the awareness of the psychological dimension of time, which reveals the anxiety caused by the anticipation of a feared event. The debt to Stoicism is clear in their framing; however, although a devoted reader of Montaigne and others, the guilt-ridden Borges considered that he himself lacked the qualities of a good Stoic, and contrary to what the philosophy proposed, he let himself be overwhelmed by his present worries about the future. In "La espera" (1977), a poem titled exactly like the short story referenced earlier, the poet is tormented by the anxieties that the approaching meeting with a woman creates in him:

> Antes que suene el presuroso timbre
> Y abran la puerta y entres, oh esperada
> Por la ansiedad, el universo tiene
> Que haber ejecutado una infinita
> Serie de actos concretos.[54]

The poet does not call her by her name and does not tell us about the nature of their relationship (Is it a long established one? Is it a first and uncertain encounter?). She is only the "esperada por la ansiedad," and her eventual arrival creates fear in the present ("el temeroso tiempo de la espera"). The time of anguish defies conventional forms of counting it ("nadie puede computar ese vértigo ... la arena no sabría numerarlos") because it is a purely subjective time that can only be measured by the physical symptoms of anxiety ("en mi pecho, el reloj de sangre mide ..."). The slowness of the endless "infinita serie ..." that goes through his mind tells us that the poet also experiences the paradox of the time of waiting: "cuando uno espera el tiempo pasa despacio; sin embargo, lo que uno siente es que pasa mucho tiempo."[55]

Borges also re-created the excruciating awareness of the passing of time that the fear of women caused in him in the poem "El amenazado" (a man

---

52 See chapter 7.
53 Borges, *OC* [1974], I, 611.
54 Borges, *OC* [1974], II, 192.
55 Bioy, *Borges*, 518.

threatened by love and desire): "Es, ya lo sé, el amor: la ansiedad y el alivio de oír tu voz, la / espera y la memoria, el horror de vivir en lo sucesivo." And, as in "La espera," the poet experiences the tormenting anxiety of the wait in his own body: "Me duele una mujer en todo el cuerpo."[56]

In "El amenazado" and "La espera," however, the poet also re-creates a mental device he uses to cope with the anxiety that the encounter with women creates in him. In the first of the poems, he explicitly refers to such devices as "talismanes":

> ¿De qué me servirán mis talismanes: el ejercicio de las letras, la vaga erudición, el aprendizaje de las palabras que usó el áspero Norte para cantar sus mares y sus espadas, la serena amistad, las galerías de la Biblioteca, las cosas comunes, los hábitos, el joven amor de mi madre, la sombra militar de mis muertos, la noche intemporal, el sabor del sueño?[57]

The "talismanes" are images, visions, memories of readings, friendships, habits, all essentially immaterial experiences on which he concentrates his attention to help him take his mind off the object of desire and fear. But although the poet tries, the mental exercise does not save him from his suffering. Borges explores the same question in another poem, titled "Talismanes," which contains another enumeration ("... Los cinco tomos de la obra de Schopenhauer ... / La memoria de una mañana. / Líneas de Virgilio y de Frost. / La voz de Macedonio Fernández ...") that is equally useless for escaping the anxiety of sex: "Ciertamente son talismanes, pero de nada sirven contra la sombra que no puedo nombrar, contra la sombra que no debo nombrar."[58] And in "La espera," the poet does not speak explicitly of talismans but describes a similar thought process that shows how during the "temeroso tiempo de la espera," he momentarily tries to forget the woman by thinking about an "infinita serie de actos concretos": "Antes que llegues, / Un monje tiene que soñar con un ancla, / Un tigre tiene que morir en Sumatra, / Nueve hombres tienen que morir en Borneo."

The "talismanes" reveal another form of Montaigne's presence in Borges's re-creation of his anxious experiences. In "Sur la force de l'imagination," the French thinker says (building upon the teachings of the ancient Stoics) that imagination is such a powerful quality that it can in itself create a reality. So, he proposes, some problems affecting human beings, such as illnesses, often are the consequence not of real physical conditions but of their "imaginations"; that is, they are manifestations of psychological troubles. One such problem, to which he dedicates most of the essay, is male sexual impotence (the "nouement d'aiguillettes"). These "shameful" problems arise because "notre âme se trouve tendue outre mesure par le désir ..." and they usually happen during the first sexual experiences "parce que, au moment de cette

---

56 Borges, *OC* [1974], I, 1107.
57 Borges, *OC* [1974], I, 1107.
58 Borges, *OC* [1974], II, 111.

première intime approche, on craint beaucoup plus d'être défaillant."[59] Thus, when this problem afflicted a newly wed friend of his, Montaigne gave him an object that, he deceptively made the troubled man believe, had special properties to overcome sexual failure. The placebo or "talisman" "venerien"[60] proved very effective. But this was not the only remedy that the French essayist offered his readers: he also observed that if some men never experienced such sexual failure it was because "ceux qui savent leurs membres naturellement dociles prennent soin seulement de neutralizer leur imagination"[61] and, thus, he suggested men should try to exercise the same mental control in their stressful amorous encounters. The presence of the "talismanes" and the poet's mental practices suggest that Borges also read Montaigne almost therapeutically, as many others did before him.[62] However, given the disappointing performance of his mental and venerian talismans, here too Borges appears as a failed Stoic.

## A Philosophy of Desire

Finally, I propose to look at a long footnote included in the second section of "Historia de la eternidad" (1936) that is both a philosophical reflection *and* a partially veiled discussion of desire, sex, and the imagination. Similar to what we have seen regarding the presence of the erotic in the exploration of eternity and time, this is another instance in which Borges's literature apparently has little to do with sex, yet a close reading of it allows us to sense an undercurrent of desire.[63] In the long footnote we see how metaphysics slides into the erotic and how the latter ends "dressed up" in philosophy; that is, we see how Borges moves in between genres and discourses, as he did in some of his best texts. And as will become apparent, Borges's speculation partially relies on two tales included in Burton's *Nights*, which shows, once again, how his erotic readings are often transformed and displaced to reappear under a somewhat different guise or context. Let us read the note:

> No quiero despedirme del platonismo (que parece glacial) sin comunicar esta observación, con esperanza de que la prosigan y justifiquen: *Lo genérico puede ser más intenso que lo concreto.* Casos ilustrativos no faltan. De chico, veraneando en el norte de la provincia, la llanura redonda y los hombres que mateaban en la cocina me interesaron, pero mi felicidad fue terrible cuando supe que esa redondez era "pampa," y esos varones, "gauchos." Igual, el imaginativo que se enamora. Lo genérico (el repetido

---

59 Montaigne, *Essais*, I, XXI, 123, 125.
60 Montaigne, *Essais*, I, XXI, 124.
61 Montaigne, *Essais*, I, XXI, 125.
62 e.g. Flaubert, *Correspondance*, 497.
63 For a very different reading of this note (from the standpoint of mathematical thinking), see Martinez, *Borges y la matemática*, 35–37.

nombre, el tipo, la patria, el destino adorable que le atribuye) prima sobre los rasgos individuales, *que se toleran en gracia de lo anterior.*

El ejemplo extremo, el de quien se enamora de oídas, es muy común en las literaturas persa y arábiga. Oír la descripción de una reina—la cabellera semejante a las noches de la separación y la emigración pero la cara como el día de la delicia, los pechos como esferas de marfil que dan luz a las lunas, el andar que avergüenza a los antílopes y provoca la desesperación de los sauces, las onerosas caderas que le impiden tenerse en pie, los pies estrechos como una cabeza de lanza—y enamorarse de ella hasta la placidez y la muerte, es uno de los temas tradicionales en las 1001 Noches. Léase la historia de Badrbasim, hijo de Shahrimán, o la de Ibrahim y Yamila.[64]

Borges placed the note at the end of a paragraph in which he highlighted the logical holes and contradictions that he saw in Plato's doctrine. However, against accepted wisdom and even his own critical look, he added this note that approvingly points out one of the paradoxical qualities that Platonic abstract "ideas" actually have: they can be more "intense" than the concrete material reality, including ... human beings. Thus, Borges gradually and tactfully slides from a logical speculation toward a psychological insight about how desire works: from his observation of "gauchos" and "pampa" he smoothly displaces his reflection toward "el imaginativo que se enamora." To illustrate this quality of Plato's doctrine, he refers to two tales included in Burton's translation. In the first, King Badrbasim, the protagonist, heard the "description" of the "beauty" and "perfection" of a princess and, thus, "fire was kindled in his heart."[65] Therefore, as Borges indicated, Badrbasim "fell in love with her on hearsay" ("se enamora de oidas") because, as the poetry included in the tale justified, "ear oft loveth ere eye survey."[66] In the other tale, titled "Ibrahim and Jamilah," something slightly different occurs: here the protagonist randomly perused a book, and while doing so, he stumbled on a "picture" of a woman of perfect beauty ("never was seen on the earth's face one more beautiful"[67]). The image "captivated his reason" and troubled him so much that he promised himself that "if the original be living, I will seek access to her; but, if it be only a picture, I will leave doting upon it and plague myself no more for a thing which hath no real existence."[68]

What unleashed the emotional response of the protagonists in both tales, then, is an image, in spoken words or painted, that may not have a "real existence" and that is no more than a representation or an archetype of a woman or female beauty (Jamilah means "beautiful" in Arabic; that is, the character literally embodies the "idea"). Thus, what triggers the sexual

---

64 Borges, *OC* [1974], I, 358. Italics in the original.
65 *Arabian Nights*, 475.
66 *Arabian Nights*, 474.
67 *Nights*, IX, 207.
68 *Nights*, 207–8.

desire of Badrbasim and Ibrahim are the spoken words or forms and colors on a page that stimulate their imaginations. This impulse literally puts the (young) protagonists in motion and sends them each on a journey that ends when they find and marry the women; that is, they realize the sexual desire ignited by an erotic discourse or an erotic picture (abstract representations) with real women because, according to Borges, "los rasgos individuales [of the women] ... *se toleran en gracia de lo anterior*" (the ideal represented in their description or picture).

Borges's insight, although distinctly articulated, is not unique, and over time its numerous modulations have resulted in beautiful compositions (perhaps the best known of them in the Western tradition is Ovid's *Pygmallion*). Thus to further illuminate the note, we may, as I argued in the introduction, follow Paul Muldoon's suggestion and place the "text in its social context, but in terms of its relation to other texts."[69] Here, then, I would like to consider two works that will help us round out the relationship between Borges's reflection and Burton's project and, more broadly, Victorian erotic literature. One of those texts is the *Kama Sutra of Vatsyayana* translated and published by Burton. While it is certain that Borges knew about this text,[70] it is not clear whether he actually read it. Yet, there are some intriguing conceptual overlappings and even similarities of phrasing between Borges's footnote and a passage of the famous Indian sex manual, which I consider worth pointing out. In a section titled "On the Different Kinds of Love," Vatsyayana speaks of, among other things, that "Love which is felt for things to which we are not habituated,"[71] that is, love that does *not* come from a real experience or habit such as, for example, sexual intercourse between two persons. On the contrary, "the love that comes from erotic arousal arises ... not in response to any objects of the senses," but "from the imagination."[72] The Hindu sage calls this type of love the "love resulting from the imagination" ("el imaginativo que se enamora," wrote Borges) and, according to Vatsyayana, it "proceeds entirely from ideas."[73] So, given the conceptual and formal similarities between the two texts and Borges's interest in Burton's work, there is a reasonable possibility that the Indian sex manual was one of the readings that alerted him to the possibilities created by the affinities between Platonic "ideas" and desire.

The other text that will help us glimpse the readings implied in Borges's insight on desire and the imagination is a work by Swinburne. The piece in question is the poem "Aholibah," which Borges highlighted as one of his "obras literalmente espléndidas."[74] In this piece the Victorian poet re-creates

69 Muldoon, *The End*, 27.
70 See chapter 4.
71 Vatsyayana, *Kama Sutra*, trans. Burton, 119.
72 Vatsyayana, *Kamasutra*, trans. Doniger and Kakar, 38.
73 Vatsyayana, *Kama Sutra*, trans. Burton, 119.
74 Borges, *BES*, 148.

a biblical allegory from the book of Ezequiel[75] with the purpose of attacking Christianity and realizing the erotic potential of the source. The poem tells the story of Aholibah, a woman who is overwhelmed by her "lust" for "strange gracious paintings" that adorned the walls of her home. The paintings portrayed "strong" and "desirable" warriors, "all girdled around the loins." Aroused by the "shapes" on the wall, Aholibah acts on her apparently uncontrollable desire:

> Thy mouth was leant upon the wall
> Against the painted mouth, thy chin
> Touched the hair's painted curve and fall;
> Thy deep throat, fallen lax and thin,
> Worked as the blood's beat worked therein.[76]

The biblical woman is one of those "imaginativo(s) que se enamora(n)" "hasta la placidez." Aholibah's erotic impulse is triggered not by living men but, as Swinburne writes, by "shapes" (or archetypes). Here too, then, "lo genérico puede ser más intenso que lo concreto."

Finally, in the note, Borges employs strategies, images, and language that we can find in erotic poetry, including his own. From the start, he opposes the "glacial" against the "intenso," a device that prepares the reader for the question that he intends to explore. In the same vein, we have an erotic description of a woman that is a partial and revealing translation of the spoken portrait heard by Badrbasim and whose Spanish rendition echoes "Arrabal en que pesa el campo" (1925), one of Borges's poems of intense desire. In effect, in this brief passage of sensual prose, Borges highlights the woman's "andar" and her "onerosas caderas," which follows closely the English source ("her hips of heavy weight ... when she walketh ..."),[77] but that also reminds us of the poet's gaze when he cruises the *arrabal* for sex and notices "las caderas que pasean la vereda."[78] But even more suggestive of the impulse that seems to guide the writing of the note is that Burton's "when she walketh, she breeds envy in the willow branch"[79] becomes in Borges's translation "el andar que ... provoca la desesperación de los sauces"; that is, he drops "envy" and chooses "desesperación," a significant shift in emphasis that depends on a word that, in the above-mentioned poem, the poet employed to express a painful desire: "la desesperación se mira en los charcos"[80] of the *arrabal* where he goes for sex. The literary devices and language employed in the note, then, also allow us to sense the impulse that guided its writing and afford us one more level

---

75 NRSVA, Book of Ezekiel, 23.1–49.
76 Swinburne, *Poems and Ballads*, vv.96–100, 217.
77 *Arabian Nights*, 475.
78 Borges, CSM, 14.
79 *Arabian Nights*, 475.
80 Borges, CSM, 14.

of understanding of the ways Borges's literature often swings back and forth between genres and discourses, between the philosophical and the erotic.

As the vitality of the language suggests, the note was more than a mere philosophical or purely literary game: it also speaks about one of the ways Borges lived his desire. Poet and friend Carlos Mastronardi observed in his diary that "Borges trata la realidad como si fuera una composición literaria"[81] and, speaking about the real women whom he desired and whose favor he unsuccessfully sought, said:

> Borges sólo busca y concibe símbolos. *Propenso a imaginar arquetipos,* admite [por ejemplo] que ... los magistrados son la justicia esencial ... como si la forma y la esencia fueran una misma cosa. *De igual modo, concede gran poder de "representación" a ciertos estilos femeninos.* La lenta señorita de tez morena que vive en el barrio de Belgrano ... [y que tiene] cierto aire de serenidad arrogante, es para Borges el más grato pasado criollo ... La alta muchacha de pelo rojizo, que frecuenta el mar ... y afronta los desengaños con admirable firmeza, le trae el recuerdo de hermosas leyendas escandinavas.[82]

Like the "terrible happiness" that came over Borges when he realized that the men in the countryside were "gauchos," the nostalgic longing that he felt for the *criollo* past fed his desire for the dark-skinned lady who became (the idea of) the tradition. So also his gusto for the Scandinavian sagas energized his love for the red-haired woman who embodied them. For Borges—as for Badrbasim, Ibrahim, or other "imaginativo(s) que se enamora(n)"—"lo genérico (... el tipo, la patria ...) prima sobre los rasgos individuales, *que se toleran en gracia de lo anterior.*"

---

81 Mastronardi, *Borges*, 83. Emphasis added.
82 Mastronardi, *Borges*, 80–81.

CHAPTER 6

# Desire and Sex in Buenos Aires
## Borges's Poetry on the *Arrabal*

In the 1920s, Borges's main literary project was to write poetry on the *arrabal* or *orillas,* the working-class neighborhoods of low one-story houses, vacant lots, and dirt roads located on the edges of the city of Buenos Aires, a transitional area where the urban and the rural worlds intermingled. In the current critical consensus, Borges's *orillas* were the landscape of a nostalgic past, a reservoir of creole traditions in which the Porteños could see themselves to better understand the cosmopolitan changes that Buenos Aires was going through in the first decades of the twentieth century. Thus, Olea Franco pointed out that Borges's "voluntad es volver literariamente al mundo criollo de la ciudad decimonónica," and Sarlo explained that "sin esa dimensión cultural, Buenos Aires moderna sería una ciudad sin raíces ... la modernidad es —también— una relación con el pasado,"[1] Because of its mythical nature, some critics have seen in Borges's *arrabal* "un espacio estético y simbólico [que] brinda experiencias espirituales" and considered its poetry as "una especie de fuga de la realidad."[2]

Although I find this consensus overall convincing, I still think that there are corners in Borges's poetry on the *arrabal* that have not been visited and I would like to argue that this (not always mythical) landscape was *also* a real "red-light" district that served as the backdrop against which he could speak about his own troubled sexuality. The reading of the poems proposed here will add, I hope, another layer of meaning to our understanding of Borges's poetry on the *orillas* and, thus, will also show another of the multiple locations of eroticism within his work.

### Sex: Not in "El Paseo de Julio"

The intersection of sex and the city in Borges's works has been considered before, but its exploration has often revolved around the presence of the

---

[1] Olea Franco, "La verdadera," 41; Sarlo "Orillero y ultraísta," 150, 151.
[2] Lefere, "Fervor," 218–19; Cajero Vázquez, "Para la lectura," 21.

Paseo de Julio in his literature, which reflects, I think, a very partial and unconvincing reading of Borges's corpus. For Adriana Bergero, "El Paseo de Julio" (a poem on a notorious brothel district in a city notorious for prostitution in the 1920s)[3] and the short story "Emma Zunz" (in which the female protagonist has paid sex on the infamous avenue) are the texts that allow her to propose that this area of downtown Buenos Aires was the urban space in which Borges lived his conflicted sexuality.[4] Jason Wilson also accords the district a (in my view unwarranted) relevance in Borges's life and poetry. For Wilson, the poem reflects Borges's encounter with the Buenos Aires of the white slave trade and his realization that he did not want this city of venal sex to be his "patria," which brought his poetic project of re-creating the city to a close.[5]

"El Paseo de Julio,"[6] a poem with more obscurities than usually acknowledged, lends itself, of course, to a different reading. Although the poet suggests he has tasted the "carne" that the district offers ("recuerdos mios, antiguos hasta la ternura, te saben"), he also hints that he is not well acquainted with it ("mi verso es de interrogación," "sólo poseo de tí una deslumbrada ignorancia," "lo entrevisto") and affirms his alienation from it ("nunca te sentí patria"). But this did not imply a negation of Buenos Aires. Actually, the poet does suggest that his "patria" is also in the city, but in another district: "mi suburbio," the one of tough carts that evoke *compadritos* and their creole cult of bravery ("de hierro y de polvo"), a tradition that he does not find in the cosmopolitan and maritime underworld of the Paseo de Julio ("fauna de monstruos," "sirena," "griegas").

In "El Paseo de Julio" we can hear Borges talking about his troubled sexuality. The district has the nightmarish quality of his sexual experiences ("Barrio con lucidez de pesadilla"), a sentiment that is emphasized by the mirrors that uncover the ugly inner-self of sexual desire ("tus espejos curvos denuncian el lado de la fealdad de las caras"). In the same vein, in a line that seems to speak to Edward FitzGerald's *The Rubáiyát of Omar Khayyám* ("I Myself am Heav'n and Hell / Heav'n but the Vision of fulfill'd Desire, / And Hell the Shadow from a Soul on fire"), he tells us that the district that promises to satiate sexual desire is "Cielo para los que son del Infierno."[7] Estela Canto's testimony on Borges's sexual troubles supports the confessional reading of this line, but directs us toward another, concurrent literary

---

3 Paseo de Julio was the old denomination of the current Paseo Colón Ave., in downtown Buenos Aires.
4 Bergero, *Intersecting Tango*, 137–38.
5 Wilson, *Jorge Luis Borges*, 85–86; Wilson, "Borges and Buenos Aires," 47.
6 First published in *Criterio*, February 21, 1929 and reproduced in *TR1*, 379–80; then included in *CSM*, 49–51, (with changes), which is the version that I use here.
7 LXVI–LXVII. In both FitzGerald's and Borges's lines, it is possible to hear Miltonian echoes "The mind is its own place and in itself / Can make a Heaven of Hell, a Hell of Heaven," *Paradise Lost*, Bk.I, vv.254–55.

influence: "[Borges] me repetía que él era Dante, que yo era Beatrice y que habría de liberarlo del infierno, aunque yo no conociera la naturaleza de ese infierno."[8]

Although the poet feels alienated from this particular red-light district, we will see that sexual desire will take him (and Borges) to the *orillas*, another space of venal or casual sex where, however, he will not escape the malaise that impregnated the Paseo de Julio ("toda felicidad, con sólo existir, te es adversa").

Desire and Sex in the *Arrabal*: Villa Urquiza and Villa Ortúzar

Borges seems to have looked for his "Heav'n of fulfilled desire" in "his suburb," in Villa Urquiza and Villa Ortúzar, two neighborhoods in the northwestern corner of the city. The first poem that I want to read is "Villa Urquiza,"[9] a sonnet that has not received enough critical attention and whose title makes reference to the neighborhood of the same name. In the first decades of the twentieth century, Villa Urquiza was a predominantly working-class settlement on the outskirts of Buenos Aires, where large plots of undeveloped land coexisted with an increasing number of recently built modest homes. It was one of those areas of the *orillas* of Buenos Aires, where the city and the country met.

Villa Urquiza occupies an easily noticeable position in Borges's poetry of the 1920s and commentators of his work usually explain the presence of the neighborhood in his literature in a biographical key that recalls two of his experiences at the time.[10] First, in the 1920s Borges went to the neighborhood to attend the literary gatherings that took place in the home of sisters Haydeé and Nora Lange (eventually, in the later years of the decade, Borges will fall in love with Nora, a love that she did not correspond). Second, it was at the Langes' that in early 1922 Borges met sixteen-year-old Concepción Guerrero and initiated a relationship that lasted until late 1924. The house of the Langes became the place where they would see each other more or less frequently. Concepción, a girl with "espléndido pelo negro repartido en dos trenzas,"[11] was the daughter of Spanish immigrants, and her father was a primary

---

8 Canto, *A contraluz*, 95.
9 Borges apparently wrote this sonnet in 1923, and it was published in Spain in the literary review *Alfar* in 1926; however, he never included it in any book, and it was only published again in *TR1*, 248. The manuscript of this poem is titled "Villa Mazzini" (the name of a section of the neighborhood of Villa Urquiza); Carlos García [2000], 19–20, reproduced the poem and listed the variants between the manuscript and the version published in *Alfar*. There is another, significantly different, poem also titled "Villa Urquiza," initially published in *FBA* (more on this below).
10 García, *El jóven Borges*, 20–21; Fine, "Villa Urquiza o la impronta"; Vázquez, *Esplendor*, 79–86; Vaccaro, *Borges* 125–27, 131–32; Williamson, *A Life*, 102–8.
11 Vázquez, *Esplendor*, 85.

school teacher; Borges described her social condition as "poor" although of a "decent" family and said that she "endured" the "hard" and "monotonous" life of the *arrabal*.¹² Many years later, Borges would also say that Concepción "era una persona sin gran cultura."¹³ Convinced that the class difference rendered Concepción unacceptable to his family, Borges never told his parents about the relationship. On the other hand, her family did know about it, and they presented some resistance, perhaps because of the age difference between Borges and Concepción, his lack of steady income, or, why not?, because of their social distance as well.

Borges fell madly in love with Concepción ("je suis amoureux, totalement, idiotement"¹⁴) and overall seems to have enjoyed a relationship that he described as of "apacible romanticismo y dulzura."¹⁵ He called her a "miracle" and thought that the words that described her well were "Beauté, *Delicia, Hermosura*."¹⁶ Borges dedicated to her the poem "Sábados," which he ended with "Tú, /que ayer sólo eras toda la hermosura / eres también todo el amor ahora."¹⁷ His relationship with the young girl also colored his vision of the neighborhood, which he articulated in the other poem, also titled "Villa Urquiza," which, like "Sábados," Borges included in *Fervor de Buenos Aires*. In this "Villa Urquiza," Borges felt "Atendido de amor y rica esperanza" and said that "La frecuente asistencia de un encanto / acuña en mi recuerdo [con] predilecta eficacia / ese arrabal cansado."

The "Villa Urquiza" published in *Alfar* has been placed before in the context of the two experiences that I just mentioned,¹⁸ a critical assumption that I would like to rethink. The sonnet re-creates a trying trip ("un... tranvía rezonga rendimiento"), on a Sunday afternoon, from downtown Buenos Aires to the distant *orillas*, where the city and the country meet ("En la borrosa linde"). The poet cannot help but observe the ugly landscape of the neighborhood ("arrabal macilento," "turbio dejamiento"), a gaze that, when it turns to the overcast sky and the rain that it announces, becomes gloomier ("apesadumbra"). And we are told that this is a working-class *arrabal* ("pobre"), a quality that compounds the grim picture of Villa Urquiza that the poet shows us.

The young working-class girls on the sidewalk smile to the visitor from downtown and hope that he will notice and respond with flirtatious remarks

---

12 "Elle souffre dans une extrême banlieu, la vie orgueuilleuse et dure et monotone et timide d'une jeune fille *bien* et pauvre," Borges, *Cartas del fervor*, 209 (emphasis in the original).
13 Vázquez, *Esplendor*, 86.
14 Borges, *Cartas del fervor*, 209.
15 Borges, *Cartas del fervor*, 224.
16 Borges, *Cartas del fervor*, 216. Emphasis in the original.
17 Borges, *FBA*, n/p.
18 García, *El jóven Borges*, 20–21; Fine, "Villa Urquiza o la impronta," 213.

("Una que otra chicuela sonríe su contento / De posibles piropos en la acera ... /"). This is a type of scene that occurs often in Borges's poetry and essays on the *orillas* and of which he hinted at its literary ancestry. In "La presencia de Buenos Aires en la poesía," he points out that one of his precursors in the re-creation of the *arrabal* was Domingo Martinto. In the essay, Borges quotes some verses of "Divagando," a poem that narrates a visit to the *suburbio*:

> Allí un grupo de mujeres,
> Viejas, jóvenes, sentadas
> En el umbral de la puerta
> O en toscas sillas de paja,
> Súbitamente interrumpe
> La alegre y confusa charla
> A la voz del organillo
> Que en la esquina, un vals ensaya.[19]

Borges says that the poem is a "narración de un desganado paseo de noche por las orillas. Es un cuadrito desdibujado, serio, de barrio,"[20] but he recognizes that Martinto "ha sabido nombrar cosas nuestras" such as "las comadritas en la acera y en el zaguán." Martinto's gaze, then, opens a possibility, which Borges fills with another type of experience. In "Villa Urquiza," the old women sitting in the coarse chairs and their domestic conversation disappear, and, instead, what we find on the sidewalk are the provocative young women willing to engage in an exchange of smiles and flirtatious remarks. The change allows us to see a different side of the *arrabal* and, thus, reveals another layer of Borges's project on the *orillas*: from a "cuadrito desdibujado, serio, de barrio" we step into an eroticized *arrabal*. The scene appears in other Borges poems and essays as well. He speaks about "alboroto de chicas," "chicuelas con su jarana y su secreteo," and, more tellingly, "la jarana de las chiruzas en el portón," which affirms the sexual and class connotations of his view of the *arrabal*: in the colloquial Spanish of Argentina in the first decades of the twentieth-century, "chiruza" referred to poor young women of creole background who were sexually available.[21] In "Villa Urquiza," then, the presence of young women on the street in a seductive pose suggests that the poet might not be simply walking but cruising. That is, from Martinto's "desganado paseo" we shift to a poem driven by the erotic energy of the visitor.

The nature of the trip to the *arrabal* is finally stated in the last four verses, in which Borges's voice becomes more audible:

---

19 Borges, *TR1*, 251.
20 Borges, *TR1*, 250.
21 Borges, *LE*, 31; Borges, *IA*, 40; Borges, *IA*, 121; Lehmann-Nitsche, *Textos eróticos*, 284.

> Lo que en las hondonadas del corazón nos arde:
>
> Urgencia de ternura, esperanza vehemente,
> Carne en pos de la carne con silencio cobarde:
> Burdo secreto a voces que unifica la tarde.[22]

The lines exhibit an intense accumulation of expressions of the sexual desire that has driven the visitor to Villa Urquiza, an accumulation that in itself suggests the anxiety that desire and sex elicit in him. One of these expressions of sexual desire is pretty explicit ("carne en pos de la carne"), but it is also true that the wording of the others may puzzle today's readers, which reminds us of the necessity of being alert to the nature of Borges's erotic language. Take "esperanza," a word well associated with Borges's literature but that often is logically read with a completely different meaning, as in his essay "El tamaño de mi esperanza" ("[A Buenos Aires] hay que encontrarle la poesía ... Ése es el tamaño de mi esperanza"). But in another context, Borges could use it to allude to sexual desire, as when, in his comment on Baldomero Fernández Moreno's "Roja inicial," a poem that Borges said was "demasiado explícito" and full of "carnalidad," he wondered (in a biographical key) whether the piece reflected the author's "esperanza o recuerdo." And the same could be said of "urgencia," a word that we find in Lugones's erotic poetry (more generally, the poem's language shows some debts to *Lunario sentimental*[23]) and that in Borges's literature denotes intense desire ("las yeguas urgentes," "urgente Afrodita").[24] On the other hand, when the poet vents his desire, he also suggests that he may be talking about an erotic experience that is shared by other men ("lo que en las hondonadas del corazón nos arde").

Neither the poet nor the people in the neighborhood dare to acknowledge what has brought him to the *arrabal*; yet, everybody (including the young girls on the sidewalk who hope for a flirtatious remark from the visitor) seems to understand what all this is about: sex is a public secret, a "Burdo secreto a voces[25] que unifica la tarde" (or "la gente," in one of its variants[26]).

---

22 Borges, *TR1*, 248.

23 As we have seen in chapter 3, in "Oceánida" (in *Los crepúsculos del jardín*), Lugones speaks of "urgencias masculinas" (*Obras poéticas*, 122); Borges anthologized the poem, although his comments to Bioy Casares indicate that he did not like Lugones's use of the term (392). In "Luna ciudadana," Lugones starts the poem thus: "Mientras cruza el tranvía una pobre comarca / De suburbio"; and in "Luna campestre," we find the adjective "macilenta," the verb "rebuzna" and the substantive "vislumbre" (Lugones, *Obras poéticas*, 286, 292, 294). On Lugones's vocabulary in Borges's *FBA*, see Cajero Vázquez "Para la lectura."

24 Borges, *OC* [1974], I, 378; I, 863.

25 Borges also uses this expression in "Jardín botánico" (in *FBA*), a poem that can also be read as part of his expression of desire and its intersection with the urban geography Buenos Aires.

26 The variant can be consulted in the transcription of the manuscript done by Carlos García, *El joven Borges*, 20.

The concept in this verse can be traced back, I propose, to Schopenhauer's *The World as Will and Representation*, in which the German philosopher says that the sexual act "is the great unspeakable, the public secret which must never be distinctly mentioned anywhere, but is always and everywhere understood"[27] ("secreto a voces"). It is illuminating to read the verse, particularly in the variant pointed out above, against "La secta del Fénix," where the phrasing of the problematic ubiquity and odd suppression of sex in society and culture is very similar ("una sola cosa —el Secreto— los une" / "[el] secreto ... unifica la gente").[28] The poet experiences the unspoken complicity implied in the "secreto a voces" with guilt ("silencio cobarde"). In the same vein, in "La secta" Borges says that the secret is "ridículo," "penoso," and "vulgar," which like "burdo" tells of the shame and disgust that the awareness of his desire produces in the poet. But the adjective used in the poem also has the ability to trigger other connotations. "Burdo" phonetically and visually evokes "burdel" (even when the meanings of the words do not allow a semantic identification), and thus insinuates that the secret (sex) that Borges talks about may involve either some sort of venality or other purely profane ("carne en pos de la carne"), casual, amorous encounters.

In short, in this poem we find an *arrabal* that does not fit well with the one we usually read in Borges's poetry on the *orillas*. Here there is no nostalgia for "la dulce calle de arrabal" ("Las calles," *Fervor de Buenos Aires*) and there are few allusions to the creole experience ("campos," "prestigio fiestero"). On the contrary, at the opening of the poem, we get a grim picture of Villa Urquiza that corresponds well with the anxiety and shame that sexual desire engendered in Borges. In this "Villa Urquiza," then, we find a gaze and an experience that is also significantly different from the one presented in the other "Villa Urquiza" that was included in *Fervor de Buenos Aires* or in other poems that allude to the neighborhood. Frankly, it is very difficult to read it against the literary gatherings at the Langes' or Borges's relationship of "apacible romanticismo y dulzura"[29] with Concepción Guerrero. How, then, to explain this other, very different picture that we see here?

One possibility is to consider this "Villa Urquiza" in the context of the sacred/profane love duality, which Borges lived as a conflictive opposition.

---

27 Schopenhauer, vol. 2, 570–71. See the previous chapter for this aspect of Schopenhauer's insight on erotic language and metaphysics.
28 Borges, *OC* [1974], I, 523. For a discussion of "el secreto abierto" as homoerotic desire, see Daniel Balderston's "Pudor." Among other things, Balderston considers Xavier Villaurrutia's "Nocturno de los ángeles," a poem permeated by a similar language and insight, including the expression "estar en el secreto" that Borges also adopted to speak about his own sexuality. For Borges's use of the expression, see his essay "El mapa secreto," *TR3*, 26–28.
29 Borges, *Cartas del fervor*, 224.

María Esther Vázquez said that throughout his whole life, Borges was an "adolescente romantico,"

> pero al mismo tiempo, era el hombre que se avergonzaba de las necesidades de su cuerpo, odiaba su cuerpo, desdeñaba la carnalidad, se despreciaba por los oscuros deseos que le encendían la sangre.[30]

Perhaps the poem analyzed here re-creates Borges's vision of the profane (and hateful) side of his relationship with Concepción and its corresponding darker view of the neighborhood, while the other "Villa Urquiza," "Sábados," and other poems project more of the sacred component of the amorous relationship.

However, there is at least one other possibility. It could be that the "Villa Urquiza" published in *Alfar* is not about Borges's relationship with Concepción Guerrero at all, but is about a type of experience that he and other contemporaries had or could have in Villa Urquiza. In this respect, it may be helpful to consider this question after listening to an anecdote told in 1987, when this poem had not yet been republished and, as far as I know, remained unknown to those who were acquainted with Borges and to scholars. According to the testimony of a Borges friend,

> Borges tenía una novia en Villa Urquiza —¿quién no tenía por aquel entonces *una novia* en Villa Urquiza?—. La hora del encuentro se había fijado para las 19. Borges, luego del almuerzo salía ya caminando lentamente rumbo a la cita. Preguntado por qué partía tan temprano, respondía: "Ya soy el que seré, ya estoy con quien estaré."[31]

Perhaps this walk to the neighborhood was one of the times that Borges went to see Concepción; regardless, the anecdote also allows us to see the anxiety that the amorous encounter elicited in Borges (a mood that is also palpable in the poem). But in this testimony, the most valuable insight is not in what it says about Borges but in what it says about the neighborhood: the anecdote hints at one of the meanings that Villa Urquiza had for young men in Borges's circle (in "Villa Urquiza," the poet does suggest that he was also speaking for others like him—"nos"). His friend said that it was common to have "una novia," an expression in which the indefinite article generally implied noncommittal, casual, or even venal sexual relationships. In some cases the expression referred to situations in which men established more or less stable relationships with part- or full-time prostitutes, and the venality of the arrangement was euphemized with the term "novia";[32] in others, this term could refer to asymmetrical power relationships in which men of a higher social status exploited the expectations of lower-class women who entered into the arrangement with the hope of marrying up

---

30 Vázquez, *Esplendor*, 337.
31 Woscoboinik, *El secreto* [1988], 198. Emphasis added.
32 Goldar, *La 'mala vida'*, 107.

or of deriving more immediate material benefits. Actually other lines by Borges can also inform us on this question of the "novias" in *las orillas*. Let us look at some verses of the 1925 "Versos de catorce" and how Borges rewrote them in 1974:

| 1925 | 1974 |
|---|---|
| I supe en las orillas, del querer *de una novia* I a punta de ponientes desangré el pecho en salmos I canté la tristona gustación de esa gloria.[33] | Y supe, en las orillas, del querer, *que es de todos* Y a punta de ponientes desangré el pecho en salmos Y canté la aceptada costumbre de estar solo.[34] |

Investigative criticism may lead to very illuminating results when close reading is not limited to a particular text but is applied simultaneously to other pages by the author under investigation. Here the comparison between two published versions of the poem uncovers the hide and seek that Borges played with the language of eroticism and, thus, reveals a lot about the meaning of the verses (and of Borges's view of the *arrabal*).[35] In this rewriting we see how the love given by "una novia" transitions into the love that "es de todos," that belongs to everybody: the woman is everybody's *novia*. In other instances, like in his comments on "La Queja" (Carriego's *"harlot's progress* Sudamericano"), Borges's use of the expression is unambiguous: "una mujer de todos" is a prostitute.[36]

Then, if we "work hard to find clues both within [the work] and outside it,"[37] as Jorge Gracia recommends, we can place the poem "Villa Urquiza" in an alternative context, very different from the one in which it has been considered until now: the predominantly working-class neighborhood was one of the areas of the *arrabal* where middle- or upper-class young men, like Borges, could go for sex. Finally, the lines from "Versos de catorce" suggest, as does "Villa Urquiza," that sex (casual or venal) is problematic: it does not satisfy ("tristona gustación") the poet and leaves him emotionally depleted ("estar solo").

Villa Urquiza was not the only place in the northern *arrabal* that Borges could visit in search of an erotic experience. Villa Ortúzar, a working-class neighborhood contiguous to Villa Urquiza, also seems to have become one of the landscapes of his troubling desire. In this case Borges also wrote two poems: "último sol en Villa Ortúzar" and "Arrabal en que pesa el campo,"

---

33 Borges, *LE*, 41. Emphasis added.
34 Borges, *OC* [1974], I, 73. Emphasis added.
35 On this method of interrogating Borges's poetry, also see Linares, *Un juego*, 134.
36 Borges, *OC* [1974], I, 127.
37 Stavans and Gracia, *Thirteen Ways*, 90.

which he defined as "un par de composiciones describidoras"[38] of the neighborhood. Here it will be the latter that will receive most of the attention, although I will first comment briefly on the former.

In "último sol en Villa Ortúzar,"[39] we find the experience of a visitor who mostly concerns himself with the comparative vastness with which the proximity of the country endows this neighborhood and with the numerous visual effects that the sunlight creates on the landscape at dusk ("la claridá que ardió en la hondura"). In this poem there is no desire driving the re-creation of the neighborhood; yet, the erotic touch is not completely absent: the poet does hear again an "alboroto de chicas," whom he places visually near "la verja herrumbrada."

"Arrabal en que pesa el campo"[40] also re-creates a trip to Villa Ortúzar, although here the visit is, pretty explicitly, about Borges's desire. As its title suggests, the neighborhood is in the *orillas*, where the country seems to penetrate the city. The poet points to the undeveloped lots ("huecos"), the long dirt streets bordered by tall trees ("callejones"), and the sunsets on the pampas that can be observed from Villa Ortúzar ("ponientes"). The place is still steeped in creole customs and values ("caña fuerte," "trucada") but the process of modernization ("fonógrafo") is turning this presumably formerly dignified rural setting into a neighborhood whose urban and working-class character and sensibility the poet despises ("dolor guarango").

As in "Villa Urquiza" here too there are young women on the sidewalk:

> En Villa Ortúzar
> el deseo varón es triste en la tarde
> cuando hay caderas que pasean la vereda
> y risas comadritas.

The poet hears the seductive laugh of the *comadritas*, the working-class women who are expected to be sexually available and who, in Borges's imaginary of the suburb, are the symmetrical counterpart to the *compadritos* ("En la frontera de los arrabales, / Vuelven a ... / ... su puta y su cuchillo"[41]). The women's bodies also catch the attention of the visitor: his gaze lands on the insinuating hips of the *comadritas* walking on the sidewalk, the "caderas

---

38 Borges, TR1, 252.
39 The poem was first published in *LE*, 31, in 1925. Borges kept it in all subsequent editions of his poetry with only one variant introduced in 1943. In its first printing the title starts in lower case.
40 Borges, *CSM*, 13–14. Borges wrote this poem in 1925, and it was first published in the literary magazine *Nosotros* in May 1926. The following year it was one of the poems by Borges showcased in the anthology *Exposición de la actual poesía argentina (1922–1927)*, edited by Pedro Juan Vignale and César Tiempo. In 1929 Borges included it in *CSM* but dropped it afterwards from all editions of his poetic work. It was only published again in *TR1*, 241, in 1997.
41 Borges, *OC* [1974], I, 949.

que pasean la vereda," which in the Spanish brothel re-created by Borges are "las combas fáciles de una moza"[42] or "las curvas peligrosas de las chicas averiadas"[43] (suggesting the wearing effects that the profession had on them).

In some confessional lines, we do hear that the search for sex in the *arrabal* is painful. Borges says that "En Villa Ortúzar...la desesperación se mira en los charcos"; that is, the street puddles unveil, like mirrors, his ugly face of unfulfilled desire (the image of the "charcos" of the quasi rural landscape of the *orillas* finds its urban counterpart in "El Paseo de Julio"'s "espejos curvos denuncian el lado de la fealdad de las caras"). His trip to the *orillas* is a mix of self-hatred and humiliation: in a line reminiscent of Mallarmé's "La chair est triste, hélas!"[44] Borges says (twice!) that "En Villa Ortúzar / el deseo varón es triste en la tarde." It is also frustrating: in Villa Ortúzar he has not been able "to taste" any "love" ("no he sabido ningún amor"), a disappointment that is barely mitigated by the creole experience that he does find in the neighborhood ("pero detrás de una trucada he puesto horas muertas").

The reading that I propose of Borges's Villa Ortúzar (and other parts of the *arrabal*) as the geography of venal or casual sex is further supported by some contemporary poetry that re-created the same experience but did it from a radically opposite standpoint. In José Portogalo's *Tumulto*, a controversial book that was banned in 1936 for its alleged pornography and politically subversive content,[45] we hear a child of immigrants and a leftist poet who apparently lived in Villa Ortúzar:

> y en Villa Ortúzar —mi barrio— el sol tutea los ojos de los niños,
> el corazón maduro de los jornaleros sin trabajo
> y las cabelleras de las muchachas pobres que van a las fábricas.[46]

This poet also sings to the sun that shines on the neighborhood, not because it colors the empty lots, the long streets, or the fences, but because it celebrates Villa Ortúzar's working class, including "las muchachas pobres que van a la fábrica." Yet, in Portogalo's poetry we also learn that not all women accepted their proletarian life, and, instead, some of them embraced (socially) higher and (morally) darker destinies. Thus an Italian immigrant's daughter with "trenzas oscuras" took that questionable path out of the *arrabal*:

> Mi hermana Genoveva fugó de nuestra casa.
> Amaba el suave roce de la seda y el oro.
> Desde entonces sus pasos quedaron en la sombra.[47]

---

42 Borges, *TR1*, 113.
43 Borges, *Cartas del fervor*, 184.
44 Mallarmé, *Poésies*, 22. The complete first line of "Brise marine" reads thus: "La chair est triste, Hélas! Et j'ai lu tous les livres."
45 Cane Carrasco, "Unity," 448–53.
46 Portogalo, *Tumulto*, 17.
47 Portogalo, *Los pájaros ciegos*, 76. Here Portogalo's re-creation of the *arrabal* is

The intended sensuality of the second verse is persuasive enough about the opportunistic or decidedly venal consummation of sexual desire that happened in the *orillas* and the class differences that made it possible ("roce" not only suggests physical intimacy but also the desire for social proximity with those who could provide access to material well-being). More telling for our reading, in another poem Portogalo loudly confronts Borges himself on this question:

> Jorge Luis Borges cantó las orillas de Villa Ortúzar pero no vió el incendio del centro de Villa Ortúzar.
> -Muchachas exangües con los sueños torcidos en los zaguanes y el sexo herrumbrado.[48]

The leftist poet appropriates and turns upside down Borges's aesthetics and imagery (in particular, the "sexo herrumbrado" that sends us back to the "verja herrumbrada" in "último sol ...") to denounce the bourgeois gaze and ethics of the visitor who comes from downtown. Borges goes to the *orillas* but he cannot see (or, better, does not want to see[49]) that the combination of poverty and sex is morally consuming Villa Ortúzar to the core.

## Of Maps, Sunsets, and Precursors

For Borges, then, the *orillas* were, yes, a mythical landscape, a historical mirror that allowed him both to sense the city of the past and to understand the current changes in Buenos Aires in the 1920s. But the *arrabal* was also the geography of casual or venal sex and, more important, of his own troubled sexuality. That is, Borges's *orillas* had an intimate and painful dimension that, for the most part, has escaped us. Actually, in his essay "El mapa secreto" Borges hinted that his private life could work as a compass to read the city into his literature. He explained how the public space of a city is, at the same time, a private one:

> He recordado estos secretos a voces, estos abiertos misterios, estas cosas públicas y escondidas, porque me parecen singularmente aplicables a Buenos Aires [...]. Para todo porteño, Buenos Aires, al cabo de los años, se ha convertido en una especie de mapa secreto de memorias, de encuentros, de adioses, acaso de agonías y humillaciones, y tenemos así dos

---

receptive to Carriego's foundational take (and his epigones') on neighborhood life. In the section on "La costurerita que dio el mal paso" we read, "Los menores te extrañan todavía, y los otros / verán en ti la hermana perdida que regresa," Carriego, *Obra completa*, 147.

48 Portogalo, *Tumulto*, 90. In this piece titled "Poema escrito en el puño de mi camisa," the poet denounces bourgeois intellectuals and the establishment: "Porque me burlo de los intelectuales y ya no leo los versos de Don Leopoldo Lugones," 88.

49 We may read a pun in these verses (the author may be banking on Borges's well-known poor sight), but Portogalo's comment is, obviously, ethical and political.

ciudades: una, la ciudad pública que registran los cartógrafos, y otra, la íntima y secreta ciudad de nuestras biografías [...] [es un] mapa personal ... [entonces hay] —una reserva central, un pudor— en Buenos Aires que no quiere que la describamos abiertamente, sino por obra de alusiones y símbolos. Claro está que para entenderlos hay que estar en el secreto.[50]

"Secretos a voces," "cosas públicas y escondidas," "encuentros," "adioses," "agonías," "humillaciones," "íntima," "pudor," "estar en el secreto": a language with echoes of Schopenhauer and that suggests that his sexuality was one of the invisible hands drawing this private map. To decipher it, the literary sleuth (or the inquisitive reader), says Borges, must learn the code of "symbols" and "allusions" with which he communicated the "secret" experiences he had in different areas of the city, including the *arrabal*. We can detect this code at work, for example, in the 1969 prologue to *Fervor de Buenos Aires*, in which he spoke about how his life had changed since the 1920s: "En aquel tiempo, buscaba los atardeceres, los arrabales y la desdicha; ahora, las mañanas, el centro y la serenidad."[51] In his youth the sunset and the *arrabal* were the time and the territory of his "desdicha," a word that, as we have seen when he referred to Boileau and others, Borges often reserved for the emotional pain created by the dissonance between his desire and his sexual troubles (see also, further below, how this word appears in his reading of Almafuerte). Now (1969) close to the end of his life, he did not feel the urge to go to the *orillas* and he remained downtown, more at ease with himself. An attentive reading of "Elogio de la sombra" may help us to understand better what had changed in his life and how in his literature different ages corresponded with different areas of the city:

> La vejez (tal es el nombre que los otros le dan)
> puede ser el tiempo de nuestra dicha.
> El animal ha muerto o casi ha muerto.
> Quedan el hombre y su alma.
> ..................................................
> Buenos Aires,
> que antes se desgarraba en arrabales
> hacia la llanura incesante,
> ha vuelto a ser la Recoleta, el Retiro,
> las borrosas calles del Once
> y las precarias casas viejas
> que aún llamamos el Sur.[52]

---

50 Borges, *TR3*, 26–28. In the same vein, in the poem "Buenos Aires," Borges says, "Y la ciudad, ahora, es como un plano / De mis humillaciones y fracasos; / ... / No nos une el amor sino el espanto: / Será por eso que la quiero tanto," *OC* [1974], I, 947.
51 Borges, *OC* [1974], I, 13.
52 Borges, *OC* [1974], I, 1017.

Sex and procreation, says Schopenhauer in *The World as Will and Representation*, "is the most marvelous of the instincts"; "Instinct is given only to animals ... but almost only in the case here considered is it given to man."[53] Borges conceived sex and eroticism in similar terms: in "La secta del Fénix," he says that the secret "ya es instintivo" or speaks of "esa bestia vergonzosa, furtiva, ya inhumana y como estrañada de sí que es un ser desnudo."[54] Thus, in old age "el animal,"[55] or his (troubling) sexual desire, "ha muerto o casi muerto"; that is, his physical decline is not a loss but a happy circumstance that has freed him from the necessities of profane love and, therefore, he does not feel anymore the urge to embark into disappointing and painful ("se desgarraba") trips to the *arrabal*. Now is the time to enjoy the sacred side of love ("el hombre y su alma"): the fulfilling spiritual relationships and the intellectual life that he can find downtown. It is, finally, the time of his "dicha."

Borges placed the re-creation of his troubling sexual desire not only in a specific location (the *arrabal*) but generally at a specific time: sunset. For Borges, the experiencing of the *orillas* changed with the hour of the day and the corresponding volume of light. When he commented on Eduardo Wilde, one of his precursors in the literature of the *orillas*, Borges said that "Wilde camina de día, cuando el sol saca los arrabales a la vergüenza pública,"[56] which implied that at sunset the growing darkness of the night started to cover that shame (in "La fin de la journée," of which Borges's comment sounds like an echo, Charles Baudelaire said that "La vie impudente" unfolds under the light of day but in the evening "La nuit voluptueuse monte / ... / Effaçant tout, même la honte").[57] Thus, in Borges's essays and poetry on the *arrabal*, the word "poniente" is the term around which he constructs erotic allusions. That eroticism in consonance with the tenor of his literary project on the *orillas* was articulated by resorting to the imagery and language of the creole tradition, which generally worked to hide in plain sight (or to deflect toward that tradition) some of its meanings. Borges speaks of "ponientes ... más apasionados que una guitarra"[58] or about "querencia de ponientes en Villa

---

53 Schopenhauer, vol. 2, 512, 540.
54 Borges, *OC* [1974], I, 524; *TR1*, 185.
55 In "Elogio de la sombra" it is possible to hear some echoes of W.B. Yeats's poem sequence "A Woman Young and Old," in which the Irish poet dealt with similar questions about the life cycle and sex, although he offers a radically different perspective on them. In particular the lines: "He fancied that I gave a soul / Did but our bodies touch, / And laughed upon his breast to think / *Beast gave beast* as much," Yeats, *Collected Works*, 280 (my emphasis). Borges knew this sequence very well: it was from here that he lifted "I'm looking for the face I had / Before the world was made," which he used as the epigraph of "Biografía de Tadeo Isidoro Cruz (1829-1874)."
56 Borges, *TR1*, 251.
57 Baudelaire, *Fleurs du mal*, 145.
58 Borges, *Inq.*, 89.

Urquiza,"⁵⁹ where "querencia" introduces a creole flavor while maintaining the meaning of love and sex (for the gaucho "querencia" is home, where his woman awaits him). He also wrote of "los ponientes machos / Color baraja criolla que he versiado en Urquiza"⁶⁰; in "Versos de catorce," he said that "I supe en las orillas, del querer de una novia / I a punta de ponientes desangré el pecho en salmos"; or told of "durezas de ponientes" that he associated with "pampas furtivas,"⁶¹ expressions all ("macho," "punta," "desangré," "durezas") that remind us of the gauchesque but also of sex, which suggests the type of experience that Borges sought (and re-created) in the *arrabal* at sunset.

Finally it is critically illuminating to look at how Borges understood that his poetry on desire and sex fit into the tradition of the literature of the *arrabal*: it was not so much Evaristo Carriego that he recognized as a precursor in this respect, but Almafuerte. In his reading of these two authors, Borges did factor in their sexuality and reflected on whether it had shaped their poetry. Borges pointed out that Carriego was "tímido" and that "no se le conocieron hechos de amor," although his "asistencia viril a la casa de zaguán rosado como una niña"⁶² was known. However, Borges noticed, in his verses Carriego made no room for himself (and his own sexuality):

> Seguramente, Carriego es el día y la noche del arrabal. La habitualidad del suburbio le pertenece [...]. Sin embargo, entre ese día y esa noche hay unas rendijas cuya pasión es demasiado vehemente para él y que en verso de Carriego no caben. Esas rendijas —durezas de ponientes y amaneceres, pampas furtivas ...— están en la voz de Almafuerte. En la desesperada voz de Almafuerte.⁶³

Borges placed the latter along with "Boileau, Swift, Kropotkin, Ruskin, Carlyle," who also suffered sexual impotence, and said that Almafuerte's "castidad no era voluntaria."⁶⁴ He admired the ethics of the poet who in "El abismo" (in which resonate words such as "humillación," "impotente," "sublimado") could look at himself thus:

> Soy la expresión del vacío,
> de lo infecundo y lo yerto,
> como ese polvo desierto
> donde toda hierba muere ...⁶⁵

---

59 Borges, *TME*, 16.
60 Borges, *TR1*, 233.
61 Borges, *IA*, 40.
62 Borges, *OC* [1974], I, 157; 118; 119.
63 Borges, *IA*, 39–40.
64 Borges, *TR2*, 197, 195. "El tema fisiológico es siempre ingrato," Borges also clarified with sad confessional precision.
65 Borges, *TR2*, 196.

In poems like this, Borges said, Almafuerte declared his "desdicha" and "la aceptación plenaria de esa desdicha."[66] His "desesperada voz" (like Borges's poetry) allowed a glimpse at what happened in the *arrabal* at sunset.

I hope the exploration of these poems will help rethink some of our currently accepted ideas about Borges and his poetry on the *arrabal*. As an example, we may need to consider other possible readings to those that propose that Borges's walks through the *arrabal* during the "atardecer hacia el horizonte, es una búsqueda de aquello que del pasado sobrevive en el presente" or that "el atardecer, el ocaso, [es el] instante perfecto para encontrar la paz anhelada."[67]

The texts highlighted here do give us also the opportunity to revise the question of desire and sex in Borges's work. Beatriz Sarlo says that "Donde Borges restaura un mundo de coraje, honor y traición, en el suburbio arrabalero, Girondo lo inspecciona con una mirada sexualizada y desacralizadora" and thus cites the latter's "Milonga": "El bandoneón canta con esperezos de gusano baboso, contradice el pelo rojo de la alfombra, imanta los pezones, los pubis y la punta de los zapatos."[68] I think that we can revise this comparison that, as has very often happened in Borges criticism, seems reflexively inclined to negate his capacity to speak about sex. On the one hand, in Borges's *arrabal* the creole tradition and sex are not mutually exclusive; to the contrary, they are intimately related. On the other hand, we could even argue that Borges's sotto voce conversation on sex (in the *arrabal* or anywhere else) tells us "more," it talks about things that Girondo's strident eroticism does not dare to speak of (as do not dare other contemporary poets such as Nicolás Olivari or the César Tiempo of *Clara Beter*): while Girondo's obvious sexualization of the city is about the display of aesthetic convictions, Borges's reticent eroticism is more than that: it is also about his own troubled sexuality.

---

66 Borges, *TR2*, 197.
67 Sarlo, "Orillero y ultraísta," 154; Olea Franco, "La verdadera," 41.
68 Sarlo, "Orillero y ultraísta," 155.

CHAPTER 7

# Stoicism and Borges's Writing of Women

Criticism has identified essentially two types of female characters in Borges's literature. On the one hand, there are a few texts in which women establish love relationships with male protagonists, such as "Ulrica" or "El congreso." On the other, more frequently, women in his literature seem to be defined by negative qualities and conflictive contexts. This last group (which is the one that has garnered most of the attention) includes women that appear to be reduced to mere instruments of men's desires ("La intrusa") or that threaten men with their criminal conduct ("Emma Zunz").[1]

Although at first glance the qualities that define these two groups seem capable of explaining Borges's representation of women, I find them insufficient. There are two problems, I think, with the way Borges's female characters have been approached. The first is that this critical consensus has been built upon a few scenes and circumstances that have acquired the status of classic moments in Borges's literature and, thus, it is based on the study of a limited number of texts, most of them narrative fictions. It is symptomatic in this respect that, for example, the French editor of Borges's works thinks that Emma Zunz and Ulrica are the only two females characters in Borges's literature,[2] which simply omits La viuda Ching and others that, even though they did not lend their names to the title of a short story, play central roles in other tales, such as "Pedro Salvadores" or "Juan Muraña." The second problem is that the analysis of these texts has not sufficiently taken into account other components of Borges's work. One of these neglected components is philosophy, which has as much influenced his thoughts about women as it has shaped other topics of his literature, including male figures or even something apparently as distant and unrelated to female characters as his conceptions of time. In other words, criticism has tended to consider women in Borges almost as a category in itself while in fact (and inevitably)

---

[1] See, for example, Pyñeiro's analysis in section IV of his *Ficcionalidad e ideología*, which represents well the general view on this subject.
[2] Borges, *OC* [2010], II, 1333.

women also bear the mark of Borges's more general philosophical and ethical preoccupations.

In this chapter, I want to propose another reading that relies not only on an analysis of Borges's short stories but also on his nonfiction prose and, to a lesser extent, on his poetry. I think that to understand how Borges writes women we have to acknowledge a continuum between his fiction and nonfiction (including prologues, dedications, public speeches, and letters), which allows us to see, for example, some common traits between a character such as Emma Zunz and the representation of his mother. The thread that unites Emma with other fictional and real women, I will argue, is an admirable and enviable Stoicism: they are virtuous women who, with valor and courage, confront the worst circumstances that destiny presents to them.

This way of thinking and writing women reflects not only Borges's preference for the Stoic tradition but also a guilty self-perception of his own masculinity: Borges did not think he was brave or morally courageous, qualities that he admired and that he imagined some women had. Therefore, the reading that I propose also reveals an ubiquitous asymmetrical relationship between women and men, in which the former appear stronger and better than the latter. This analysis will give us an additional perspective on Borges's complicated relationships with women.

## Borges's Stoic Imaginary

Borges's literature is traversed by several of the classic topics of Stoicism, an important aspect of his oeuvre that, to the best of my knowledge, has received no attention. The opening of this new interpretive path required the sampling of Borges's repertoire of Stoic readings and, in particular, I had to become acquainted with authors such as Seneca and Michel de Montaigne; knowledge that, in turn, made visible the ubiquitous but not always obvious presence of the doctrine in Borges's texts. That is, the reading of what Borges read has worked like a detective's magnifying glass that has the ability to uncover the clues of previously unnoticed literary and philosophical influences.

Given the variety of forms that the doctrine takes in Borges's literature and the fact that this question is virtually unknown among his readers, in the next few pages I will introduce the main characteristics of Borges's Stoic imaginary, which will provide a useful context for the main subject of the chapter. Among the questions treated by Stoicism that we find in Borges's literature are the importance of courage and moral integrity in confronting the hardships of destiny and achieving virtue, death as the key moment of life, the role of generosity and favors in personal relationships, and cyclical time (I review these topics in the corresponding sections of this chapter). The presence of the Stoic doctrine in Borges's writings is noticeable on several levels, from central concepts in a short story or a poem to passing critical comments about some of his favorite authors (for example, Bernard

Shaw, Lawrence of Arabia, and Quevedo were "hombres austeros" who knew how to explore "las posibilidades retóricas ... del valeroso estoicismo"[3]).

The articulation of Stoicism in Borges's work follows a logic (as often happens with other ideas) in which individuals closely correspond with nations, races, religions, or other communities to which they belong, with the result that individual figures end up as exemplars or types that demonstrate the qualities previously attributed to those collective identities. Thus, as the critical comment that I just quoted suggests, Borges believed that the Stoic doctrine was a fundamental component of the British and Spanish cultures (more on the latter below). With a similar generalization, however, he denied that quality to the Italian people, whom he considered too emotional and plaintive.

For Borges, Stoicism was one of the fundamental traits of Argentine culture too. At the beginning of "El matadero," Esteban Echeverría had quoted Epictetus's well-known maxim "*sustine, abstine* (sufre, abstente)"[4] and thus planted in Argentine literature this philosophical school. Similarly, in the first pages of *Facundo* (1845), Sarmiento pointed out that "[había] en el carácter argentino, cierta resignación estoica para la muerte violenta," which was proven by "la indiferencia con que [los gauchos] dan y reciben la muerte."[5] José Hernández too, according to Borges, recognized that quality: Martín Fierro was of "índole estoica,"[6] a trait revealed by the "coraje que no ignora que el hombre ha nacido para sufrir."[7] The tradition included Almafuerte, "de incorruptible y dura virtud"[8] and whose work reflected the "aceptación valerosa de [la] desdicha";[9] that is, he had stoically accepted his sexual impotence.

Courage and the capacity to endure suffering were not the only evidence of the stoic ethics of Argentines. Friendship (and conversation as its best manifestation) was another such quality. The subject was carefully pondered by Cicero in *On Friendship*[10] and more famously realized by Montaigne who, for example, thought that the literary form of his philosophical reflections in *Les Essais* and their tone reflected well that they had been conceived as a conversation with his dead friend Étienne de La Boétie.[11] In Argentina the

---

3 Borges, *BES*, 135.
4 Echeverría, *La cautiva/ El matadero*, 101.
5 Sarmiento, *Facundo*, 24.
6 Borges, *OC* [1974], IV, 87.
7 Borges, *OCC*, 563–64.
8 Borges, *IA*, 36.
9 Borges, *OC* [1974], IV, 17.
10 "La naturaleza no prefiere nada en soledad," Cicerón, *Sobre la amistad*, chapter 88; "Conviene que se añada...cierta dulzura en las conversaciones y el trato, condimento nada insignificante de la amistad," Cicerón, *Sobre la amistad*, chapter 66.
11 "Parce que c'était lui, parce que c'était moi," Montaigne, *Essais*, I, XXVIII; "l'exercise le plus fructueux et le plus naturel de notre esprit c'est, à mon avis, la conversation,"

importance of this Stoic value and its practice was revealed by Estanislao del Campo's *Fausto*, a poem in which "lo esencial es el diálogo, la clara amistad que trasluce el diálogo."[12]

In addition, two other traits reflected the centrality of Stoicism in Argentine culture, which not coincidentally Borges pointed out in "El escritor argentino y la tradición" (1953). One of them was modesty and decorum in speech and writing, a style of expression that corresponded with Stoic ethics. Seneca said that "speech that aims at the truth should be unaffected and plain" and judged that "just as a man of wisdom should be *modest* in his manner of walking, so should his speech be *restrained*, not impetuous."[13] In Argentina that precept was realized, among others, by poet Enrique Banchs. In 1928 Borges proposed that it was in "el estoicismo argentino de un poema de Enrique Banchs" and not in "las efusiones italianas de los tangos" that we could find the (true) "argentinidad"[14] and, decades later, he reiterated the argument in "El escritor argentino y la tradición": while tango lyrics dramatically and unashamedly exhibited the emotional pain of men who lost women, in *La urna* (1911) "al hablar de esa mujer que lo había dejado," "al hablar de ese gran dolor que lo abrumaba" Banchs remained within the boundaries of "el pudor argentino, la reticencia argentina."[15]

Argentina was also "cosmopolita," a word that Borges used "en el primitivo y recto sentido de esa palabra que los estoicos acuñaron."[16] Stoics created the concept to signify that individuals did not belong to a city, a country, or even a language and that, on the contrary, they were "ciudadanos del cosmos, ciudadanos del orbe, del universo."[17] Victoria Ocampo, for example, had "esa interpretación generosa de la palabra cosmopolita...[que] significa la generosa ambición de querer sensibles a todos los países y a todas las épocas."[18] The founder of *Sur*, Borges summarized, understood that "nuestro patrimonio es el mundo."[19] Similarly, when in "El escritor Argentino y la tradición"

---

Montaigne, *Essais*, III, VIII; "J'aurais choisi plus volontiers [the genre of letters instead of the essay]...si j'avais eu à qui parler. Il m'aurait fallu, comme je l'ai eue autrefois, une certaine forme de relations qui m'attirât," Montaigne, *Essais*, I, XL.

12 Borges, *OC* [1974], I, 187.
13 Seneca, *Letters on Ethics*, 121, 123. Emphasis added.
14 Borges, *TR1*, 366.
15 Borges, *OC* [1974], I, 269. Among other things, Borges's Stoic preferences may *partially* explain his own inclination to reticence and decorum but we may also suspect that Stoicism came handy to justify an aesthetic choice that had wider roots in the literary traditions that he knew, his own personal experiences, and the historical context in which he wrote.
16 Borges, *OC* [1974], IV, 82.
17 Borges, *BES*, 326.
18 Borges, *BES*, 327. Some men admired by Borges shared that quality with Ocampo: education made Henry and William James true "cosmopolitas—ciudadanos del mundo en el sentido estoico de la palabra," Borges, *OC* [1974], IV, 94.
19 Borges, *TR3*, 87.

he famously asked "¿Cuál es la tradición argentina?" he gave an answer of undeniable Stoic pedigree: "debemos pensar que nuestro patrimonio es el universo"[20] ("My city and fatherland is Rome; as a human being, it is the universe,"[21] said Marcus Aurelius).

Of course, in Borges's imaginary the identification between the Argentine tradition and Stoicism worked both ways and somehow implied the "Argentinization" of the ancient doctrine: thus Borges characterized Socrates, the most representative of the Stoic heroes, as "un criollo viejo."[22]

Borges's Stoic imaginary had other characteristics that it is necessary to note. On the one hand, he created it with a specific and consistent vocabulary that included words such as "valeroso," "duro," "arduo," "recto," "primitivo," "sufrido," "austero," "rudeza," "firmeza," and "sereno." On the other hand, for Borges, the generations that founded Argentine Stoicism and their heirs also defined the times and spaces where that ethic was practiced. In the ideal nineteenth-century creole society conceived by Borges, not only the elites but also the common people were endowed with that quality; however, that was not the case in twentieth-century Argentina because those ethics were alien to the popular classes, comprising foreign, mainly Italian, masses. In modern, post-immigration Argentina, Stoic values survived primarily among the descendants of patrician families and in the suburbs populated by tough knife fighters of creole background. The attribution of such ethics to the creole masses reflected a certain Stoic orthodoxy: philosophers in this tradition (particularly Seneca and Montaigne) believed that virtue was more common among the lower classes because their daily wants and hardships prepared them better for adversity.[23] Thus, in Borges's imaginary, the *arrabal* of Buenos Aires was the Stoic space par excellence, and it is not a coincidence that in 1928 he chose the title "Séneca en las orillas"[24] for one of his explorations on the ethics of that area of the city. Also in *El Tango* Borges presented gauchos and their descendants of the arrabal as instinctive practitioners of the stoic doctrine. He explained that "los *compadres*,"[25] who lived in poverty and were used to "las durezas y sinsabores de [la] vida," "se propusieron como

---

20 Borges, *OC* [1974], I, 273–74.
21 Marcus Aurelius, *Meditations*, 6.44. In his preparatory notes and rough draft for the essay Borges does twice mention the stoics in reference to their concept of destiny as a corolary of the perfect organization of nature but the documentary evidence does not explicitly link them to the two questions discussed here; for an analysis of the manuscripts, see Balderston, "Detalles."
22 Bioy, *Borges*, 457. "Socrates was the chief Saint of the Stoics throughout their history," Russell, *Western Philosophy*, 253.
23 Seneca, *Selected Letters*, 128, 143; Montaigne, *Essais*, II, XXXV, 903.
24 Review *Síntesis*, then republished in *Sur* (1931) with the same title; it was also included in *Evaristo Carriego* (1930) with the title "Las inscripciones de los carros."
25 *compadre/compadrito*: working men of creole origins, descendants of gauchos, often thugs and criminals, who engaged in knife fights.

ideal el de ser valientes."²⁶ To support his thesis he quoted *Martín Fierro* and told the story of a peon:

> En el *Martín Fierro* leemos: 'Amigazo, pa' sufrir han nacido los varones'. Y Adolfo Bioy Casares me contó el caso de un peón de estancia, a quien tenían que hacerle una operación inmediata, de urgencia, y muy dolorosa. Le explicaron que iba a sentir mucho dolor, hasta le ofrecieron un pañuelo para que él lo mordiera mientras estaban operándolo, y entonces este hombre dijo, *sin saber que estaba diciendo una frase digna de los estoicos, digna de Séneca*: 'Del dolor me encargo yo'. Y sufrió la operación sin que se notara ningún cambio en su cara. Es decir, se había propuesto ser valiente y logró serlo.²⁷

Borges's poetry on the *arrabal* and the men who lived in it also reflects well his conception of their ethics: he speaks about the "duro arrabal," the "valerosa chusma" whose "austero oficio era el coraje," the *compadre* who "muere y ... no se queja," another "de valor sereno" who "murió como si no le importara," and that "el destino no hace acuerdos / y nadie se lo reproche" (while he qualifies *compadritos* as "fatales").²⁸

Finally, and to conclude with this overview of Borges's Stoic imaginary, it is important to know that his interest in the ancient doctrine also influenced his reading of Spanish Peninsular literature and his understanding of the relationship of the latter with the Argentine tradition. To see this question it is helpful to remember that in "Otro poema de los dones" (1963) (a piece itself imbibed in the doctrine—more on this below) Borges thanks destiny

> Por Séneca y Lucano, de Córdoba,
> Que antes del español escribieron
> Toda la literatura española²⁹

That is, the Stoicism of the Cordoban Seneca (and his nephew Lucano) was at the origin of and fundamentally molded Peninsular literature. In effect, Borges's personal canon of Spanish literature, in which we find Jorge Manrique, Fray Luis de León, Quevedo, and, perhaps above all, Fernández de Andrada,³⁰ was largely organized by the presence of the doctrine in the

---

26 Borges, *ET*, 52–53.
27 Borges, *ET*, 53–54. Emphasis added.
28 Borges, *OC* [1974], I, 949, 955, 957, 961, 969.
29 Borges, *OC* [1974], I, 937.
30 "Cuánto más complejo es este autor que Quevedo, Góngora, Lope, y que el mismo Fray Luis," Bioy, 899. The attribution of authorship to the "Epístola moral a Fabio" was uncertain for about three centuries but the enigma was solved in the first decades of the twentieth century (by, among others, Dámaso Alonso). However, Borges was either unaware of or unconvinced by the arguments presented by scholars and continued to consider it as anonymous, which fitted perfectly in the Stoic aesthetics of modesty of speech and self-effacement of the poem: in "Otro poema de los dones"

works of those authors ("¿Por qué es tan lindo el poema de Manrique? No solo por los versos: por su ética. La ética es importante en todo; también en literatura"[31]). For Borges, then, beyond the obvious fact of the language, the common Stoic doctrine revealed one more dimension (this time ethical) of the Spanish ancestry of the Argentine tradition and future studies could perhaps consider the hypothesis that Borges conceived his poetry on the arrabal (e.g. *Para las seis cuerdas* [1965]) not just within the creole heritage but also as a late Transatlantic incarnation of his personal Peninsular and Stoic canon.[32]

After this introduction to Borges's largely overlooked modulation of Stoicism, then, we can begin to address the main subject of the chapter. If the Stoic doctrine was defined around a restrictive idea of masculinity, nonetheless it did save a place for women, particularly in its most classic moment, when Seneca wrote specific essays on this topic (for example, "Consolation to Marcia" and "Consolation to Helvia"). This side of the tradition was not omitted by Borges and, on the contrary, as we will see from now on, he relied on it to write (almost obsessively) the symmetrical female counterpart of his very masculine Stoic imaginary.

As a first step in investigating this question it may be helpful to remember Mastronardi's annotation that I quoted in chapter 5. In his diary he registered the cases of two women who Borges liked. One of them was a read-headed woman who went to the sea often and who had a stoic personality ("se abstiene de toda coquetería y afronta los desengaños con admirable firmeza"[33]), a combination of traits that turned her into a figure out of an Icelandic saga. The other was a "lenta señorita de tez morena" who represented "el más grato pasado criollo" and who possessed the same "serenidad"[34] exhibited by brave knife fighters ("de valor sereno"), qualities that, according to Borges, also defined the "sentimiento criollo" of William H. Hudson's novels, made of the "aceptación estoica del sufrir y [la] serena aceptación de la dicha."[35]

Borges, then, was attracted to stoical women. But equally important, Mastronardi's annotation also prepares us methodologically for their study.

---

he thanks destiny "Por aquel sevillano que redactó la Epístola Moral/ Y cuyo nombre, como él hubiera preferido, ignoramos" (*OC* [1974], I, 937) and in one of their conversations he told Bioy "Qué bien que el poema haya quedado anónimo. Es como si el destino hubiera complacido al autor," Bioy, *Borges*, 898.

31 Bioy, *Borges*, 1033.
32 An early insinuation by Borges of his conception of the relation between the two traditions and the role of ethics in it in "Las coplas acriolladas," *TME*, 80–88. It is evident that in this assessment of Spanish culture, Borges took into account the philosophical and critical trends from the first decades of the twentieth century that explored the "senequismo" or the Stoics' ethics present in its poetic tradition, including Jorge Manrique, Quevedo, Fernández de Andrada, and Unamuno; see Zambrano, "Pensamiento."
33 Mastronardi, *Borges*, 81.
34 Mastronardi, *Borges*, 81.
35 Borges, "La tierra cárdena," *TME*, 41.

As we have seen, Borges lives through literature, and his view of the women around him is no exception. The "real" women whom he encounters in his life are "arquetipos" or "representan" literary and cultural traditions. That is, as he reads them, he experiences and writes them. This has the effect of blurring the boundaries of the literary genres where he displays his Stoic imaginary, which is evident in the similarity of his formulations of women in texts as varied as the dedication of a book, a public speech, or a short story. Then, I propose, Borges's women must be explicated by looking at the whole spectrum of genres and types of texts that his literature offers, from a tale and a poem to a letter.

Brave Women (Cowardly Men)

According to Stoics, the supreme being and creator (called Nature, God, or Zeus) was omniscient and rational and, therefore, the world was perfectly organized. This concept justified the idea of "destiny" or "Providence," which implied that everything that happened (to the minutest of details) was part of the universal plan or design and that the creator not only had wanted it this way but also knew it would happen exactly in that form. Thus, everything that occurred was in harmony with the rest of nature and, however terrible an event seemed to be, it was never bad. Therefore, it did not make sense to complain about destiny, and it was useless to resist it or to try to escape from it. Wise people accepted it and faced it, because they understood that the challenges presented by fate were an opportunity to demonstrate one's own worth. Stoic virtue, then, demanded bravery and moral courage to deal with the adversities posed by destiny.

In Stoicism, virtue was never monopolized by men. Actually there was a long tradition of the celebration of women who possessed this quality, including Seneca's and Marcus Aurelius's mothers, whose sons made sure posterity would remember them.[36] More importantly, in a variant of this question, Stoics recorded stories of brave women and commented on them. For example, Montaigne devoted a chapter to "Des trois bonnes femmes" (which some modern French editions title "Sur trois femmes *valereuses*"[37]), while Seneca was convinced that women had "just as much aptitude [as men] for noble actions ... they endure pain and toil as well as [men] do"[38] and praised some "whose evident courage has won them a place in the ranks of great men."[39] In Stoics' texts, these heroines usually know how to accept the death of loved ones without demonstrating their suffering or are the women who in the midst of wars, invasions, and despotic regimes, show their bravery,

---

36 "Consolation to Helvia," Seneca, *Dialogues and Essays*, 163–87; Marcus Aurelius, *Meditations*, Bk. I.
37 Emphasis added.
38 Montaigne, *Essais*, II, XXXV; Seneca, *Dialogues and Essays*, 68.
39 Seneca, *Dialogues and Essays*, 182.

while men reveal themselves to be cowards. One of those typical women was, as Seneca pointed out, "the wife who, forgetful of her own weakness ... exposed her own life to dangers."[40]

This aspect of the doctrine had one of its literary realizations in nineteenth-century Argentina, more precisely in Echeverría's "La cautiva." As far as I know, critics have not related the poem to Stoicism and have not considered it as one of the references that Borges necessarily had recourse to in the writing of his female characters (with the exception of the prostitute in "La noche de los dones").[41] With his quotation by Epictetus in "El matadero," Echeverría invokes the Stoic tradition, and it is not a coincidence that "La cautiva" was largely organized around the topics treated by the doctrine. María, the protagonist of the composition, embodies the archetype of "the wife who, forgetful of her own weakness ... exposed her own life to dangers," as Seneca underscored ("salvar quisiste a tu amante," says Echeverría). As happens with Stoic heroes and heroines, it is destiny that tests María's worth ("arrostrando del destino / la rigorosa crueldad," "tu vivir predestinado"), who shows that she is as good as men ("tu varonil fortaleza"). And, as usually happens in Stoic narratives, if the woman has no choice but to rely on her own courage, it is because the man she is with has revealed himself to be inadequate for the difficult circumstances that they face ("ella infunde a su flaqueza [la de Brian] / constancia allí y fortaleza"; "Yo en nada puedo valerte," says Brian).[42]

Borges's mother shared some qualities with María. In the dedication of his *Obras completas*, Borges speaks of "la memoria de los mayores ... la carga de los húsares del Perú y el oprobio de Rosas—, tu prisión *valerosa*, cuando tantos hombres callábamos."[43] The praise for Leonor's courage goes hand in hand with the reproach to cowardly men (including the son) who did not speak up. With her behavior ("valerosa"), the woman shows that she is a true heir of the nineteenth-century patrician elite, a genealogical maneuver that allows the author to establish a clear symmetry between Rosas's dictatorship and Perón's "segunda dictadura," when Borges's mother was briefly arrested for protesting in the streets. In the dedication there is another similarity with "La cautiva" that I want to point out because it reveals, I think, the imaginary in which Borges locates both the figure of his mother and his most important

---

40 Seneca, *Dialogues and Essays*, 186.
41 Borges does allude to Echeverría's poem with his character, precisely nicknamed "la cautiva" in his "La noche de los dones," which is pretty clear and that has been noted before; however, it has not been examined in the context of Stoicism. But more important and more generally, I refer to the similarities between the ethics of Echevarría's María and those of many, if not most, of Borges's female characters or the real women he wrote about.
42 All the quotations from "La cautiva" in this chapter in Echeverría, *La cautiva/ El matadero*, 11–94.
43 Borges, *OC* [1974], I, 9. Emphasis added.

female character, Emma Zunz. Borges recalls the "*oprobio* de Rosas—tu prisión valerosa" and among the challenges that destiny has posed for Emma, he includes "el auto de prisión, el *oprobio*,"[44] a noun that Echeverría uses to allude to the Rosista barbarism that threatens the "mujer sublime" ("Huye tú, mujer sublime, / y del *oprobio* redime / tu vivir predestinado").

Norah, Borges's sister, also achieved virtue, and her circumstances too are narrated by resorting, even more clearly than in the case of the mother, to the topics of Stoicism:

> Durante la segunda dictadura, hacia mil novecientos cuarenta y cuatro [*sic*], padeció un mes de prisión por razones políticas; para no afligir a mi madre, le escribió que la cárcel era un lugar lindísimo. Aprovechaba el obligado ocio para enseñar dibujo a sus compañeras de encierro, que eran mujeres de la calle.[45]

Seneca said that "great men delight ... in adversity, just as brave soldiers delight in warfare,"[46] a moral quality that in this case allows the daughter to cheer up the mother, although it is the former who suffers prison; in addition, she turns the difficult moment into an opportunity for art and teaching ("Son dulces los empleos de la adversidad,"[47] said Borges, quoting Shakespeare, who also read Montaigne). Norah's proximity to prostitutes, who in Borges's imaginary were the symmetrical female counterpart to *compadritos* (I address this matter further below), suggests his efforts to place his sister in the landscape of the *orillas*, a space that he reserved for creole Stoicism. Norah was also more determined and courageous than her brother "Georgie":

> Norah en todos nuestros juegos, era siempre el caudillo; yo, el rezagado, el tímido y el sumiso. Ella subía a la azotea, trepaba a los árboles y a los cerros; yo la seguía con menos entusiasmo que miedo. En la escuela el contraste se repitió. A mí me intimidaban los chicos pobres y me enseñaban con desdén el lunfardo básico de aquellos años ... Mi hermana, en cambio, dirigía a sus compañeras. ... Durante toda la adolescencia la envidié porque se encontró envuelta en un tiroteo electoral y atravesó la plaza de Adrogué, un pueblo del Sur, corriendo entre las balas.[48]

As in the case of Leonor, bravery defines Norah, a quality that reveals, once again, that she is a true twentieth-century heir of the creole past (he calls her a "caudillo"). As in his portrait of his mother, here too Borges blames himself when he emphasizes "el contraste" between his intrepid sister and his own fear; between the fact that Norah leads her classmates, while he is intimidated by the *compadritos* of the future (working-class children). Equally

---

44 Borges, *OC* [1974], I, 564. Emphasis added.
45 Borges, *TR3*, 184.
46 Seneca, *Dialogues and Essays*, 10.
47 Borges, *TR2*, 265.
48 Borges, *TR3*, 182–83.

important, in a maneuver similar to the one attempted with the prostitutes in the paragraph quoted earlier, Borges suggests that Norah even goes "orillera," to the extent that, on her way, she participates in an electoral skirmish among *compadres*.

Borges also commended "la valentía" of another descendant of the patrician elite, Victoria Ocampo. In a text of evident Stoic pedigree titled "Un destino," Borges recalled her arrest during Perón's administration and underlined the same attitude that he celebrated in his sister when she faced a similar adversity:

> la fortaleza y casi la alegría con que sobrellevó el rigor de la cárcel, cuando la suerte, siempre tan generosa con ella, quiso que también conociera la desventura honrosa y el sacrificio personal.[49]

In Borges's fictions, too, women exhibit a bravery and moral courage that men do not have. Thus, in the story "La viuda Ching, pirata," we hear that Mary Read, another pirate, "declaró una vez que la profesión de pirata no era para cualquiera, y que, para ejercerla con dignidad, era preciso ser un hombre de coraje, como ella" and when "uno de sus amantes fue injuriado por el matón a bordo Mary lo retó a duelo, y se batió con él a dos manos ...."[50] In "Hombre de la esquina rosada," the Lujanera (a woman from the *orillas* of Buenos Aires) has to remind Rosendo (her man) that he is expected to be brave (in their neighborhood, says the narrator, "cuanto más aporriao, más obligación de ser guapo"). The scene is reminiscent of the well-known episode involving Arria and Paetus, referred to by several Latin texts and commented on by Montaigne: Paetus does not have the courage to commit suicide and, therefore, Arria stabs herself in the chest, then pulls the dagger out and places it in her husband's hand while she famously pronounces: "Paete, non dolet"[51] ("Paetus, it does not hurt"). Similarly, the Lujanera "le metió la mano en el pecho y le sacó el cuchillo desenvainado y se lo dio con estas palabras: —Rosendo, creo que lo estarás precisando." When the man refuses to fight, the woman, disappointed and outraged, denounces him: "nos hizo creer que era un hombre."[52]

But it is in "Pedro Salvadores"[53] that Borges more neatly writes a Stoic woman. The protagonist of the story is the wife, and if she does not appear in the studies that have explored Borges's female characters it is, perhaps, because the title may have deterred critics. The brief text is based on a historical event that occurred during the Rosas years: Salvadores, a Unitarian persecuted by the *caudillo* Rosas, hid himself in the basement of his home for 9 years and was only able (or dared) to emerge from his subterranean exile

---

49 Borges, *TR3*, 87.
50 Borges, *OC* [1974], I, 306.
51 Montaigne, *Essais*, II, XXXV, 904, 905.
52 Borges, *OC* [1974], I, 331.
53 The story and all its quotations in Borges, *OC* [1974], I, 994–95.

after the *caudillo* was overthrown; in the meantime, his wife had managed to convince their families, friends, and authorities that the husband had escaped to Uruguay. The exceptional episode was registered by nineteenth-century memorialists and writers, although Borges suggests it was his grandfather who told him about it.[54]

In the story, when the *mazorca* (Rosas supporters) arrives at their home, Salvadores barely has time to hide himself, while it is his wife who confronts the violence of the soldiers and is harassed. Borges says that it is then that "principia verdaderamente la historia" because at that moment begins the long confinement to which Salvadores will be reduced by his own cowardice. It is in that decade-long solitude that the woman shows her moral courage, as before she displayed her bravery. First, she accepts with integrity the poverty caused by her husband's "absence" and works to support the man, even when she has to humiliate herself and sew uniforms for the troops of the dictator ("Ganó el pan de los dos cosiendo para el ejército"). In addition, like other women celebrated by the Stoic tradition who proved their virtue while losing their honor (they preferred to yield to the sexual desire of their husband's enemies to save the life of their men[55]), Salvadores's wife too does not hesitate to lose her personal reputation to protect her husband. In effect, during those 9 years she bears him two children but "la familia la repudió, atribuyéndolos a un amante" and, so, she has to wait several years to recover her honor: "Después de la caída del tirano, le pedirían perdón de rodillas." In the same Stoic vein, although the wife is the one who suffers more, she is also stronger and keeps up the man's morale: "Para que no la dejara sola, su mujer le daría inciertas noticias de conspiraciones y victorias." Finally, Borges says that Salvadores "acaso era cobarde y la mujer lealmente le ocultó que ella lo sabía," a conjecture that seeks to confirm her moral superiority and that is reminiscent of Montaigne's observation at the beginning of his essay on Stoic heroines: "Comme les pères cachent leur affection envers leurs enfants, elles, de même, cachent habituellement la leur envers leur mari pour garder une attitude respectueuse et décente."[56]

In spite of the title, the true protagonist of the story is the valiant woman who appears as a female archetype of creole Stoicism.[57] It is interesting to note that the behavior of Salvadores's wife is almost identical to that of Norah Borges: although they are the ones who endure the worst consequences of political adversities, it is they who morally support other members of their families (one gave false news of possible conspiracies and military victories, and the other tells her mother "que la cárcel era un lugar lindísimo"), a

---

54 According to Bioy, Borges learned about the episode from Eduardo Gutiérrez's *El puñal del tirano*.
55 Montaigne, *Essais*, III, V, 1051.
56 Montaigne, *Essais*, II, XXXV, 901.
57 Borges says that her maiden name was Planes, which suggests that she was a relative of the composer of the Argentine national anthem.

new symmetry between the nineteenth and the twentieth centuries and between the "first" and "second" dictatorships. These similarities suggest the possibility that one of the texts might have served as a source for the other, at the same time that they highlight the artificiality of both and the porosity of the boundaries that formally separate their genres.

This is even more evident if we note that there are some common elements between "Pedro Salvadores" and another apparently very different text, "El incivil maestro de ceremonias Kotsuké No Suké," which, like the former, has not been explored by critics who are interested in Borges's female characters. However, I think it can illuminate the way Borges has written Stoic women, including Emma Zunz, as we will see in the next chapter. For the time being, I only want to highlight the similarity of a circumstance that we find in the two plots. The tale narrates the history of a brave Japanese warrior who is willing even to lose his own life to achieve justice and to honor the loyalty that he has sworn to his lord. To reach his goal, he goes so far as to feign a scandal that, once again, relates to illicit sex: "Se dejó arrebatar por los lupanares … se codeó con rameras … despidió a su mujer y al menor de sus hijos, y compró una querida en un lupanar, famosa infamia,"[58] which implies his momentary public disgrace but that, in reality, conceals his true virtue. This is also the case of Salvadores's wife who, to realize her noble purpose, when she is accused of being unfaithful to her husband, does not contradict the accusation and pretends to accept it, which in itself implies that she has actually engaged in such a relationship. And in the same way that her relatives would later kneel down before her to beg her pardon, a man who trod on the Japanese warrior and spit on him to punish his pretended moral fall, later, when the sham is finally revealed and he understands the true integrity of the warrior, "[ofreció] satisfacción" to him and "cometió harakiri."

## How to Die

Borges's women also know how to die and, thus, they embody one of the fundamental precepts of the doctrine. Montaigne said that "La mort est l'action la plus remarquable de la vie humaine"[59] and that the purpose of philosophy "n'est pas autre chose que s'apprêter à la mort."[60] Like Seneca and other Stoics, the French essayist believed that one of the benefits of virtue is that it allows us to disdain death and face it with courage: "c'est une grande chose que mourir honorablement, sagement et avec fermeté."[61] On the other hand, death is ruled by destiny and, therefore, it never arrives too early or too late but when universal design indicates.

---

58 Borges, *OC* [1974], I, 321–22.
59 Montaigne, *Essais*, II, XIII, 738.
60 Montaigne, *Essais*, I, XX, 100.
61 Montaigne, *Essais*, II, XIII, 743.

Stoic narratives include several famous "honorable" deaths, some of them suicides. Two of the classic examples were the deaths of Seneca and Socrates, who with exemplary calmness and firmness carried out the order to kill themselves. Borges was clearly interested in the latter's death. He once highlighted:

> Es interesante señalar que Sócrates ... no se quería despedir patéticamente. Echó a su mujer y a sus hijos, quería echar a un amigo que estaba llorando, quería conversar serenamente.[62]

And in one of his conversations with Bioy, Borges compared the death of the Greek philosopher with that of Christ:

> Si comparás la muerte de Sócrates y la de Cristo, no hay duda de que Sócrates era el más grande de los dos. Sócrates era un caballero y Cristo un político, que buscaba la compasión. También en las sagas [nórdicas] se describen muertes mejores. El que dijo: "Sí, ahora se usan esas espadas anchas," parece infinitamente más sereno, más valiente, más noble que Cristo con su efecto teatral, falsamente grandioso, de "Perdónalos, no saben lo que hacen."[63]

The serenity commended by Borges reflected the courage implicit in the acceptance of destiny and, on the contrary, the exaggeration of emotions revealed the absence of valor. "Pity," according to Seneca, was "the defect of a small mind," it was usually "seen in the worst specimens of humanity"[64] and, therefore, to try to avoid death by resorting to it or any other means was not honorable.[65] For Borges, then, Socrates or the heroic characters of the Nordic sagas proved to be more courageous, more noble, than Christ, and by extension, their respective cultural traditions were ethically superior to the Christian one ("mucho mejor son los estoicos," he also told Bioy). On the other hand, his comments on Socrates allow us to understand the way Borges himself described similar moments. He pays attention to "descriptions" of those final moments and "compares" them, because, like Seneca and Montaigne,[66] he thinks that the form of death reveals the ethics with which the individual lived the whole life that is about to end.

If death, even suicide, were welcomed and honored by the Stoics, it was because it also meant the end of misfortunes, a liberation from the suffering (whatever its form) inherent in life. This is what we read in, for example, "La cautiva," which contains a creole version of Arria's and Paetus's suicide that I mentioned earlier. In the third part of the poem, precisely titled "El puñal," María warns her faltering husband that rather than be captured

---

62 Borges, *OC* [1974], IV, 177.
63 Bioy, *Borges*, 1367.
64 Seneca, *Dialogues and Essays*, 215.
65 Seneca, *Dialogues and Essays*, 129–30.
66 Seneca, *Dialogues and Essays*, 136; Montaigne, *Essais*, I, XX, 110.

again by the barbarians, they will take their own lives: "Cuando contrario el destino / nos cierre, Brian, el camino, / antes de volver a manos / de esos indios inhumanos, / nos queda algo: este puñal."

Borges, however, was not capable of following the precepts on suicide. In the story "Veinticinco de agosto, 1983" (1983), an older Borges reflects, along with a younger double, upon a failed attempt to take his own life, which apparently occurred at some point between the early 1930s and the year 1940. The older Borges says, "Los estoicos enseñan que no debemos quejarnos de la vida; la puerta de la cárcel está abierta. Siempre lo entendí así, pero la pereza y la cobardía me demoraron."[67] Ashamed, and perhaps also lamenting at not having done it, he confesses that he has not learned to die and suggests that, although he is a convinced reader of the doctrine, he did not consider himself a good practitioner of it.

Borges's grandmother, however, did know how to die, and it is easy to note that the narration that the author wrote of her death is shaped by Stoic precepts:

> estaba muriéndose en Ginebra, yo no le había oído nunca una mala palabra, tenía apenas un hilo de voz, era hija del coronel Suárez que comandó la carga de Junín, en el Perú, estaba muriéndose y todos la rodeábamos también y nos dijo, "déjenme morir tranquila," y después la mala palabra que yo nunca le había oído antes, entonces sentimos que era una mujer valiente. "Caramba, era la hija del coronel Suárez," dijo mi padre."[68]

The anecdote told by Borges has points in common with one of the most notable examples of virtuous deaths narrated by Montaigne (the episode lends the title to one of the essays). In the event, which occurs on the island of Zéa, "une femme de grand prestige" dies surrounded by her family while she serenely describes to them the gradual death of her organs and extremities, until she finally instructs her daughter to close her eyes once she is dead.[69] As I said earlier, Montaigne describes this and other exemplary deaths because he is convinced that the virtue of their forms corresponds to the life that is ending, an insight that Borges also shared. In effect, the attitude of Mrs. Acevedo before death allows the narrator to underline that she was a brave woman and to suggest that her virtue was the expression of nineteenth-century patrician and creole Stoicism. The doctrinal and fictional components of the narration of this death become more evident if we note that this was not the only one that Borges told in this form. The references to Ricardo Guiraldes, for example, show well that such scenes form part of Borges's Stoic imaginary. He said that the author of *Don Segundo Sombra* "representaba el mejor tipo de señor argentino" and that Guiraldes died after "una agonía que sobrellevó con firmeza, con la firmeza

---

67 Borges, *OC* [1974], II, 380.
68 Vaccaro, *Borges*, 312–13.
69 Montaigne, *Essais*, II, III, 431–48.

de sus duros troperos y domadores."[70] That is, on the one hand, Borges writes Guiraldes's death with the vocabulary chosen for the creation of his Stoic imaginary ("firmeza," "duro"); on the other hand, as Mastronardi well observed, the individual Guiraldes becomes a "type" that "represents" the national version of the doctrine. Actually, Borges narrated more of these deaths. Like Guiraldes, "[Beatriz Viterbo] murió después de una imperiosa agonía que no se rebajó un solo instante ni al sentimentalismo ni al miedo";[71] this is the way Borges's *orilleros* die too: one *compadre* "murió como si no le importara," and another "muere y ... no se queja."[72] And this was also the case with the author's father: "Murió con impaciencia de morir, pero sin una queja."[73]

## Generous Women

In *De Beneficiis,* Seneca reflected on the question of "favors" or "gifts" and on other aspects of reciprocity in Roman society. His goal was to encourage citizens to be generous, and therefore, in his essay, he thought through the ethics that should guide these types of exchanges. The Cordoban philosopher said that when one makes a present or renders a service, the material object or the help offered are not relevant in themselves and say nothing about the generosity of the person giving or helping. The key question is to understand what the action means for he who performs it, that is, what really matters is the attitude with which the favor is granted or a certain object given. In the same vein, for the exchange to be beneficial to society, the recipient too must accept it in the right manner and show his gratitude accordingly.

Borges was very interested in this aspect of the doctrine, which is evident in the several texts that he devoted to "los dones."[74] One of those is "Variación" (1970), a poem written in verses reminiscent of Book I of Marcus Aurelius's *Meditations,* where the emperor recalls his personal debts to all those who prepared him for life. In a similar form, in his poem Borges thanks, for example, his Stoic grandmother: "Doy gracias por aquella señora anciana que, con la voz muy tenue, dijo a quienes rodeaban su agonía 'Déjenmé morir

---

70 Borges, *TR3,* 164, 165.
71 Borges, *OC* [1974], I, 617.
72 Borges, *OC* [1974], I, 969, 968.
73 Borges, *OC* [1974], II, 12. In another version of his father's death, Borges says that he died "al cabo de una morosa y dura agonía, que sobrellevó con sonriente resignación y con una secreta impaciencia," *TR3,* 162. This quality was also shared by some of the writers that most interested him, such as Henry James, who, when he was about to die, said "ahora, por fin, esa cosa distinguida, la muerte" (*OC* [1974], IV, 94); similarly, Robert L. Stevenson "guardó hasta el fin ... la voluntad de sonreír," *OC* [1974], IV, 505.
74 "Poema de los dones," "Otro poema de los dones," "La noche de los dones," Borges, *OC* [1974], I, 809, 936; II, 41–44.

tranquila' y después la mala palabra, que por única vez le oímos decir."⁷⁵ And in the same ethical vein, he also says:

> Doy gracias por aquel viejo asesino, que en una habitación desmantelada de la calle Cabrera, me dio una naranja y me dijo: "No me gusta que la gente salga de mi casa con las manos vacías." Serían las doce de la noche y no nos vimos más.⁷⁶

Borges does not approve of the killings carried out by Don Nicolás Paredes (to whom he seems to allude here), but he understands that the *orillero* learned to accept his destiny ("como todos los hombres a morir, el compadre se resigna también a matar"⁷⁷). The good qualities of the man go even further: he was austere and poor ("una habitación desmantelada") and, in spite of it, he still was generous ("una naranja" was all he could give). Borges feels honored not by what he is given but by Paredes's generosity and, more generally, because the latter achieved virtue. On the other hand, Borges also follows Seneca's advice: he knows the value of the *compadre*'s gesture and he does not forget about it: he thanks him (with a poem).

The virtue of some of Borges's women is similar to that of Paredes: they are generous, and they know how to give. For example, "cuando era muy niña, Norah no aceptaba una golosina si no me daban la mitad ... suelo juzgar a las personas por la inteligencia y el valor; Norah, por la bondad."⁷⁸ He also saw that quality in his mother: "Yo recibía los regalos y yo pensaba que no era más que un chico y que no había hecho nada, absolutamente nada, para merecerlos ... Desde entonces me has dado tantas cosas,"⁷⁹ including the example of her creole virtue. Victoria Ocampo also "fue extraordinariamente bondadosa"⁸⁰ with Borges. Although Borges said that they "nunca fueron amigos íntimos," Ocampo offered him her literary patronage:

> Yo no era nadie, yo era un muchacho desconocido en Buenos Aires, Victoria Ocampo fundó la Revista *Sur* y me llamó, para mi gran sorpresa, a ser uno de los socios fundadores. En aquel tiempo yo no existía, la gente ... me veía como hijo de Leonor Acevedo, como hijo del Dr. Borges, como nieto del coronel, etc. Pero ella me vió a mí, ella me distinguió, cuando casi no era nadie ... y luego recibí aquel premio internacional [Formentor, en 1961] ... todo eso lo debo también a Victoria Ocampo.⁸¹

The influential woman, who could easily count on the loyalty and support of well-known and established writers, nevertheless made the gift of recognition

---

75 Borges, *BES*, 73.
76 Borges, *BES*, 73.
77 Borges, *TR2*, 324.
78 Borges, *TR3*, 183.
79 Borges, *OC* [1974], I, 9.
80 Sorrentino, *Siete conversaciones*, 176.
81 Borges, *BES*, 329–30.

to the young and unknown Borges, who thought he did not deserve so much generosity. The image that Borges presents of his relationship with the powerful Victoria reveals the same asymmetry that we find more generally in his relationships with women: it reminds us of the disparity of his filial relationship with Leonor, from whom he also received undeserved "gifts," and, perhaps more importantly, it echoes "el contraste" that he underlined between Norah's bravery and his timidity and cowardice.

## Stoicism and Sex

In "Otro poema de los dones" (1963), Borges is grateful also for things that, however, he prefers not to be specific about: "los íntimos dones que no enumero,"[82] that is, the amorous gifts. Nonetheless, years later Borges did choose to mention the "gifts" related to love and sex. In effect, in some of his fictions the main characters and their sexual experiences seem to have been written following some Stoic precepts. In *De Beneficiis* Seneca praises not only those who intentionally look for ways to help others but also those who, although they did not seek such opportunities, take advantage of unexpected occasions to offer their favors.[83] This is what "la cautiva," the prostitute in "La noche de los dones" (1975), does. When the boy flees from the threatening presence of Juan Moreira and his bandits and, inadvertently, hides himself in an unoccupied bedroom in the brothel, the woman steps up to the virgin teenager and, aware of what it would mean for him, makes herself sexually available for free: "yo estoy aquí para servir,"[84] she says. For his part, as a devotee of the doctrine, the protagonist understands the true value of the favor that he received: as an adult he still remembers with gratitude the night when the woman made him the "gift" of initiating him sexually.

This use of the Stoic doctrine, then, presents us with a prostitute who is not necessarily a morally reprehensible figure and, on the contrary, seems to share some good qualities with other women written by Borges. After all, as Seneca also observed, anybody, independently of condition or social status, can bestow favors and, thus, demonstrate her or his virtue. Moreover, he says, "the very value of the service [exalts the person's] condition."[85]

The fact that a Borges prostitute exhibits Stoic qualities should not come as a surprise. In *De Beneficiis* Seneca says that it is not sufficient to simply render a service or to give a material object to the person in need. To contribute to the well-being of another person and to demonstrate virtue, the action of giving has to be accompanied by gestures of generosity and kindness that make the recipient of the "gift" understand that the favor reflects a special and unique relationship of friendship and consideration. To illustrate this

---

82 Borges, *OC* [1974], I, 937.
83 Seneca, *Moral Essays*, I, VII.2.
84 Borges, *OC* [1974], II, 43.
85 Seneca, *Moral Essays*, III, XXVIII. 1–2.

idea, Seneca resorts to the figure of the "courtesan" ("meretrix") who, although she has sex with several men in exchange for material benefits, establishes an intimate and personal relationship with each of her customers that somehow makes them feel special.[86]

"Ulrica" (1975) is another tale of sex in which the ethics that Seneca proposed in *De Beneficiis* are noticeable. The story, also included in *El libro de arena*, works as the symmetrical counterpart to "La noche de los dones." The piece tells about the brief and circumstantial amorous encounter between a young woman and an old man for whom the episode could be his last love adventure and, therefore, like the boy in the brothel, he feels fortunate: "Para un hombre célibe entrado en años, *el ofrecido amor* es *un don* que ya no se espera."[87] The sex is certainly as casual and anonymous as that experienced by the boy in the brothel: "No incurrí en el error de preguntarle si me quería. Comprendí que no era el primero y que no sería el último. Esa aventura, acaso la postrera para mí, sería una de tantas para esa resplandeciente y resuelta discípula de Ibsen."[88] However, the protagonist is grateful for the careful intimacy that, like Seneca's courtesan, the young woman offers him.

As I explained before, the world of *compadritos* is ruled by the Stoic ethics that, in Borges's imaginary, also regulate the lives of their symmetrical female counterpart, the prostitutes of the *orillas* ("En la frontera de los arrabales, / [los compadritos] Vuelven ... / ... a su puta y su cuchillo"[89]). Thus, in their characterization we can observe, more or less discreetly, other concepts of the doctrine. For example, in one of his re-creations of the *orillas* Borges mentions the "tristes lupanares de las afueras" and refers to the "prostitutas inocentes como animales,"[90] a comparison that is based on Seneca's reflections on virtue. The philosopher said that virtue is taught and learned, and that good is a quality that depends on reason, hence children and animals cannot know it. However, and for the same reason, they cannot know or be evil either. That is, they are morally neutral, innocent ... like prostitutes.[91] In the case of the "cautiva" in "La noche de los dones," this quality is suggested indirectly: the woman says that "no [sabe] llevar la cuenta del tiempo,"[92] which alludes to another aspect of the doctrine that Borges quoted often: "Ya Séneca observó que los animales viven en un presente puro, sin antes ni después."[93]

---

86 Seneca, *Moral Essays*, III, I, XIV.4.
87 Borges, *OC* [1974], II, 18. My emphasis.
88 Borges, *OC* [1974], II, 18.
89 Borges, *OC* [1974], I, 949.
90 Borges, *TR2*, 323.
91 In a similar fashion, in the poem "El guardián de los libros," he also compares Tartar warriors to morally neutral animals: "usaron y olvidaron a las mujeres / y siguieron al Sur, / inocentes como animales de presa / crueles como cuchillos."
92 Borges, *OC* [1974], II, 42.
93 Borges, *CS*, 49.

As we have seen in Mastronardi's diary, Borges was attracted by the Stoic personality of some women, which suggests that Stoicism had for him an erotic appeal too. María Esther Vázquez, who in the 1960s maintained a close romantic relationship with the sexagenarian Borges, said that a type of women that he liked were, precisely, "aquellas que soportaban con entereza y alegría duras desgracias sin quejarse y como despreciando sus penas,"[94] a preference that can be detected early in his life in a description of Concepción Guerrero, his first great love of the 1920s: "Elle souffre dans une extrême banliue, la vie orgueuillesse et dure et monotone et timide d'une jeune fille *bien* et pauvre."[95] The brief portrait of the beloved woman is almost an archetype of Stoic virtue: she "suffers" and her life is "hard" ("suffer and endure," said Epictetus) but, as Seneca advised, she accepts her situation with pride because it "is not what you endure that matters, but how you endure it."[96] It is not superfluous nor coincidental that Borges notes Concepción lives in the *arrabal* ("dans une extrême banliue"), the Argentine setting of the doctrine that a few years later (in 1928, when he published "Séneca en las orillas"), Borges would claim more explicitly and definitely for Stoicism.

Stoic ethics was a quality that Borges also saw in Sylvina [sic] Bullrich, a writer he fell deeply in love with and with whom he had a brief relationship in the 1940s.[97] In his review of *La redoma del primer ángel* (one of Bullrich's books) in 1944 Borges said:

> A la convicción de que nuestra vida es atroz, une Sylvina [sic] Bullrich la convicción de que nuestro deber —nuestro imposible pero inevitable deber— es la felicidad y el coraje. Ese valeroso estoicismo (el de ciertas páginas de *Martín Fierro*, el de nuestro injuriado Almafuerte) es inherente a todos sus libros, aunque los propósitos ocasionales hayan sido otros.[98]

Bullrich believes, according to Borges, that fate will pose challenges and that instead of complaining about our problems we must welcome the opportunity to test ourselves and demonstrate our virtue ("Nothing ... seems to me more unhappy than the man who has no experience of adversity"[99]). This "valeroso estoicismo," Borges thinks, "es inherente a todos sus libros," that is, independently of their topics or of the author's intention in each of them, her works reflect it because it is a trait of her personality. These Stoic ethics, as the invocations of *Martín Fierro* and Almafuerte imply, squarely place

---

94 Vázquez, *Esplendor*, 256.
95 *Cartas del fervor*, 209. Emphasis in the original.
96 Seneca, *Dialogues and Essays*, 5; Seneca also said, "a man on good terms with poverty is rich," Seneca, *Selected Letters*, 4.
97 Years later Borges would tell Bioy that at some point he thought about "llevarla a casa" and "vivir siempre con ella," Bioy, *Borges*, 992; Vázquez, *Esplendor*, 178.
98 Borges, *BES*, 269.
99 Seneca, *Dialogues and Essays*, 7.

this descendant of the nineteeenth-century patrician elite within the literary tradition of creole Argentina.

The Stoic doctrine was, in addition, one of the means used by Borges to express his desire and the frustration and anxiety that it provoked in him. This can be observed in "La noche cíclica" (1940), a poem dedicated to Bullrich. The composition is organized around the idea of eternal return, and it is worth looking at because, among other things, it is a good example of the variety of zones that Stoicism occupies in Borges's oeuvre. The poem has been read in tune with the question of cyclical time, but commentators do not seem to have fully noticed its relationship with the Stoic doctrine and the importance that it had for Borges, let alone the ways in which this philosophy shaped his perception and writing of women.

Borges published the poem for the first time in *La Nación*, in October 1940, and three years later, when he included it in the anthology of his poetry titled *Poemas [1922–1943]* (1943),[100] he dedicated it to Bullrich. The fact that initially the poem came out without the dedication suggests the possibility that Borges may not have written it for her. However, it is important to underscore that, contrary to what happened with some of his other texts, where Borges suppressed or changed the dedicatees, in this case, once he inscribed it to Bullrich he never revised his decision,[101] and the dedication has been maintained until today in his *Obras completas*. That is, he clearly associated her with that particular text. Moreover, what Borges added in 1943 implies a rewriting that resignified the text and, therefore, the poem cannot be read ignoring the dedication. The identification of Bullrich with "La noche cíclica" was probably a result of the way Borges lived his passion with her but, more important, I think, is the fact that the author saw this woman as an exemplary Stoic and that, therefore, he wanted to express his love for her with a poem coined in that philosophical tradition (a gesture similar to the one he made toward Victoria Ocampo: to honor her, he wrote a text saturated with the doctrine and titled "Un destino," as I pointed out earlier in this chapter). In any event, and independently of whether his love experience with Bullrich influenced the decision to write the poem, "La noche cíclica" generally allows us to understand the way in which Borges resorted to the doctrine for the expression of desire and the anxiety that it provoked in him.

Before we get to the poem, though, we must sensitize ourselves so we will be prepared to solve some of its inevitable riddles. With this purpose in mind, then, I will succinctly review essays, lectures, and poems where Borges explored the question of cyclical time. We can start with the essay "La doctrina de los ciclos" (1934), where he quotes a classical source that says

---

100 All the quotations from the poem are in *Poemas* [1943], 164–66; the variants in *OC* [1974], I, 863–64.
101 On Borges's practice of dedicating (consecutively, not simultaneously) the same text to different people or of suppressing them, see Vaccaro, *Borges*, 421–22.

that "*si hemos de creer a los pitagóricos, las mismas cosas volverán puntualmente*" and then, Borges explains:

> En la cosmogonía de los estoicos, *Zeus se alimenta del mundo*: el universo es consumido cíclicamente por el fuego que lo engendró, y resurge de la aniquilación para repetir una idéntica historia. De nuevo se combinan las diversas partículas seminales ... de nuevo cada minuciosa noche de insomnio.[102]

That is, although he points out that the idea originated with Pythagoras, for Borges cyclical time and the repetition of history are Stoic concepts ("los arduos alumnos de Pitágoras" in the first line of the poem, then, are not the Pythagoreans but the Stoics, which is suggested by the adjective "arduo").[103]

In another respect, from the quoted paragraph we can conclude that Borges associates the idea with two other questions. On the one hand, to illustrate circular time he says, "de nuevo cada minuciosa noche de insomnio": that is, the repeated nights of insomnia, a problem that affected Borges for many years. This repeated insomnia is the form in which he experiences cyclical time or a sensation similar to it. In the same vein, in another passage of the essay where he revisits the presence of the concept in Friedrich Nietzsche's work, he also suggests an equivalence between the idea and sleeplessness, and to justify the philosopher's interest in cyclical time, he points out that the German "suffered from" the same problem.[104] Thus, Borges tries a biographical interpretation of Nietzsche's adoption of the idea, a perspective that is implicit in his own association of this aspect of Stoic metaphysics with the experience of insomnia.

Why this association? Permanent vigil and the impossibility of sleeping make the same images, sensations, and experiences return, night after night, to the insomniac's mind. It is a situation whose repetition causes the feeling of being in a labyrinth without a way out. This is the image that we find in Robert Burton's *The Anatomy of Melancholy* (1621), a work that devotes many pages to the problem of insomnia and which Borges quotes in "La doctrina de los ciclos." Burton speaks about melancholic people who suffer from sleeplessness and says, "They could spend whole days and nights without sleep ... [they are in a] labyrinth of anxious and solicitous melancholy meditations, and cannot ... leave-off, winding and unwinding themselves."[105] For Burton, insomnia in itself is a labyrinth with no apparent exit, which is

---

102 Borges, *OC* [1974], I, 387. Italics in the original.
103 In the note on the poem for the poetry anthology in English prepared by N. T. Di Giovanni in 1972 and prefaced by Borges, the idea of cyclical time is explicitly attributed to the Stoics, Borges, *Selected Poems (1923–1967)*, 296.
104 Borges, *OC* [1974], I, 389.
105 Burton, *The Anatomy of Melancholy*, Partition 1, section 2, memb.2, subsection 6, 247. Although Borges mentions Burton's work and quotes a passage from it, he makes no specific reference to this section of the book.

the way Borges thinks about cyclical time: he calls it the "laberinto circular de los estoicos."[106] That is, cyclical time is one of the forms that the labyrinth of insomnia takes.

On the other hand, in the paragraph quoted earlier, Borges qualifies the nights of insomnia as "minuciosas," an adjective that, as I pointed out in chapter 2, generally denotes an extreme and almost obsessive, disgusting bodily awareness, which provokes self-hatred. In the poem "Insomnio" (1936), written two years after the essay, we find the same associations between insomnia, the repellent sensation of his own body, and the impossibility of escaping from such an experience: the poet says "en vano quiero distraerme del cuerpo" and mentions, for example, "los rumbos minuciosos de la muerte en las caries dentales,"[107] thus using the same adjective to convey the repugnance that arises in him. In Borges this repulsive physical experience often includes sex (Emma Zunz's sexual initiation is a "minuciosa deshonra"). In the same vein, as in the passage quoted earlier, in another attempt to illustrate the Stoic concept, Borges says that "de nuevo se combinan las partículas seminales," an adjective that in its most current meaning refers to the semen that will again form the same people or animals.[108] That is, and to present a first and partial conclusion, insomnia is the form in which Borges lives cyclical time, and in turn, the Stoic concept offers a conceptualization of the experience, which is associated with a disgusting bodily awareness, including the one produced by sex.

In the same essay on cyclical time, to illustrate the suffering caused by insomnia, Borges quotes, as I said before, *The Anatomy of Melancholy*: "*El no dormir* (leo en el antiguo tratado de Robert Burton) *harto crucifica a los melancólicos.*"[109] In this passage Burton says that melancholic people do not sleep "by reason of their continual cares, fears, sorrows,"[110] preoccupations that may have several causes. One of them is the desire experienced by people who have fallen in love. To illustrate this type of vigil, Burton refers, among others, to Dido's desperation for Aeneas ("Unhappy Dido could not sleep at all, / But lies awake and takes no rest: / And up she gets again, whilst care and grief, /And raging love torment her breast,"[111]) in which we not only find the suffering caused by passion but also the feeling of repetition provoked by insomnia ("again"). To summarize, then, in Borges's literature, the cyclical time of Stoics offers a conceptualization of the experience of insomnia, a condition that may be the consequence of desire and passion.

---

106 Borges, *OC* [1974], IV, 166.
107 Borges, *OC* [1974], I, 859.
108 "Seminal" in this context can also allude to "semilla," that is, to the "original" elements that repetition makes it possible to unite again, to form, say, water or any other natural matter, not necessarily living creatures.
109 Borges, *OC* [1974], I, 389. Italics in the original.
110 Burton, *The Anatomy*, second partition, section v, memb. I, subsection vi, 251.
111 Burton, *The Anatomy*, third partition, memb.III, sec.2, 134.

Having reviewed and specified the idea of cyclical time in Borges, then, we can look at "La noche cíclica." Not only is the poem inspired by the Stoic concept, but Borges also designed it around that idea: the text starts and ends with the same line ("Lo supieron los arduos alumnos de Pitágoras"), that is, the last line returns to the point of departure, and thus, it creates in the reader a feeling of circularity. As Borges once said, "es cíclico el poema también ... se muerde la cola."[112]

The circularity of the poem makes us feel that, in effect, things repeat themselves, but what truly returns, as the title and one line indicate, are the nights, more precisely, the nights of insomnia ("Volverá toda noche de insomnio: minuciosa"). "La noche cíclica" is, then, another poem on insomnia.

To allude to the Stoic concept coined in classical Antiquity and to create a setting for it, Borges resorts to characters, myths, and places from the corresponding historical period, such as "Pitágoras," "Afrodita," "tebanos," "ágoras," "centauro," "lapita," "Roma," "minotauro." These references locate the poem in the realms of history and philosophy and, thus, turn the poem into an erudite text; erudition that attracts the imagination of the reader and, to some extent, draws our attention away from the more autobiographical lines on the experience of insomnia and desire. That is, the classical allusions work toward the depersonalization of the poem and somehow soften its confessional side. "La noche cíclica" is not a dramatic monologue, but it does exhibit Swinburne's strategy to speak about love and sex, as is the case too with "Endimión en Latmos," "La secta del Fénix," and "El incesto."[113]

In addition to the dedication, which itself expresses desire for a woman, the poem contains lines that allude more or less explicitly to love and sex. For example, the reference to "la urgente Afrodita de oro" in the first stanza suggests, with the adjective "urgente," that the experience that the poet wants to communicate includes an erotic dimension; and, in a circular mode, the penultimate line alludes again to the impossibility of escaping the desire that causes insomnia: "Vuelve a mi carne humana la eternidad constante."

After the first two stanzas, where, as I said, the poet introduces the doctrine of cycles and illustrates it with allusions to Classical culture, in the third stanza we hear the poet talking about himself:

> Volverá toda noche de insomnio: minuciosa.
> La mano que esto escribe renacerá del mismo
> Vientre ....

[112] Carrizo, *Borges*, 284.
[113] The Pre-Raphaelite influence on the poem could also include Rossetti, who wrote about similar topics in "Insomnia" and "Spheral Change" (the title "Noche cíclica" seems to echo those compositions); in these poems the poet also obsessively thinks about a woman whom he loves but who cannot live with him, Rossetti, *Collected Poetry*, 233–34.

Here Borges tells us, as he did in the essay written six years earlier, what the "laberinto circular de los estoicos" or "La noche cíclica" are really about: it is the insomnia that, night after night, he cannot escape. It is, then, an autobiographical line and conveys to us the personal experience of the poet. In the following sentence ("La mano que esto escribe renacerá del mismo vientre"), however, in what seems to be in contradiction to the confessional mode of the previous line, the poet offers us another repetition that, instead, would have the purpose of illustrating once more the concept that inspired the poem: the hand of the poet would come out again from his mother's "vientre"; that is, his personal history will also be repeated.

However, there is nothing to indicate that, inevitably, the "vientre" is the mother's; our most common assumption, in a first reading, makes us associate "renacerá" and "vientre" with mother. But it is precisely the fundamental absence of the unequivocal that all poetry implies that encourages a different reading of those lines. Let us see. The previous line says that the repeated "noche de insomnio" is "minuciosa"; that is, it implies an experience with his own body, including sex, that is disgusting and arouses self-hatred, but that repeats itself time and again. The adjective "minuciosa" inevitably reaches, by contiguity, the following line: "La mano que esto escribe renacerá del mismo vientre"; that is, the hand that reappears can be what turns the night into "minuciosa." "La mano que ... renacerá" is an experience the poet feels with his own body and, therefore, the "vientre" it emerges from could be his own. In another respect, "renacer" is a metaphor because, strictly speaking, the hand cannot be born twice: therefore, we could think that while writing "renacerá" the author also wanted to suggest, for example, "volverá a emerger" or "volverá a levantarse." If we consider these possibilities, we could think that each "minuciosa" night, the hand would emerge or rise from the poet's own abdomen ... to try to placate his desire, which is the cause of the insomnia.

The insomnia that repeats itself, says the poet, "Noche a noche me deja en ... los arrabales," the landscape of Stoic creole *compadritos* but also a zone of venal and guilty sex that the poet cruises, driven by his desire. The walks through the streets of the city, like the solitary and "minuciosa" nights, are, however, insufficient: "el tiempo que a los hombres / Trae el amor o el oro, a mí apenas me deja / Esta rosa apagada ..." or a frustrating, loveless sex without the woman that he really longs for. The elusive love and the desire that cannot be satisfied are the causes of the insomnia and, thus, prolong the "laberinto circular" from which the poet cannot escape: "Vuelve a mi carne humana la eternidad constante."

"La noche cíclica" is, then, not only a poem that explores a metaphysical concept but also a confessional text of love and desire. The philosophical idea around which the author organized the poem reflects, to some extent, the importance of the Stoic doctrine in Borges's literature, but it also speaks about a personal experience: the insomnia, caused, in part, by desire. On the other hand, the dedication in itself highlights Borges's will to express his love for Sylvina Bullrich, an exemplary Stoic woman, in the keys of that tradition, thus illuminating the erotic possibilities of the doctrine and the appeal of the women that he identified and had in mind when he wrote it.

Asymmetries and Another Influence:

As we have seen, Borges generally established emotional and moral asymmetrical relationships with women, an imbalance that may also extend to their different physical prowess. In the cases of his mother and sister, Borges highlights their valor and moral strength, while he blames himself for his cowardice and weakness ("cuando tantos hombres callábamos," "yo la seguía con ... miedo," "a mí me intimidaban los chicos pobres"). Similarly, while Sylvina Bullrich seemed to display a "valeroso estoicismo," Borges confesses with "horror" that he is not more than an exemplar of Sebastián, the character in *La redoma del primer ángel* who "es incapaz de toda redención moral o intelectual";[114] and the same logic is noticeable in the explanation of the relationship between the influential Victoria Ocampo and the childlike and unknown author. We find these differences between women and men in his fiction as well. When another pirate insults Mary Read's lover, the latter is incapable of defending his own honor, and it is the woman who takes the matter into her own hands; Salvadores is a coward both morally and physically, in marked contrast with the courage of his wife, a situation that is repeated in the relationship between Rosendo Juárez and the Lujanera, a woman who does have the tough qualities that life in the *orillas* demands. Love and sexual relationships are also unbalanced. In "La noche de los dones" the boy is "tímido" and "tiembla," while the *cautiva* reassures him, saying, "Acercate, que no te voy a hacer ningún mal";[115] and in "Ulrica" it is the woman who dictates the rules of the amorous encounter: "El milagro tiene derecho a imponer condiciones."[116]

These asymmetries, as we have seen, are organized by the logic of Stoicism, and the positions of men and women in them are partially determined by their proximity to or distance from the values proposed by the doctrine. Borges conceives and narrates these uneven relationships as a "contraste" (the word he uses in the explanation of his relationship with Norah), which suggests that the contrast could also reflect a logical and narrative game in which the portrait of a woman implies, by opposition, his own.

The explanation of the contrasts and asymmetries between men and women in Borges's writings may also require taking into account a last text that should also be considered among his influences, both literary and personal. I refer here to the novel *El caudillo*, published in 1921 by Jorge Guillermo Borges, father of the author. The novel narrates the passionate and

---

114 Borges, *BES*, 268.
115 Borges, *OC* [1974], II, 43.
116 Borges, *OC* [1974], II, 18.

tragic relationship between Dubois, a Frenchman, and Marisabel, a young creole woman and daughter of a *caudillo* from Entre Ríos. Several of the philosophical questions and readings that are pretty visible in the novel are the same ones that interested the younger Borges throughout his whole life and that appear time and again in his works. For example, in tune with the Stoic tradition and its modulation by Montaigne, Dubois says:

> El triunfo de las circunstancias adversas se basa en nuestras flaquezas, en la falta de virtud en nosotros que les da su fuerza. Montaigne ... maquinalmente se palpó los bolsillos donde el libro favorito solía estar.[117]

In the same vein, other passages of father's novel seem to anticipate Georgie's writing of women. In the final chapter, when a group of followers of the *caudillo* come to kill Dubois, we read that Marisabel's "manos febriles"

> descolgaron del muro la escopeta de caza. Entregándola a su amante le dijo con voz ronca: defiéndete. *De los dos, suyo el espíritu más fuerte* ... Fue Marisabel que les salió al encuentro ... haciendo de su cuerpo una barrera. El tropel de los hombres se detuvo atónito ... *Dubois indeciso* no atinaba a la acción ... arrojó al suelo la escopeta y se cruzó de brazos pero ... allí estaba Marisabel. Una oleada de sangre le coloreó el rostro ... *Marisabel enloquecida les increpaba indómita.*[118]

The scene very explicitly proposes the same "contraste" between the woman's courage and the man's hesitation and cowardice that Jorge Luis wrote about throughout his work: "de los dos, suyo el espíritu más fuerte." In addition, it follows rather closely Arria's and Paetus's story commented on by Montaigne and it anticipates the episode of the Lujanera and Rosendo in "Hombre de la esquina rosada" (1933), even in some of the details (the man throws down the weapon, the woman is ashamed of him). Passages such as the two quoted here, then, suggest that in his writing of women Borges reworked and distilled preoccupations and questions that he somehow "inherited" from his father, who, after all and as the son said, had initiated him in philosophy and was a "devoto de Montaigne"[119] as well.

But we can think that these asymmetries are also a transmutation of his experiences with women. Estela Canto said that for Borges, "la mujer [era] un ídolo inalcanzable, al cual no se atrevía a aspirar,"[120] which in itself suggests also an emotional impotence of sorts. Other evidence indicates even a certain degree of defenselessness: Borges himself said that the woman who had inspired him to create the character of Beatriz Viterbo (one of the Stoics who knew how to die):

---

117 Borges, J. G., *Caudillo*, 127.
118 Borges, J. G., *Caudillo*, 152. Emphasis added.
119 Borges, *TR3*, 164.
120 Canto, *A contraluz*, 81.

me maltrataba ... y cuando a un hombre una mujer lo maltrata siente inmediatamente un gran respeto por ella, ¿no? Es una forma de coquetería, también, maltratarlo a un hombre. Quizás sea la mejor forma de coquetería, porque una mujer dulzona generalmente es desagradable, eh, una mujer servil es intolerable, en cambio una mujer que se da cuenta de que uno es bastante insignificante, uno ya la mira con cierto respeto.[121]

Borges, then, was attracted to women who established asymmetrical relationships with him, similar to the ones we find in his work; and his preference could arguably go to the point of emotional abuse (which is corroborated by other evidences of mistreatment by women[122]). Finally, Julio Woscoboinik too noticed Borges's emotionally uneven relationship with women and considered it a trait of his personality: "Borges fue siempre un niño-grande, un grande-niño. Las relaciones que estableció con las distintas mujeres que figuraron en su vida, tienen las características propias de las filiales."[123]

---

121 Borges, *Borges para millones*, 75.
122 Helft on his mother's and Bullrich's mistreatment, *Postales*, 30–31, 82; Canto on his mother's, *A contraluz*, 231; Vázquez on Bullrich's, *Esplendor*, 178; Bioy on Canto's, Bioy, *Borges*, 240, 94.
123 Woscoboinik, *El secreto* [1988], 47.

CHAPTER 8

# "Emma Zunz":
# Sex, Virtue, and Punishment

So far my reading of Borges's women has not included, except for few earlier references, Emma Zunz, his best-known female character and the one who has been fundamental in the explanations tried by critics. "Emma Zunz" is a short story of classic detective format that tells the tale of a young Jewish Argentine woman whose father was betrayed by his business partner, Aarón Loewenthal. The latter embezzeled money from their firm but falsely accused Mr. Zunz of the crime. Apparently unable to defend himself, the innocent victim goes into exile in Brazil, where he dies in shame and solitude. Loewenthal's treason is devastating for the family, and its economic ruin forces Emma to take a job as a worker in the factory of her father's enemy. Thus, Emma decides to settle accounts with the scoundrel (now also her boss), and with this goal in mind, she carefully prepares a plan that will allow her both to punish Loewenthal and to avoid any legal consequences. The subtle plot conceived by the 19-year-old woman includes losing her virginity, which she does when she pretends to be a prostitute and has sex with a foreign mariner (a complete stranger to her).

Most of the interpretations of the story have revolved around the scene of Emma's sexual intercourse with the sailor, and critics have focused on the thoughts of the narrator on the sex life of her parents. In his psychoanalytical reading, Julio Woscoboinik asserts that Emma's revenge is motivated by the guilt caused by her parents's sexual relationship; Beatriz Sarlo's interpretation says that Emma's experience with her own body makes her aware of the sexual violence her father inflicted on her mother, which gives her revenge a second, additional motivation; for their part, Aguilar and Jelicié understand Emma's vengeful plan as an opportunity for the young woman to imagine an incestuous sex act with her own father; and Edwin Williamson proposes that the story shows a woman "trapped in a labyrinth of sexual strife."[1] Without ignoring this influential scene, Josefina Ludmer, however, reads the

---

1 Woscoboinik, *El secreto* [1988], 143–53; Sarlo, *La pasión*, 126–29; Aguilar and Jelicié, *Borges va*, 104; Williamson, *A Life*, 304.

text in a political key and proposes that Emma's revenge represents "todas las justicias," [2] including the one deserved by women and the working class (the worker settles accounts with the boss). Finally, Edna Aisenberg places the short story within the Hebrew tradition and tells us that Emma, contrary to other female characters in Borges's literature, is a combative and militant woman, qualities with which the Kabbalah also endowed female incarnations of God.[3] The best-known and most accepted interpretations, then, focus on her revenge and sex (with ever rising levels of guilt) and have created around Emma a halo of quasi pathology and violence that reveals her to be a "resentful," "manipulative," and "vengeful" woman,[4] qualities that, at least for some critics, reveal the "misogynistic" nature of Borges's tale.[5]

The story has a rather unusual quality for Borges's literature in the scene where sex is pretty explicit. Critics have often seen this explicitness as a rare opportunity to investigate sex in Borges's work, which, somewhat paradoxically, has complicated the understanding of the character (and the tale). It is not sex or even its form ("la cosa horrible") that defines Emma. The key question is what she intends to do with it, which requires us to evaluate the character within Borges's interest in ethics. The story is organized around concepts such as fate and the necessary courage to confront it, the virtue implied in it, and the problems of passions, revenge, and justice, upon which classic Stoicism reflected and that were later revised by other philosophers, as Schopenhauer did with his idea of "punishment." As we will see, Emma may be included among the Stoic women of Borges's literature.

This reading requires a somewhat different methodological approach. Students of Borges usually read "Emma Zunz" in relation to other works that deal with women or sex; however, I think that it is fundamental to *simultaneously* place it among the texts where Borges addressed the ethical questions mentioned above, which may or may not include women. Thus, if we read it in dialogue with some apparently very different texts that, however, deal with virtue, revenge, justice, and punishment, such as "El incivil maestro de ceremonias Kotsuké No Suké," "Pedro Salvadores," or even Borges's dedication of his *Obras completas* to his mother, we may be able to observe patterns and changes in the treatment of certain problems and characters and, thus, shed light on some aspects that have been overlooked by the current critical consensus.

Origins of the Short Story and a Literary Source (The Book of Judith)

As a first step, I would like to look at the origin of the story and its literary sources, because they will allow us to think of the tale in a broader context.

---

2 Ludmer, *El cuerpo*, 363.
3 Aizenberg, *Borges*, 133–39.
4 Pyñeiro, *Ficcionalidad*, 141.
5 Williamson, *A Life*, 303.

In the epilogue to *El Aleph* Borges says that it was Cecilia Ingenieros who gave him the "argumento espléndido"[6] of "Emma Zunz," an attribution that seems to have been tinged with amorous motivations[7] and that must not be taken as an exhaustive and complete acknowledgement of literary influences. Moreover, in 1949, in the review of *El Aleph* that Estela Canto wrote for *Sur*, she questioned this literary debt because, she thought, Borges had significantly changed Ingenieros's initial plot.[8] This is plausible because the story shares important common elements with "El incivil maestro de ceremonias Kotsuké No Suké" (1934) and with "Pedro Salvadores" (1969), tales that Borges published before and after "Emma Zunz" (1948). Later in the chapter I point out some of their common elements.

In addition, Borges's story exhibits significant parallels with a biblical tale that seems to have worked as one of its sources: I refer to the book of Judith, a Hebrew narrative that for centuries attracted the interest of many commentators, writers, and painters (including Michelangelo, Caravaggio, Artemisia Gentileschi, Dante, and Lope de Vega). In this section, first I will briefly review the biblical tale and afterward I will compare "Emma Zunz" to this book from the Apocrypha.

The biblical text tells the story of a Hebrew village (Bethulia) that is under siege by the Assyrians, who await the right moment to launch their final attack. In that extreme situation the "courage" of the Hebrew leaders "failed" them and they started to consider that "it would be better for [them] to be captured"[9] and enslaved instead of seeing how the invaders killed their wives and children. It is then that Judith, a beautiful and chaste widow who continued to be faithful to her dead husband, told the fearful men that they should thank God because he "is putting us to the test."[10] Thus, to liberate the village the woman conceived a plan that she kept secret and that she essentially executed alone.[11] Judith took off her modest garments and dressed herself in beautiful clothes and flashy jewelry to "entice the eyes of all the men who might see her."[12] When night arrived she left the village without being

---

6   Borges, *OC* [1974], I, 629.
7   Borges liked Cecilia Ingenieros and in the 1940s flirted with her (Bioy, *Borges*, 457). Years later Borges would characterize the plot as "un don" by Ingenieros (Carrizo, *Borges*, 234), thus placing her in the category of women who were generous with him. In the same vein, in the form of the attribution itself, we can observe the asymmetry that Borges believed he established with other women: in the epilogue to *El Aleph* he says that Ingenieros's "argumento espléndido" was "[muy] superior a su ejecución temerosa," *OC* [1974], I, 629. That is, the attribution was motivated by love and is not a simple acknowledgement of a literary debt.
8   Canto, "Jorge Luis Borges," 97.
9   *NRSVA*, Book of Judith. 7.27.
10  *NRSVA*, Book of Judith, 8.25.
11  Her maid will follow her but has no real participation in the action, although she does appear in some of the pictorial representations of the story.
12  *NRSVA*, Book of Judith, 10.4.

noticed and walked into the Assyrian camp, where she introduced herself as a traitor: "I am a daughter of the Hebrews but I am fleeing from them ... [I want] to see Holofernes [the Assyrian chief] to give him a true report; I will show him a way by which he can go and capture" the whole country.[13] The value of the information that she promised and her seduction did their work and aroused the admiration and desire of the Assyrian leader: "You are not only beautiful in appearance but wise in speech."[14] Eventually Holofernes invited Judith to his tent with the intention of having sex with her. However, the warrior failed in his attempt because he drank too much and fell asleep. That was the opportunity that Judith had looked for with her plan: then she took Holofernes's own sword (which was hanging on one of the bedposts) and decapitated him (a scene that painters have classically re-created in gory detail). Thus Judith achieved the liberation of her people. When she returned to the village, she told the Hebrews that "it was my face that seduced him,"[15] but she clarified that in spite of being alone with Holofernes in his tent he could not have sex with her ("he committed no sin with me, to defile and shame me").[16] She was praised by all because "[she] risked [her] own life,"[17] and to thank her, one of the men "threw himself at Judith's feet."[18] In the celebrations that followed the liberation of the village, Judith marched at the head of the women "while all the men of Israel followed,"[19] singing that the powerful enemy had fallen "by the hand of a woman" and not "by the hands of young men."[20]

As we can see, Judith was a heroine who Seneca or Montaigne could have easily inducted into the pantheon of virtuous women who faced the challenges posed by Providence with courage and sacrifice, while the hesitant and fearful men turned out to be cowards. That is, the tale also exhibits the type of asymmetrical relationship that Borges felt he established with women and that he often re-created in his literature, which could be one explanation for why he was interested in this biblical book.

There are clear similarities and parallels between the story of Judith and "Emma Zunz" that suggest that the biblical tale may have been one of Borges's sources. To begin with, the fact that Emma is Jewish seems to hint at such a literary debt; moreover, the name of the character is an abbreviation of her father's "Emmanuel," which in Hebrew means "savior,"[21] the role actually played by Judith. But, in addition, the similarity of facts and circumstances

13 *NRSVA*, Book of Judith, 10.12, 10.13.
14 *NRSVA*, Book of Judith, 11.23.
15 *NRSVA*, Book of Judith, 13.16.
16 *NRSVA*, Book of Judith, 13.16.
17 *NRSVA*, Book of Judith, 13.20.
18 *NRSVA*, Book of Judith, 14.7.
19 *NRSVA*, Book of Judith, 15.13.
20 *NRSVA*, Book of Judith, 16.5, 6.
21 Williamson, *A Life*, 303.

that make up the plots of both tales is pretty apparent: destiny that requires courage and audacity / seduction and sex / simulation of betrayal and of being an informer / access to the enemy's personal space and assassination with his own weapon.

Emma's life is also at the mercy of the ups and downs of Providence or destiny, which puts her to the test (the story "está gobernada por un terrible destino," said Bioy Casares[22]). Loewenthal's embezzlement and his false incrimination of Emma's father imply a change of fortune: "los antiguos días felices"[23] are gone, and now she must suffer her father's exile, a new situation of poverty, and "el auto de prisión, el oprobio"[24] ("el auto de prisión, el oprobio" of this story carries echoes of "el oprobio de Rosas—tu prisión valerosa"[25] that Borges recalls in his dedication of the *Obras completas* to his mother and that suggests the type of character the author had in mind). Emma will try to redress the injustice by resorting to her audacity and courage. The situation in which the young woman finds herself is, actually, a classic of Stoicism. For example, in his essay "On Providence," Seneca says, "How can I know with what strength of mind you would face poverty, if you abound in wealth? How can I know what fortitude you would show in the face of disgrace, dishonor, and the hatred of the people, if you grow old to the sound of cheers, if you attract an irresistible popularity ... ? ... disaster is the opportunity for true worth."[26]

To carry out her plan Emma erases the signs of her chastity, as Judith did, and pretends that she is a different type of woman: in spite of being a virgin, she behaves like a prostitute to attract and seduce men. And thus, she finds a way of losing her virginity, which she does for her father ("el muerto que motivaba el sacrificio").[27] However, in spite of having sex with the sailor, Emma remains a virtuous woman. Reflecting on the ethics of women's sex, Montaigne said that the key point was their will: if a woman does not do it because of lust—that is, voluntarily—then she does not lose her chastity and virtue, because what really matters is what happens in her mind and not what she does with her body. Therefore the French essayist praised the virtue of those women who, even when they "aimait mieux son honneur que sa vie," yielded "au desir forcené d'un mortel ennemi pour sauver la vie de son mari";[28]

---

22 Bioy, *Borges*, 89. Bioy's comment refers to the movie based on the story, for which Borges co-authored the script with the director Leopoldo Torre Nilsson (Aguilar and Jelicié, *Borges va*, 102–4); the movie version emphasizes the importance of destiny in several ways: e.g. in two different places in Buenos Aires Emma meets an unknown man who offers her "barquillos del azar."
23 Borges, *OC* [1974], I, 564.
24 Borges, *OC* [1974], I, 564.
25 Borges, *OC* [1974], I, 9.
26 Seneca, *Dialogues and Essays*, 10–11.
27 Borges, *OC*, I, 566.
28 Montaigne, *Essais*, III, V, 1051.

that is, they were "unfaithful" to help their husbands.[29] In Emma's case, then, we can think that the "temor casi patológico" and the "asco"[30] that sex aroused in her underscores the virtue ("el sacrificio") of what she was willing to do for her father (in the book of Judith we also read that "all sacrifice ... is too little").[31] This is, precisely, what was emphasized in the program issued for the premiere of the movie based on the story (*Dias de odio*, 1954): Emma "afrontó la más horrenda de las verguenzas para cumplir su juramento" of punishing the man who had wronged her father.[32] In addition, Emma does not prostitute herself because she tears up the money that the sailor gives her in exchange for sex. That is, in "Emma Zunz," sex does not imply an ethical failure of the woman, as was also the case for Judith who, although she seduced the man, was not "defiled" or "shamed" by him.

Like Judith, Emma also pretends to betray her own (the workers) and to be an informer: Loewenthal "esperaba el informe confidencial de la obrera Zunz."[33] The trick allows her to get to the private place of her enemy (the office of the boss) and, as the biblical heroine did, kill the villain with his own weapon, which was also left temporarily unattended in a piece of furniture (this time not the bedpost but the "cajón" of a desk).

Finally, there is another common element between the book of Judith and "Emma Zunz." Commentators of the biblical episode have underlined that part of the interest created by this tale is due to the moral ambiguity of the woman: Judith seduces, lies, and kills, a reprehensible behavior in itself but one that the justice of her ultimate goal (the liberation of her people) renders acceptable.[34] Borges's character exhibits a conduct similar to Judith's: Emma also seduces, lies, and kills.

However, there also is a very important ethical difference between the biblical narrative and Borges's story: in Emma's case it is not so clear that her behavior can be excused by her ultimate purpose. The clarification of this problem depends on how we understand Loewenthal's assassination: what did Emma intend by it? Was it justice? Or revenge? The answer has fundamental consequences for the characterization of the protagonist and, therefore, for the interpretation of the story. Because of its relevance for the explication of the text I will devote most of the remaining of the chapter to this problem.

---

29 Here, differing with classic Stoicism, Montaigne accepts Saint Augustine's criticism in *City of God*, Bk.I, chaps.18–19. Stoics would have expected the woman to commit suicide rather than lose her honor.
30 Borges, *OC* [1974], I, 565, 566.
31 *King James Bible*, Book of Judith. 16.16.
32 Aguilar and Jelicié, *Borges va*, 104.
33 Borges, *OC* [1974], I, 567.
34 *NRSVA*, "Apocrypha," 32.

## Revenge and Justice (in Japan)

In 1953, while the cinematographic version of "Emma Zunz" was being filmed, Borges told Bioy, with apparent disgust, that the story "está basado en la idea de la venganza, que yo no entiendo,"[35] an opinion that he would essentially repeat years later in interviews ("Ese cuento ... a mí no me gusta porque es un cuento de venganza. Y yo descreo de la venganza"[36]); a characterization of the tale that we must inevitably question if we remember that barely four years earlier, in the epilogue of *El Aleph*, Borges had praised his "argumento espléndido." In addition, this evaluation does not quite correspond with the actual text of the short story, which is more complex than what this type of synthesis can account for: the tale does speak about "odio" and "vengar" but also about "justicia," "justicia humana," "justicia de Dios," and "castigar."[37] More important, Borges's evaluation of the story as one of "revenge" contradicts another evidence of what he seems to have had in mind when he wrote it: in the typescript of the first draft (very close to the final version) that he gave Ingenieros, he wrote her a note that said that the tale "también podría titularse *El castigo*,"[38] an alternative title that in itself is an explication of the text and that, as we will see later, is not exactly "revenge." The context of his comment, then, suggests that it was intended not so much as an explication of his short story but as an opinion on the movie.[39]

We also need to remember that "Emma Zunz" is not the only one of Borges's short stories that addresses the problem of revenge and justice: in the "El incivil maestro de ceremonias Kotsuké No Suké" we find a similar treatment of these problems and, to the best of my knowledge, he never denounced that story. I think it would be helpful to look at some aspects of this tale because it can help us understand Emma's ethics. The story, originally published in 1934 and set in Japan, re-creates the historical case of Kotsuké, infamous courtier who, with his calculated offenses and manipulations, induces an honorable feudal lord, Takumi, to defend his honor, which inevitably requires an act of violence on the part of the latter. Both know that the Emperor will condemn such violence and that it will be punished with a

---

35 Bioy, *Borges*, 89.
36 Carrizo, *Borges*, 234.
37 Borges, *OC* [1974], I, 567.
38 Borges, typescript of first draft of "Emma Zunz," 5 v. I learned of the existance of the typescript in Balderston, "Una lógica simbolica," but I have worked with a copy of it acquired at the Harry Ransom Center at the University of Texas (Austin).
39 The purpose of this type of interventions by Borges often was to steer readers in a direction that is not necessarily what he seemed to have intended when he wrote the texts, giving them a meaning they could not have had before: for instance, with similar maneuvers Borges tried to make of his "Poema conjetural" one of the first manifestations of anti-Peronism, when it was actually written and published when that political movement did not even exist, see De la Fuente, "Conjectures."

death sentence, but Takumi has no choice. The royal decision arrives quickly, and Takumi is ordered to kill himself; in addition, his family is ruined and falls into poverty and his 47 loyal vassals are disbanded. However, the latter swear to punish the vile Kotsuké, knowing that if they succeed in killing him they also will be condemned to death, as their lord had been. But the certainty of their own death does not deter them, and for a long time they "[planean] con toda precisión"[40] (as Emma also did) the punishment and do not spare any effort to achieve their goal. Finally, after they manage to kill the infamous villain, they receive the anticipated death sentence of hara-kiri, which they carry out with pride and without lamentations.

The story is based on a well-known historical event, and Borges's literary source was the narration of the episode by A. B. Mitford in his *Tales of Old Japan* (1871).[41] According to Mitford, the great reputation of the forty-seven warriors was due to the fact that they embodied better than anybody the values of "loyalty," "honor," "sense of duty," "faithfulness," and "justice."[42] According to the English writer, when the warriors captured the villain, their leader explained to him:

> our master was sentenced to hara kiri, and his family was ruined. We have come to-night *to avenge* him. As is the duty of faithful and loyal men. I pray your lordship to acknowledge the *justice* of our purpose.[43]

The "revenge," then, was "just" because with it they fulfilled the vow of loyalty that tied them to their unfortunate lord (even when he was already dead). That is, in Mitford's explanation, "revenge" and "justice" are not opposed or mutually exclusive. This is also the case in Borges's version: although he calls the warriors "sangrientos capitanes" and "vengadores," he qualifies the event as a "glorioso episodio" and "proyecto vindicatorio" and says that the samurais executed an "apropiada venganza" that was of "estricta justicia."[44] Revenge, which in this case is the consummation of "preciosas lealtades,"[45] is not, then, at odds with justice and virtue.

The exploration of the literary source that Borges used for the tale included in *Historia universal de la infamia* not only sheds light on the question of revenge and justice but also illuminates other aspects of "Emma Zunz." At the end of his narration, Mitford reproduces the documents in which, to justify their conduct, Takumi's vassals invoked the teachings of Confucius, in whose ethics filial respect and obligations are fundamental. In one of the documents, they say that they avenged their lord because otherwise they

---

40 Borges, *OC* [1974], I, 321.
41 Borges himself listed the source at the end of *Historia universal de la infamia* (1935), *OC* [1974], I, 345.
42 Mitford, *Tales*, 18, 20, 33, 32.
43 Mitford, *Tales*, 32. Emphasis added.
44 Borges, *OC* [1974], I, 322, 321, 320, 321, 320, 322.
45 Borges, *OC* [1974], I, 320.

"could not without blushing repeat [Confucius's] verse 'Thou shalt not live under the same heaven nor tread the same earth with the enemy of thy father or lord.'"[46] Mitford also explains that the Chinese philosopher "affirmed [as one of the filial obligations] the duty of blood-revenge in the strongest and most unrestricted terms."[47] One of the obligations of honorable vassals or children is to avenge their lord or father. Whoever honors this principle fulfills a duty and, therefore, is just. It is hard not to see in Mitford's text, which Borges had used in one of his first narrative attempts, another of the sources for "Emma Zunz," which is a story of filial loyalty and punishment. In the movie script, co-authored by Borges, this is even more clear: when Emma is about to kill the man who ruined her family, she says, "Debo cumplir con mi deber"; and in a similar tone, in the program prepared for the premiere of the movie, it is explained that the young woman made her sacrifice to "cumplir su juramento."[48]

Before I continue with the exploration of the problem of revenge and justice, and given the space that I allot in my explication to a story not of women but of warriors, I want to underline a methodological question that I mentioned at the beginning of the chapter: to explicate a story such as "Emma Zunz," it is not only helpful but also necessary to look at a tale apparently as different as "El incivil maestro ..." and, even, its literary source because of the way Borges worked and created his texts. As Carlos Gamerro has explained, Borges often treats the topics that interest him in successive approximations; sometimes they are similar, sometimes they are contradictory.[49] We can think, then, about a long process (14 years in between the two stories) of trial and error, of changes of setting and narrative choices: first Borges would have explored justice and revenge in a tale of Japanese warriors that remained very close to the original source (Mitford), and later he would have distilled some materials from that source to use in a story of classic detective format whose plot roughly followed the book of Judith. The thread that connects the two tales is not made of the gender of the protagonists but of the problems of revenge, justice, and virtue.

## Schopenhauer and *"El castigo"*

Now let us return to "Emma Zunz" and see what, concretely, the story talks about. After Emma has sex with the sailor, the narrator says that with the sex act, "ella sirvió para el goce y él para la justicia,"[50] and when she kills Loewenthal, she says, "He vengado a mi padre."[51] As in the case of the

---

46 Mitford, *Tales*, 39.
47 Mitford, *Tales*, 40.
48 Aguilar and Jelicié, *Borges va*, 104.
49 Gamerro, "Borges y los anglosajones," 39.
50 Borges, *OC* [1974], I, 566.
51 Borges, *OC* [1974], 567.

samurais, here revenge and justice are not at odds: revenge can be just and is not necessarily ethically wrong.

But, in addition, the text also tells us that Emma considered herself "un instrumento de la justicia" and that she thought that her plot "permitiría a *la justicia de Dios* triunfar de *la justicia humana*."[52] What Emma thinks in this respect, I propose, reflects Borges's reading of Schopenhauer and, therefore, to understand what those types of justice mean (and what their relationship is with revenge), it is necessary to closely review the arguments of the Idealist philosopher; that is, we must read the text that Borges read.

In *The World as Will and Representation,* Schopenhauer considers the two types of justice that we find in the story: temporal justice ("justicia humana") and eternal justice ("Justicia de Dios").[53] Temporal justice administered by the State regulates relations among citizens. Its goal is not to penalize what has already occurred but to deter other citizens from committing crimes in the future. On the contrary, if the criminal is penalized for the deed committed and the penalty seeks to cause a pain similar to the one experienced by the victim with the purpose of alleviating the latter's (or their kin's) suffering, then it is not justice but revenge, which is immoral and useless to society. Thus, temporal justice is concerned with the future, and revenge is focused on the past. In this affirmation of justice and rejection of revenge, Schopenhauer agrees with Seneca, from whose essay "On Anger" he quotes. The Stoic philosopher famously rejects the idea of revenge (because it is motivated by the base passions of anger and hatred) and maintains the superiority of justice.[54]

But in addition, says the German Idealist, there is an "eternal justice" that regulates the world as a whole. According to his metaphysics, the world is "the Will," which is the ultimate reality, one and indivisible. Human beings cannot know this ultimate reality because they live in a dimension of appearances and phenomena where, for example, they experience their lives as individuals and not as what they truly are: one part of that whole that is the Will or the ultimate reality. The Will has no use for temporal justice and finds ways of regulating itself through eternal justice: "the world itself is the tribunal of the world."[55]

In the world conceived by the Idealist Schopenhauer, individuals are no more than illusions or phenomena, and all of them are part of the ultimate and indivisible reality; which implies that there is no difference between the criminal and the victim and, therefore, the crime is committed against the whole of which the criminal is also part; that is, it is also committed against the criminal himself ("Tormentor and tormented are one,"[56] says

---

52 Borges, *OC* [1974], I, 567. Emphasis added.
53 Schopenhauer, vol.1, 334–359.
54 Schopenhauer, vol.1, 349; Seneca, *Dialogues and Essays*, "On Anger," Bk.III.
55 Schopenhauer, vol.1, 352.
56 Schopenhauer, vol.1, 354.

Schopenhauer). Therefore, in the realm of eternal justice, revenge is also useless.

However, says the German philosopher, it is possible to observe the inclination of human beings to take justice into their own hands, which usually ends in revenge. This happens because most people do not know enough philosophy to comprehend the Will and, therefore, to understand how far eternal justice can reach. Nonetheless, most people somehow, obscurely and remotely, do intuit eternal justice, which can be seen in the use that religions make of myth to communicate its existence and to remind us of the uselessness of revenge: for example, in the Bible we read, "Vengeance is mine; I will repay, saith the Lord."[57]

In both the realms of temporal and eternal (or God's, for most people) justice, Schopenhauer denounces and rejects revenge. However, in a last moment of his argument, the Idealist philosopher considers a few exceptions that he places in another category and that he justifies. As we saw above, Schopenhauer thinks that although most people cannot know eternal justice, almost all of them intuit it and instinctively sense that it exists. It is because of this that, exceptionally, we can see cases that reflect the intention of bringing eternal justice into the realm of human experience. In almost perfect correspondence with the arguments of "El incivil maestro de ceremonias" and "Emma Zunz," Schopenhauer explains that those exceptional cases occur when individuals are ready to risk their own lives to avenge a crime or an offense that made them "profoundly indignant."[58] Generally these punishing actions are private; that is, they are executed by individuals and not by States, and their purpose is not to enforce the law; on the contrary, they usually are aimed at deeds that States cannot or do not want to punish and for which States disapprove private punishment. In these cases, Schopenhauer points out, we can observe that individuals look for their oppressors for years, until they finally assassinate them, and afterward, the murderer himself is executed, as he knew well would happen. When carefully evaluated, says Schopenhauer, "that mania for retaliation" is "very different from common revenge,"[59] which selfishly seeks to mitigate the suffering of the victim (or his kin) by causing a similar pain to the criminal. On the contrary, these exceptional cases deserve *"to be called not so much revenge as punishment"*[60] because "the wrath which drives such a man so far beyond the limits of self-love [self-preservation], springs from the deepest consciousness that he himself is ... the Will";[61] since the Will is in all individuals, the person executing such punishment feels that his responsibility includes not only the present but also the future, and nothing

---

57 "Rom.12, 19" cited in Schopenhauer, vol.1, 358.
58 Schopenhauer, vol.1, 358.
59 Schopenhauer, vol.1, 358.
60 Schopenhauer, vol.1, 358. My emphasis.
61 Schopenhauer, vol.1, 359.

in the world is indifferent to him. That is, in these cases wrath and hatred, violence and revenge, are not motivated by a purely personal and selfish interest but, somewhat paradoxically, by generosity and altruism. When the individual affirms the Will with his own sacrifice, he hopes that the crime will not occur again and seeks to deter all potential criminals by showing them "a revenge against which there is no wall or defense"[62] (as was the case in the episode in Japan) "as the fear of death [or another sacrifice] does not deter the avenger."[63] Schopenhauer concludes,

> It is a rare, significant, and even sublime trait of character by which *the individual sacrifices himself*, in that he strives *to make himself the arm of eternal justice*, whose true inner nature he still fails to recognize [although he does intuit it].[64]

Emma too sees herself as "un instrumento de la justicia" and hopes that her stratagem will allow the "justicia de Dios" (Emma is not a philosopher and she intuits the Will in the mythical language of religion) to defeat the "justicia humana" (Loewenthal's crime has gone unpunished by the State). The virtue of her hatred and action lies in the fact that to achieve justice she was willing to expose herself to the terror and repugnance that sex aroused in her, which went beyond what she could tolerate ("the individual sacrifices [her]self"). So, what Emma carried out is not actually "revenge" but "punishment." The reading of what Borges read, then, allows us to understand the information found in the typescript of the first draft of the story regarding the alternative title that Borges considered for it: he told Cecilia Ingenieros that "también podría titularse *El castigo*,"[65] which in itself, we now understand, implied an explication of the tale and of its main character.

Sex ("la cosa horrible") is the form that virtue takes in Emma. Like Judith, for whom "all sacrifice ... is too little," or like those women evoked by Montaigne, who lost their honor to the lust of their husbands' enemies and, thus, saved their families, the young woman too confronted destiny with courage and sacrificed herself to achieve the justice that her family deserved but that her father was incapable of obtaining.

To further understand Emma's ethics and the quality of her figure, it is also necessary to take note of an element regarding sex that is common to this tale, "Pedro Salvadores," and "El incivil maestro de ceremonias Kotsuké No Suké": the simulation of illicit sex in the construction of the virtue of the characters. The last two tales show sacrifices motivated by loyalty toward a husband and a feudal lord, and in both stories, duty requires the sacrifice of personal reputation and dignity, which occurs through the simulation of illicit sex: Salvadores's wife tolerates the repudiation of her in-laws and tacitly

---

62 Schopenhauer, vol.1, 359.
63 Schopenhauer, vol.1, 359.
64 Schopenhauer, vol.1, 359. Emphasis added.
65 Borges, "Emma Zunz," typescript of first draft, 5 v.

pretends that her children are born out of an extra-marital affair to protect her husband; and the Japanese warrior pretends a weakness of character to deceive his enemy and approach him, a faked moral fall that involves buying a prostitute and living with her. Similarly, Emma's extreme sacrifice implies a double simulation involving illicit sex: first she pretends to prostitute herself and later she feigns a rape (Loewenthal does not attack her). The fact that the simulation of illicit sex appears in other characters (female and male) is another reason to place "Emma Zunz" not only in the series of Borges's women but also among texts that explore ethical questions such as virtue.

## Imperfect Virtue and Ambiguity

Although Schopenhauer generally agrees with Seneca in his rejection of wrath and revenge, to some extent he revises classic Stoicism and shows us that "vengeance" is not necessarily wrong and that there are some exceptional cases ("punishment") that may actually contribute to the common good, as justice does. Numerous textual evidences show that the German philosopher's argument convinced Borges, and in addition, it is clear that the justification of wrath (and passions) attempted by Schopenhauer overlaps with Borges's idea of the imperfection of human virtue, which he also tried in the story.

The principles of "la justicia humana" and "la justicia de Dios" have guided the preparation of the plan and a great deal of its execution, but the narrator says that at the end, "Las cosas no ocurrieron como había previsto Emma Zunz," because once she was face to face with Loewenthal, "más que la urgencia de vengar a su padre, Emma sintió la de castigar el ultraje padecido por ello. No podía no matarlo, después de esa minuciosa deshonra."[66] In spite of all the arguments that Emma has tried to justify the punishment of the man who ruined her family, in the crucial moment of its execution the hatred aroused by her sexual intercourse with the sailor, for which Loewenthal is not responsible, interferes in the action. This spurious passion does not cancel the justice of the punishment, but somehow pollutes it and shows us that Emma's virtue is not so pure as her family loyalty seemed to suggest.

Emma's imperfect moral quality is not an accident: her virtue is not perfect simply because, in spite of what classic Stoicism proposed, it cannot and it should not be. Early in the execution of the plan, Borges proposes a reflection on this ethical problem. After having sex, Emma tears up the money that the sailor gives her, and the narrator says that "Romper dinero es una impiedad, como tirar el pan ... un acto de soberbia ...."[67] The phrase is a variant of one by Antonio Conselheiro that Borges quotes on other occasions,

---

66 Borges, *OC* [1974], I, 567.
67 Borges, *OC* [1974], I, 566.

as in "Tres versiones de Judas" (1944), where he says that for the Brazilian heretic "la virtud era una casi impiedad,"[68] because only God can aspire to or achieve the moral perfection demanded by such an idea. That is, human virtue can only be imperfect. Thus, in "Tres versiones de Judas," Borges says that "la culpa" and "la virtud" can go hand in hand: for example, "en el homicidio [también participa] el coraje."[69] According to Borges, he who more convincingly revised the idea of Stoic virtue was Almafuerte, whom he qualified as a "renovador de los problemas de la ética."[70] In "El misionero," a poem that interested Borges, we read, for example, that "No hay caridad verdadera que no se enferme o que no se manche" or, more appropiately for Emma's story: "Fui grande en el soñar y fui pequeño / El día de la acción, y eso me pierde ... / ¡Pero, no quiero yo que se recuerde / Que ya es una virtud tener un sueño!"[71]

The presence of passion in a short story on punishment and justice can be explained not only because of Borges's consistent interest in ethical questions but also, it is possible to argue, because it offered a literary opportunity. Borges's comments on *Martín Fierro*, I propose, help understand this aspect of "Emma Zunz." He said that one of the great qualities of the figure created by José Hernández is "su imperfección y complejidad," which explains why some readers consider him "justo" while others see him as "vengativo" or "un malvado":

> Esta incertidumbre final es uno de los rasgos de las criaturas más perfectas del arte, porque lo es también de la realidad. Shakespeare será ambiguo, pero es menos ambiguo que Dios. No acabamos de saber quién es Hamlet o quién es Martín Fierro.[72]

Punishment and justice mixed with passion, then, are the materials with which Borges creates Emma's "imperfección" and "complejidad," an ethical ambiguity that leaves us with an "incertidumbre final" typical of "las criaturas más perfectas del arte" and that opens the possibility of endless interpretations.

---

68 Borges, *OC* [1974], I, 516. Antonio Conselheiro, "el heresiarca de los sertoes," "sintió que la virtud es una vanidad, una 'quasi impiedade,'" Borges, *TR2*, 324.
69 Borges, *OC* [1974], I, 516.
70 Borges, *TR2*, 199.
71 Almafuerte, *Obras completas*, 209, 222. In a conversation with Bioy, Borges also quoted, "No hay oficio menos pulcro / que el oficio de vivir," Bioy, *Borges*, 1182.
72 Borges, *OCC*, 563.

CHAPTER 9

# "La intrusa":

# Incest and Gay Readings

"La intrusa"[1] tells the story of Cristián Nilsen and his younger brother Eduardo, two hardened cattle and cart drivers from the Southern *orillas* of Buenos Aires, a landscape inhabited by other famous Borgesian *compadritos* (like the Iberra brothers, who also show up here). The two Nilsens live alone, and their relationship is one of exceptional friendship and solidarity. However, this tough but ideally harmonius brotherhood is put to the test when the older brother brings Juliana Burgos, presumably a former prostitute, to live with him in the house. After a while the younger brother too falls in love with the woman, which the older notices. Eventually, Cristián offers to share Juliana sexually with Eduardo, which strengthens the latter's bond with her. Thus, the presence of the woman in their home turns the relationship between the Nilsens into one of sexual rivalry and jealousy. To end the conflict, they sell Juliana to a brothel; yet, they cannot stop desiring her, and now the two of them secretly visit Juliana there. It is then that to terminate their sexual competition, Cristián, the older, kills Juliana. In the final scene, relieved because the threat that the woman represented to their ideal friendship and brotherhood was over, the two men embrace and console each other.

The story carries an epigraph that is a laconic biblical citation: "2 Reyes, I, 26." The reference corresponds to the Greek Bible (Septuagint), but in the traditional Hebrew Bible (after the Reformation better known in the West than the Greek Bible) that book is titled "2 Samuel." The reference created confusion because, while the Hebrew Bible does have a book titled "2 Kings," its first chapter does not have 26 verses, which led some readers to think that the citation was one of Borges's famous literary hoaxes. However, it is not: in the Hebrew Bible "2 Samuel, I, 26" is the verse that tells about the archetypical friendship of David and Jonathan and that, for example, in the King James Version reads, "I am distressed for thee, my brother Jonathan: very pleasant hast thou been unto me: thy love to me was wonderful, passing the love of

---

[1] The story and all quotes from it in Borges, *OC* [1974], I, 1025–28.

women."[2] With the epigraph, as we will see, Borges alluded to the nature of the Nilsens' exceptional friendship and the love they felt for each other.

The story has received significant critical attention. Beatriz Sarlo has considered it within the tradition of crime literature; J. B. Hall says that is a "riddle" and "an extended exercise in ambiguity ... enigmatic, baffling, and ironic"; Donna Fitzgerald reads the story within Borges's Jewish imaginary and as a representation of Argentina's post-colonial conflicts between main stream Christian tradition and "the other."[3] But a great deal of the criticism has been interested in exploring "La intrusa" in relation to expressions of sexuality in Borges's literature and women's positions in it. For Edwin Williamson, the story represents "Borges's experiences of being split—torn between honour and desire—whenever he fell in love with a woman. And it is also about the pain involved in having to sacrifice the woman so as to regain a measure of intergrity."[4] In *A Contraluz* Estela Canto said that the relationship between the two brothers represented the harsh and aggressive one between Borges and his mother; but more important, she also said that the story was "básicamente homosexual."[5] Carlos Hugo Christensen's 1981 movie based on Borges's text also interpreted the relationship between the brothers as gay love and thus contributed significantly to the establishment of what is perhaps the most influential critical trend in relation to this particular text.[6] For Daniel Balderston, "La intrusa" is the work where "Borges expresa más claramente ... [el] 'pánico homosexual,'" and the woman, who is sacrificed to "el deseo incestuoso" of the two brothers, is the mediator of their desire and "permite el funcionamiento del deseo homosexual."[7] Adrián Melo essentially seconds Balderston's gay reading and speaks of a story of explicit "contenido homoerótico."[8] Aguilar and Jelicié, concurring with this trend, say that in the story "la homosexualidad ... es incestuosa."[9]

These works have definitely contributed to sharper readings of Borges's story and, by implication, his literature more generally. Yet, there are relevant questions that have been overlooked or that need to be revisited. In the following pages, I will explore some aspects of Borges's creative process that, on the one hand, will help reconsider some of the questionable certainties proposed by influential gay interpretations and, on the other, will make possible a biographical reading of the text as an incest of the second type (explained in chapter one).

---

2 In the NRSVA it reads: "I am distressed for you, my brother Jonathan; greatly beloved were you to me; your love to me was wonderful, passing the love of women."
3 Sarlo, "Orillero y ultraísta," 187–94; Hall, "The David," 22; Fitzgerald, "Borges."
4 Williamson, *A Life*, 359–60.
5 Canto, *A contraluz*, 230.
6 Aguilar and Jelicié, *Borges va*, chapter 9.
7 Balderston, "Dialéctica," 67–68.
8 Melo, *Historia de la literatura gay*, 299.
9 Aguilar and Jelicié, *Borges va*, 131.

Before I get into the analysis of the story itself, I think it is necessary to point out two questions regarding, on the one hand, Borges's writing practices, and on the other, his conception of literature and interpretation. In relation to the former, the evidence shows that he often cautiously tested his work before it was published and frequently shared his ideas and plots with friends, looking for their reactions and feedback. This was the case with "La intrusa" too, a text that he said "haunted [him] for some thirty years."[10] Before it came out, he shared and discussed it with Estela Canto and Bioy Casares, as we will see below.

In relation to his conception of literature and interpretation, it is clear that Borges frequently and purposely wrote texts that encouraged and facilitated a multiplicity of readings. In an interview on French radio in 1964 (two years before he published "La intrusa"), he said that "Quand aux interprétations, je crois qu'elles peuvent être multiples ... Si les interprétations sont multiples, tant mieux."[11] During the same interview he also explained that

> Un livre qui veut durer, c'est un livre qu'on doit pouvoir lire de plusieurs façons. Qui, en tout cas, doit permettre une lecture variable, une lecture changeante. Chaque génération lit d'une façon différente les grands livres. Inutile de parler de la Bible. C'est évident.[12]

So he had a motivation and a model for this aspect of his Arte Poetica: a work that wanted to be part of the canon, and to remain in it, had to lend itself to many interpretations. Religious texts such as the Bible, that were subjected over time to endless and even contradictory readings, possessed precisely that quality. Borges also articulated this view of literature by evoking Kabbalistic readings of the Old Testament:

> Isaac Luria declara que la eterna Escritura
> Tiene tantos sentidos como lectores. Cada
> Versión es verdadera y ha sido prefijada
> Por Quien es el lector, el libro y la lectura.[13]

It is important, then, to keep in mind how Borges tested his work and his deliberate intent to create multiple interpretations.

## A Biographical Reading and the Incest of the Second Type

Let us now look at "La intrusa." In the story, Borges said that the Bible "era el único libro que había en la casa" of the Nilsens, a hint about the main source of the tale. In effect, the narrative is largely based on the story of Cain and Abel, whose basic contents it is helpful to remember. The first

---

10 Borges, *Doctor Brodie's Report*, 124.
11 Charbonnier, *Entretiens*, 118–19.
12 Charbonnier, *Entretiens*, 133.
13 Borges, *OC* [1974], II, 133.

two children of Adam and Eve were an agriculturalist (Cain) and a herder (Abel) who both decided to honor God with the product of their labor. But the Lord showed preference for Abel and not Cain:

> And the LORD had regard for Abel and his offering, but for Cain and his offering he had no regard. So Cain was very angry ... The LORD said to Cain, "Why are you so angry ... ? ... sin is lurking at the door; its desire is for you, but you must master it." Cain said to his brother Abel, "Let us go out to the field." And when they were in the field, Cain rose up against his brother Abel and killed him.[14]

The biblical story is one of violent brotherly competition for the Lord's favor. Envy or jealousy is a "sin" that "desires" Cain and, although the Lord tells him that he must learn to control it, he cannot and kills his brother.

Borges was interested in the story and explored it in three poems[15] before he published "La intrusa"; in two of them he acclimated it to the same geographical and social landscape in which he would set the short story. Thus, in his poem "El tango" (1958), he told about the Iberra brothers (the other pair of *compadritos* that appear in the tale)

> ¿Y ese Iberra fatal (de quien los santos
> Se apiaden) que en un puente de la vía,
> Mató a su hermano el Ñato, que debía
> Más muertes que él, y así igualó los tantos?[16]

In his "Milonga de dos hermanos" (1963), Borges more extensively re-created the conflict motivated by "la soberbia" of the older Iberra, whose pride in his courage and his ability with the knife led him to kill his younger brother. In this case Borges concluded the poem by saying "Es la historia de Cain / Que sigue matando a Abel,"[17] thus very explicitly making the competition between the two *compadritos* a re-creation of the chapter in the book of Genesis.[18]

In "La intrusa" Borges also speaks of "la rivalidad latente de los hermanos" and says that that "sin saberlo, estaban celándose." Even in some details of the story, Borges follows the biblical text: in the latter we read, "Cain said to his brother Abel, 'Let us go out to the field.' And when they were in the field ...," he killed him, while in "La intrusa" the setting of the ending takes a very similar form: the older brother also invites the younger to go out to the fields: "Cristián le dijo: Vení ... El campo iba agrandándose ... Orillaron un pajonal ... Hoy la maté."

---

14 *NRSVA*, Genesis 4.4–4.8.
15 In addition to the poems discussed here, see "El" (1961), *OC* [1974], I, 898.
16 Borges, *OC* [1974], I, 888.
17 Borges, *OC* [1974], I, 956.
18 This also shows that he wrote the "mitología de puñales" for the *orillas,* resorting to basic narratives.

But there is certainly a fundamental difference between the two stories, which Borges very explicitly underscores:

> Caín andava por ahí, pero el cariño entre los Nilsen era muy grande —¡quién sabe qué rigores y qué peligros habían compartido!— y prefirieron desahogar su exasperación con ajenos ... con la Juliana, que había traído la discordia.

Borges, then, rewrites the ending of Abel and Cain's story: he eliminates the object of their desire and, thus, instead of competition destroying the kinship tie, this most important of alliances prevails over jealousy and survives. That is, he rewrites the story from the book of Genesis by resorting to a story of brotherly love also found in the Old Testament: David and Jonathan's. This is not only suggested by the epigraph but by the origin of the strong bond between the Nilsens: "¡quién sabe qué rigores y qué peligros habían compartido!" which alludes to the common military experience of the Hebrew heroes. Borges, then, puts into practice a multiple and contradictory reading of the Old Testament where we find two opposing stories that contain two different assessments of kinship ties. In a way, Borges does in "La intrusa" what he did with *Martín Fierro* in "El fin": he rewrites a classic text changing the ending and thus creating alternative readings and ethical implications.

But the change involves not only the outcome but also the matter of the competition. It is not about God's favor or pride over courage: now it is competition for the same sexual partner. What could have been Borges's stimulus to take this new direction in the rewriting of the biblical story? The biblical text itself opens the possibility to imagine that it could have been a woman who caused the dispute between Cain and Abel: the brothers compete for (God's) love, and the Lord says that "sin is lurking at the door; its desire is for you," in which the words "sin" and "desire" (in the context of the book of Genesis) can easily summon ideas of sex and women. A similar possibility is also contained in "Milonga de dos hermanos" where Borges defines the Iberras as "Hombres de amor y de guerra";[19] that is, we might think that after exploring in poetry the warring life of *compadritos*, he used narrative to explore their erotic life. But the subject and the tone of the story also correlates with some of Borges's readings. The tale does explore "la crispatura trágica"[20] of eroticism as Borges found it in Del Mazo's *Los vencidos* and, in particular, exhibits points of contact with the poem "Incontaminado." In both texts we have the sexual competition and jealousy between siblings ("has envidiado el lecho que ocupa tu hermana" / "se estaban celando") and the same qualification of the sex that occurs in such relationships ("goces bestiales" / "sumisión bestial"); indeed, like Del

---

19 Borges, *OC* [1974], I, 955.
20 Borges, *TR1*, 134.

Mazo's erotic pieces, "La intrusa" also shows "la realidad violenta" of sex in Buenos Aires.[21]

However, for Borges the intersection of kinship ties and sex was more than a literary device: it related to experiences that had hurt him and continued to bother him until the end of his life. They were a significant part of his personal history, and it should not surprise us to find them in one of his short stories. A substantial aspect of "La intrusa" is, indeed, written with biographical materials, which allows it to be read as a re-creation of an incest of the second type. If for a moment we forget about the given names of the two brothers and instead think of them as "el mayor" and "el menor," as Borges repeatedly also calls them, it is quite possible to see that the relationship between them and the sharing of the woman easily reminds us of what we know of Borges's traumatic sexual initiation and the role his father played in it. In order to show the similarity of the relationships between the Borgeses and the Nilsens, I will highlight a few of the parallels between Estela Canto's recollections and the text of the short story. If we tolerate the inevitable differences between a memoir and a fictional text with a specific plot and language, we will be able to appreciate the similarities. Thus, from Canto we learn that "su padre le había ordenado acostarse con una mujer" and that "Le dio una dirección y le dijo que debía estar allí a una hora determinada. Una mujer le estaría esperando."[22] In the story, when "the older" makes the woman sexually available to "the younger," the narrator says, "El tono era entre mandón y cordial," which both matches the imperative attitude of Borges's father and, at the same time, suggests something of the affection that must have existed between the two. In Canto we also read that Borges thought that "Si esa mujer estaba dispuesta a acostarse con él era porque había tenido *ya* relaciones sexuales con su padre,"[23] while in the story "the older" tells "the younger" "Ahí la tenés ... si la querés, usala." In both cases the sexual availability of the women is decided by the older men, which, from the standpoint of the younger men, implies the objectification of the women and the impersonality of their sexual relationships. Canto also says that Borges thought that "La mujer que se le ofrecía era una mujer que él iba a *compartir* con su padre,"[24] while the narrator of the story directly says, "desde aquella noche la compartieron." Finally, the overall circumstances of Borges's traumatic sexual initiation and "La intrusa" also match in the following respect: it was "the older" Borges who conflictively brought the woman into the relationship with his son, while in the story we read that "el menor ... no había rechazado la participación, pero ... no la había dispuesto." Some of Borges's own comments on the story also hint at the sifting of biographical content into the text:

21 Borges, *TR1*, 134.
22 Canto, *A contraluz*, 116.
23 Canto, *A contraluz*, 116. Emphasis in the original.
24 Canto, *A contraluz*, 116. Emphasis in the original.

"LA INTRUSA": INCEST AND GAY READINGS 193

> There's a fact I would like you to notice. There are three characters and there is only one character who speaks ... only one of the characters speaks directly, and he's the one who's the leader of the story. I mean, he's behind all the facts of the story. He makes the final decision, he works out the whole thing, and in order to make that plainer, he's the only character whose voice we hear throughout the story.[25]

"The leader," the only one who speaks, is "behind the facts of the story ... he works out the whole thing," as Borges's father did in his sexual initiation, an affair in which the son apparently did not have a say either.[26] Moreover, the form of the explanation itself suggests that "La intrusa" is not about the Nilsens and Juliana: he refers more generally to "characters" without naming anybody and hints that the story is telling another (hidden or parallel) situation that he wants "to make ... plainer" and somehow be understood ("There's a fact I would like you to notice").

Investigative criticism, with its evidence from in and outside the text, allows us to see the biographical materials that went into the writing of "La intrusa": the sentiments and insights of how men respond to a situation of sexual competition and to an incest of the second type come from Borges's experience. In her memoir, referring to what Borges told her about his sexual initiation, Canto said that "allí estaban las imágenes que surgían en su mente,"[27] which suggests how readily and permanently available to him was the traumatic memory of the event. In "La intrusa," Borges does write another text for the "mitología de puñales" that he wants to re-create, a mythology that parallels and echoes the one in the Bible, but in this literary project for the *orillas* we can still read his sexual biography. And, inevitably, we have to consider the possibility that he might have chosen to write the story this way so he could speak about his own history. The tale can be read as a transmutation of his experience, as is the "sham Chinese poem" "El guardián de los libros." Here too "la sustancia autobiográfica, la personal, está desaparecida por los accidentes que la encarnan"; that is, the competition between father and son is partially blurred by the exigencies of the biblical plot about a rivalry between siblings. Yet, we can still sense that the biography of the author "es como corazón que late en la hondura," whose beatings can be observed with the x-rays of investigative criticism. Certainly, for some the transfiguration may be too oblique a way for Borges to talk about his sex, but we have to remember that in the 1950s and 1960s, when he wrote the story, his traumatic sexual initiation (unlike his sexual impotence) was unknown to most and its own incestuous characteristics made its public discussion off-limits.

---

25 Borges, *Jorge Luis Borges: Conversations*, 31.
26 "Borges fut sommé par son père d'accomplir pour la premiere fois un acte sexuel," *OC* [2010], II, 1434.
27 Canto, *A contraluz*, 116.

## The Objectification and Anonimity of Women and Sex

In her memoir, Estela Canto said that one of the traits of the story that bothered her was that "la mujer apareciera como un objeto inerte."[28] Her comments anticipated an influential critical trend that proposed that the story exhibits a misogynist treatment of female characters in which the defining trait is the objectification of Juliana. The textual evidence in this respect is conclusive and has been aptly presented before in other studies.[29] However, sometimes it is hard to tell to what extent critics read the evidence as identical to Borges's worldview and what role they accord to the literary demands of the text in shaping the often-cited passages. Therefore, here I am interested in analyzing some of the components that may explain the quality with which women and heterosexual relations appear in "La intrusa": in this section, then, I will look at biographical materials and purely literary factors, the latter including both intellectual influences and the demands that this particular text of fiction imposed on the writer.

As I said, critics have consistently called our attention to the "objectification" of Juliana. According to the narrator, she was "una cosa," a characterization of the woman that fits logically into the behavior of the main character and his decision to make her sexually available to his brother: "si la querés, usála." This level of objectification implies a negation of Juliana's humanity and identity, which places her within the spectrum of the anonymous female characters that consistently appear in Borges's re-creations of sex. In "El Evangelio según Marcos," in which a young woman is sexually initiated, we read that she "No dijo una sola palabra ... Cuando se fue ... Espinosa pensó que ni siquiera sabía cómo se llamaba";[30] in "Ulrica" (1975), after having sex, the male protagonist of the story realized that "No supe su apellido y tal vez no lo sabré nunca";[31] and anonymity is also one of the characteristics of Emma Zunz's sexual initiation with the sailor: "El hombre, sueco o finlandés no hablaba español."[32] "La intrusa" does not tell, as do the other texts just quoted, the story of a single sexual encounter, and therefore the credibilty of a plot in which the contact between the men and the woman is an extended one requires the naming of the character. Yet, in the story, sex is essentially impersonal ("atendía a los dos con sumisión bestial"), casual, and venal, as in the other texts. Thus, after giving the female character a name, Borges still tries to erase her individuality and, pretty explicitly, to render her anonymous: the narrator says that the brothers "no pronunciaban el nombre de Juliana, ni siquiera para llamarla." In this way of representing the experience of casual and venal sex there is a definite biographical

---

28  Canto, *A contraluz*, 230.
29  A discussion of this interpretive trend is in Leone, "An Inventory," 167–70.
30  Borges, *OC* [1974], I, 1071.
31  Borges, *OC* [1974], II, 17.
32  Borges, *OC* [1974], I, 566.

component: Estela Canto said that one of the traumatic aspects of Borges's sexual initiation was that the prostitute he had been ordered to have sex with was "una mujer que él ... no conocía."[33]

This analysis also allows us to see the broader influence of Borges's sexual biography on his literature. All the texts that I just mentioned re-create moments of casual and venal sex, as do most (if not all) of the others that speak of sexual or erotic encounters: "La noche de los dones," "Casa Elena," "Paréntesis pasional," "Villa Urquiza," "Arrabal en que pesa el campo," etc. If this is so, it is because, as the evidence of his life shows, his sexual experiences were largely of that nature. A way of testing the relation between Borges's life and his literature that my argument implies is to look at the number of texts by Borges that explore sexual intercourse in the context of an emotionally deep and extended love relationship (which in his life did not happen), and we will find almost ... none;[34] an absence that in itself highlights how important was his sexual biography for his writings and how much, when it comes to desire and sex, his literature cannot avoid a biographical reading.

But to have a more comprehensive (and reasonable) understanding of the relations between men and women in "La intrusa," we have to consider Borges's imaginary of the *arrabal*. As we have seen, the *orillas* were the landscape of Stoicism, and this story is also written in that key. Thus, reflecting on the specific rhetoric that he created for that landscape in the story, we read about "el duro suburbio" and that in it, "un hombre no decía, ni se decía, que una mujer pudiera importarle, más allá del deseo y la posesión, pero los dos estaban enamorados. Esto, de algún modo, los humillaba," a statement that echoes the Stoic precepts that deplored that men should be dominated by emotions and express them, and recommended serenity and reason to govern passions. That is, the *compadrito* masculinity (and relation with women) that the passage helps construct is also shaped by Borges's Stoic imaginary. Borges's will to highlight the ethics that guide the characters is manifested also in details: in the decisive moment when the two brothers discussed the fate of Juliana, the woman, instead of showing any anxiety regarding her future, "se acostó a dormir la siesta," as did the two gauchos in "El otro duelo" before their execution.[35] As good Stoics, both the woman and the two men accepted their fate with serenity.

The fact that Borges could give the same ethical qualities to female and male characters reveals one of the ways he conceived the mythical *arrabal* that he re-created in texts such as "La intrusa." In Borges's imaginary, the "suburbio" is populated by the archetypal and symmetrical figures of the "compadrito" and the "puta." While paid sex is the behavior that turns women of the *arrabal* into prostitutes, knife fights is what transforms men from the *orillas* into *compadritos*. The lives of these two archetypical figures

---

33 Canto, *A contraluz*, 116.
34 "El congreso" and the "Villa Urquiza" in *FBA* might be the exceptions here.
35 Borges, *OC* [1974], I, 1060.

are ruled by a Stoic destiny and fate, which implies that in the *orillas*, sex and knife fights do not depend on free will but on an impersonal force that often puts prostitutes and *compadritos* in contact with strangers. Thus, in the symmetrical *arrabal* created by Borges, anonymity is also part of the experience of the *compadritos*. As an example, in "Milonga del forastero," the knife fight takes place between two men who did not know each other before and did not have any personal relationship:

> Nunca se han visto la cara
> No se volverán a ver
> ----------------------------------
> Ya quedó tendido un hombre
> Que muere y que no se queja.
>
> Sólo esa tarde se vieron.
> No se volverán a ver.[36]

The poem parallels even in its wording "La noche de los dones" (1975), a tale of sex in a *criollo* setting in which a series of unforeseen events (his destiny) lead a boy to his initiation. The main character tells of the encounter with the prostitute thus: "No volveríamos a vernos y no supe nunca su nombre."[37] Thus, anonymity in casual and venal sex is not only a reflection of Borges's biography but it is also constructed with the Stoic concepts that Borges chose for the *arrabal*.

In "La intrusa," then, casual and venal sex are also ruled by Stoic fate and, as in the case shown above, its formulation also echoes other Borges texts: while Eduardo Nilsen brought home a nameless woman "que había levantado por el camino," in "Ulrica" the narrator explains the sexual encounter by saying that "nuestros caminos se cruzaban"; similarly, while in the poem on the *compadrito* "Jacinto Chiclana," Borges speaks of "aquella muerte casual,"[38] the Nilsens had sex in "juergas casuales."

Fate and anonymity also colored Borges's perception of some of his experiences with women. When in 1967 (a year after "La intrusa" came out) he was about to marry Elsa Astete Millán, and was almost as scared as the boy in "La noche de los dones," he told Bioy: "Pongo mi destino en manos de una desconocida."[39] Stoicism, then, also helped him make sense of his love life, which in a dialectical turn of a screw, he could eventually use to write his texts.

---

36 Borges, *OC* [1974], II, 183.
37 Borges, *OC* [1974], II, 43.
38 Borges, *OC* [1974], I, 959.
39 Bioy, *Borges*, 1204.

## Gay Readings

Several critics have attempted gay readings of "La intrusa" and have argued that it is in this story that we found the clearest expressions of homoeroticism in Borges or that it is here that he most clearly insinuates his worries about homosexuality and his homosexual panic. The story definitely calls for such readings; yet a number of them have been based on some problematic assumptions about the text and the author that end up limiting our understanding of the story. To reconsider this influential critical trend, it is necessary, as I explained at the beginning of my analysis, to keep in mind Borges's interest in creating a multiplicity of interpretations for his works and his practice of testing his writings with friends.

Let us start with the latter. In *A Contraluz* Estela Canto devoted a short chapter to the story, saying that "Fue en el cincuenta y tantos cuando Borges me habló por primera vez del tema de este cuento."[40] On that ocassion

> Me expuso el argumento ... Le dije que el cuento me parecía básicamente homosexual. Creí que esto —él se alarmaba bastante de cualquier alusión en este sentido— iba a impresionarle. No fue así ... Para él no había ninguna situación homosexual en el cuento. Continuó hablándome de la relación entre los dos hermanos, de la bravura de ese tipo de hombres, etc.
>
> De todos modos no escribió el cuento inmediatamente y la idea siguió dándole vueltas en la cabeza. No la abandonó ... él tomaba bastante en cuenta mis opiniones ...
>
> Borges veía el cuento de una manera muy distinta a como yo lo veía.[41]

Her testimony has several very illuminating elements that are relevant to an understanding of the story. The conversation occurred many years (perhaps a decade) before the publication of the narration. Canto, whose comments Borges usually took into account, told him that for her the story was "básicamente homosexual." Borges, however, understood the story very differently ("de una manera muy distinta a como yo la veía"): for him there was not any "situación homosexual." In spite of the controversial feedback, Borges did not drop his idea but continued to think about the story for several years. In short, even before writing it down, Borges knew the story lent itself to a gay reading.

Borges also shared his idea with Bioy Casares. In 1964 (two years before it came out) Borges told him a plot that was essentially the same that we read in the published text. The story was about "dos hermanos muy unidos" that desired the same woman, who was killed by the older of the brothers when their love for her threatens their bond ("ya nada nos separará"). Borges also told his friend: "Deberías escribirlo vos. Lo vas a escribir mejor que yo. Yo no

---

40 Canto, *A contraluz*, 229.
41 Canto, *A contraluz*, 230.

lo veo del todo."[42] The annotations in Bioy's diary do not mention anything about homosexuality and implicitly suggest that he saw the story as the author apparently did. In addition, Bioy's diary confirms that Borges struggled with the story and that he was hesitant about it.

Beyond the usual doubts that Borges (like any other author) could have had about his own works, it is quite likely that Canto's feedback compounded them and must have been a factor in his hesitations and the long time that it took him to publish the story. But, more important, the trial balloons that he displayed before his trusted friends also offered him two contradictory responses to his text; that is, they gave him two different readings of the story, which, I want to propose, may explain why Borges included the epigraph that associates "La intrusa" with the biblical narrative of David and Jonathan. In the nineteenth century, their story was a way of alluding to homosexual love, as most critics that have tried gay readings on Borges's tale have explained. In this respect the best-known invocation of the story is Oscar Wilde's statement in the 1890s, when he was tried for his relationship with Lord Douglas:

> "The Love that dare not speak its name" in this century is such a great affection of an elder for a younger man as there was between David and Jonathan, such as Plato made the very basis of his philosophy, and such as you find in the sonnets of Michelangelo and Shakespeare.[43]

Borges, of course, knew about Wilde's statement, and Canto's memoir allows us to understand why he used it. In itself, the decision to publish the story after so many years of hesitations implies that he finally accepted that his text could be read in a gay key and, moreover, with the inclusion of the epigraph, he seems to have been willing even to encourage the possibility of such a reading.

It was a possibility but not the only reading that the tale allowed, as his disagreement with Canto makes clear and Bioy's diary implies. The story can also be interpreted as a story of brotherly friendship and love without necessarily implying homoeroticism, which is precisely why, I also want to suggest, Borges chose the epigraph. And it is here that we need to revise the certainties proposed by gay readings. The fact that Wilde's trial is such a classic moment in the use of the biblical narrative has unjustifiably convinced Borges's critics that the epigraph can only be understood in a gay key. That is, critics have read Borges's use of the biblical lines only in relation to the best-known case of it, while they have disregarded the wider nineteenth-century historical context that offers diverse forms of reference to it and against which the epigraph of "La intrusa" can also be contrasted. Thus, current criticism has missed the fact that since the late eighteenth century, two competing trends in the reception and interpretation of the relationship

---

42 Bioy, *Borges*, 1019.
43 http://law2.umkc.edu/faculty/projects/ftrials/wilde/Crimwilde.html, accessed April 15, 2016.

between David and Jonathan had developed. The most influential of the two, in which we have to inscribe Wilde's famous statement, "read the David and Jonathan narrative in connection with ancient Greek and Roman texts, Michelangelo, Shakespeare, and Walt Whitman, all of whose writings ... were drawn upon as support for a positive, ennobling same-sex eroticism."[44] But the biblical narrative was also read as an example of "spiritual friendship between persons of the same sex ... as models of Christian manliness and manly friendship."[45] A good example of this second and today much less known trend was, for example, the use of David and Jonathan by John Keats. In a letter written to a friend, the poet expressed his deep love for his younger brothers and explained it as a consequence of being orphaned and other difficulties that they went through together from an early age:

> My love for my Brothers from the early loss of our parents and even for earlier Misfortunes has grown into a affection "passing the Love of Women"—I have been ill temper'd with them, I have vex'd them—but the thought of them has always stifled the impression that any woman might otherwise have made upon me.[46]

Here the biblical story served to illustrate Keats's relationships not with one but with all of his brothers, and to express the solidarity and the sense of obligation created by common hardships and kinship. Keats chose to privilege his family ties over the attraction he could have felt for women because he knew that a love relationship implied a new allegiance that would compete with his family ties and, possibly, be detrimental to the well-being of his younger brothers. That is, Keats's use of David and Jonathan parallels the story of the Nilsens and easily matches Borges's and Bioy's interpretation of "La intrusa." This shows that the use of the biblical narrative in nineteenth-century England responded not to one but to at least two different understandings of it. James Harding, who tracked down the many uses of the figures of David and Jonathan, has underscored the indeterminacy that they carried with them:

> The metaphor of David and Jonathan could be invoked equally by those in the know to specify a sexual bond between the two men in question, and by those not in the know to specify a non-sexual, but, nevertheless, deep emotional bond between them. "David and Jonathan" is a reversible figure, which makes the interpretation of its reception a complex and ultimately indeterminate matter.[47]

That is, the story of David and Jonathan is an especially slippery one that was subjected to more than one interpretation, which was exactly what Borges

---

44 Harding, *The Love*, 289.
45 Harding, *The Love*, 288–89.
46 John Keats to Benjamin Bailey, 10 June, 1818, in Keats, *The Major Works*, 399.
47 Harding, *The Love*, 281.

often sought for his texts. Therefore, reading the epigraph as an unequivocal allusion to gay love omits half of the traditions of interpretation to which Borges had access and, more important, creates obstacles for other readings of his short story. With the epigraph, then, Borges proposed that "La intrusa" could be either a story of gay love *or* one of brotherly friendship.

Daniel Balderston has said that the epigraph "hace creíble una lectura gay del cuento," and Adrián Melo indicates that "el contenido homoerótico del cuento queda explicitado en el párrafo de la Biblia que Borges eligió como epígrafe,"[48] two examples that show that the reference to the biblical narrative has been fundamental for gay readings of "La intrusa." Independently of the fact that it is not the only possible reading of the epigraph, it is clear that the interpretation of the tale as one of homoerotic incestuous desire has largely depended on a gay reading of the epigraph, and we can imagine that, had Borges not included the epigraph, it would have been far less clear that the tale could lend itself to such readings. Certainly, the text of the story itself exhibits elements (such as the misogynistic treatment of the woman, the woman as a mediator of homoerotic desire, the final embrace of the brothers) that would still make it possible to attempt them (as Estela Canto did); but it is also undeniable, as the above quotations implied, that in the absence of the epigraph, the argument would be significantly weakened. Which is what gives relevance to *the form* of the epigraph: Borges does not actually quote the verses that tell the story of David and Jonathan, and the citation is a tricky one that plays with variations in biblical traditions generally unknown to common readers and that may lead even curious ones to dead ends. That is, the form of the epigraph meant that many (if not most) of the readers could miss the allusion to David and Jonathan and therefore would not be able to associate the story with them.[49] Therefore, while Borges included the biblical story, he also limited the readers' access to it, a strategy that had at least two effects: on the one hand, even in the case of well-informed readers, he did not openly associate his work with homosexuality and, at the same time, he tilted the field of interpretation in favor of alternative readings that did not depend on or gained little from the biblical narrative. That is, in the game of competing readings, he was not impartial and favored his over, say, Estela's gay one.

In spite of all that we have considered so far, his decision to publish a story that he knew could be interpreted as gay love, as well as, more importantly, his gesture of encouraging such reading with the epigraph, seems to contradict what we know about him in terms of his fear of homosexuality and his avoidance of the topic in his conversations, as a reader, and as a writer. So, how to explain his choice? Although we will never know for certain, we

48 Balderston, "Dialéctica," 68; Melo, *Historia de la literatura gay*, 299.
49 In the English edition published in 1972, however, Borges cited the Hebrew Bible and even quoted a part of the verse "passing the love of women," making it more accessible and direct, Borges, *Doctor Brodie's Report*, 63.

still can explore some possible answers. With regard to the story, we should consider that he liked it, that it fit in his project on the literature of the *orillas*, and that he might have also kept it as a way of talking about his conflicted relationship with his father, all motivations that might have counted in his decision to publish it. But the gesture of including the epigraph is different and speaks of a will to somehow address, even if indirectly, the topic of homosexuality. Why? By way of a possible answer, I want to offer a speculation that considers the twin questions of Borges's ambitions as a writer and his awareness of the historical dimensions of literary canonization. I am aware that the speculation that follows may be too influenced by the relevance that Borges still commands 30 years after his death and, thus, it may be too tainted by teleological assumptions. Still, I think it is worth considering.

Let us look at the first question. As a writer, Borges expected great recognition. He aspired to occupy an outstanding place in literature and hoped that his work would survive the test of time and remain in the canon. I know this is far from the image of a Borges disdainful of honors that many readers have in mind and that he himself with his casual kindness patiently constructed, but there is plenty of evidence that goes against that public humble persona. For instance, Bioy Casares's diary is full of conversations and gestures that, more or less explicitly, indicate his (and their) preoccupation with making it into the canon and staying there.[50] But it is the diary of Carlos Mastronardi that offers perhaps the best anecdote to appreciate Borges's literary ambitions. One night, on one of their walks through Buenos Aires, they talked about Anatole France, who early in the twentieth century had enjoyed very high prestige (in 1921 he was awarded the Nobel Prize) but whose reputation after he died in 1924 had entered a free fall, to the extent that by mid-century very few writers read him or cared about his literature. It was then that Borges told Mastronardi: "Lo decisivo es tirar el primer siglo, salir indemne de esa prueba inmediata ... Rebasados los primeros cien años, las cosas marchan solas."[51] The biggest challenge for dead writers was to remain relevant during the first century after their deaths; then, as the cases of the great names in Western literature demonstrated, the built-in inertia of a major reputation (the accumulation of criticism, public celebrations, educational curricula, etc.) would take care of it. The enormity of the ambition that the statement reveals may lead us to think that Borges was joking, but Mastronardi did not think so, and the conversation made him more aware of Borges's aspirations: "la voluntad de gloria y perduración es asombrosamente fuerte en él."[52]

Which takes us to the second question: Borges's awareness of the historical dimensions of literary canonization. As we have seen at the beginning of this chapter, in his 1964 interview on French radio Borges said that "un livre que veut durer" must be able to stand a multiplicity of readings because "chaque

---

50 e.g. Bioy, *Borges*, 275–77.
51 Mastronardi, *Borges*, 67.
52 Mastronardi, *Borges*, 64.

génération" will read it in a different way. And, indeed, this applied also to the sexual politics of literature, which he felt were changing: although homoeroticism and gay love were still in the margins, their expressions were slowly but steadily becoming more acceptable, bolder, even expected. To understand this trend in Argentina and Borges's perception and reaction to it we can go back, for example, to 1948, when in *Muerte y transfiguración de Martín Fierro* Martínez Estrada suggested, invoking the new knowledge of "psicólogos y psycoanalistas,"[53] that Fierro's relationship with Cruz had not been a simple spiritual friendship but a homoerotic bond. The possibility of homosexuality among gauchos opened by Martinez Estrada's speculation, if not necessarily approved by Borges, did not go unnoticed by him.[54]

In addition, numerous annotations in Bioy's diary show that between the 1950s and the early 1970s the changing politics of sex in literature was a source of anxiety and homophobic assessments by Bioy and Borges. I will show several of those instances chronologically because they roughly convey a sense of process and because in their variety, they illuminate the multiple forms that the two friends' preoccupations took. In 1957, for example, Bioy recorded that "Borges ... reprueba la homosexualidad como tema literario,"[55] disapproval that, however, showed that it was an issue that deserved their consideration. Along these lines, in a comment that we now know had implications for "La intrusa," in 1963 Borges told Bioy, "La amistad, uno de los mejores temas de la literatura, *ya* no puede tratarse; porque sugiere pederastia."[56] In the same vein, in 1965, when the two friends were preparing *Crónicas de Bustos Domecq*, in which the leading character is a pedantic man of letters, Bioy wrote:

> En los últimos trabajos debí contener a Borges para que no precipite a nuestro autor en el abismo de la más satisfecha pederastia. Sospecho que mis descripciones de los últimos *exploits* de algunos colegas que se besuqueaban en público tienen la culpa de que Borges quiera someter a nuestro héroe a tal desventura.[57]

Apparently, Borges wanted to create a character that was in tune with current literary mores and he thought that contemporary public displays of same-sex desire and love among writers and critics would serve such a purpose. That is, his intentions implied a historical gaze on the question (it was new; it reflected a change) and suggested that, even if derisively, he could consider the possibility of including homosexuality in his literature. This same historical perspective is also clear in a 1970 comment, when he referred to a younger generation of Argentine writers as "el malón de los pederastas"

---

53  Martinez Estrada, *Muerte y transfiguración*, 89.
54  Bioy, *Borges*, 1229.
55  Bioy, *Borges*, 303
56  Bioy, *Borges*, 940. Emphasis added.
57  Bioy, *Borges*, 1084.

and asked Bioy, "¿Qué otra cosa son los jóvenes?"[58] This anxiety about the changing place of gay love in literature obviously included Bioy. In 1972, thinking about Argentine gay authors and critics, he wrote:

> Bianco, Juan José Hernández, Pezzoni y tantos otros, tratan de que pase algo así en nuestra época y en nuestra literatura. Si prevalecen, una historia de amor, para no ser deleznable, tendrá que ocurrir entre hombres. Ay de mis libros.[59]

All the evidence, then, indicates a homophobic anxiety about the new and emerging aesthetic and political criteria which they thought could eventually be extended to literature. Borges and Bioy looked at the new trend from a historical perspective and tried to assess what it meant then and could mean in the future for their own works and reputations. In the case of Borges, in addition, it is important to remember that the time frame of these annotations essentially coincided with his rise to international fame and that they paralleled his expectations of recognition.

Therefore, it is in this context that we might understand Borges's decision not so much of publishing the story but of including the epigraph. Estela's comments bothered him and created doubts, but, I want to speculate, they also helped him see an opportunity to engage with an uncomfortable issue that he thought was decisively beginning to shape the literature of the future and, thus, could perhaps help keep his work relevant. He feared and hated the new trend but he feared and hated more becoming irrelevant and not making it into the canon of the future. Aiming at this goal did not demand that he give a whole new direction to his literature but a discreet and difficult-to-find epigraph, a low-risk and limited literary gesture that, given the indeterminacy of the biblical story, could also be denied. So, if this was one of his motivations, he succeeded: more than any other of his texts, it has been "La intrusa" that has attracted gay readings, and today studies of gay literature in Argentina cannot avoid the story. That is, Borges has made it to our conversation. As I said before, this speculation may look to be too influenced by our present perspective on his relevance; yet if we understand (and accept) his immense literary ambitions, some of his apparently contradictory and zigzagging behaviors become more intelligible, and this speculation, more reasonable.

Finally, I want to briefly consider Borges's intervention in the 1981 controversy that surrounded Carlos Hugo Christensen's movie *La intrusa*, which was based on the short story. The movie was censored by the Argentine dictatorship, and Borges publicly supported the government's decision. But before I get into some of the details of this episode, it is important to make a clarification. Works that addressed this question have often conflated what

---

58 Bioy, *Borges*, 1331.
59 Bioy, *Borges*, 1441.

Borges said about his story during the controversy with his writing of the text, as if they were basically the same.[60] However, I think that we have to distinguish Borges's creative process in the 1950s and 1960s from his reaction to the reception and interpretation of his story in Christensen's movie of the early 1980s. The two are certainly related, but they are different.

Christensen, an Argentine gay director residing in Brazil, acquired the rights to the story in 1975 and finished the movie in 1981.[61] Early that year Borges attended a preview and apparently was satisfied with it. However, in the following months the movie ran into problems with the government. The official censors objected to explicit moments of homosexuality and incest and, in particular, to a scene of nudity and sex that showed the two brothers and the woman together. Christensen publicly rejected the government's intervention and did not agree to introduce changes, which meant that the movie was not shown in Argentina. It was in this moment that Borges intervened in the controversy: in an article titled "Sí a la censura" he denounced Christensen's gay interpretation of his short story ("no se trata de una versión libre sino de una versión distorsionada") and sided with the censors (and the dictatorship). To justify his position he said:

> en la película de Christensen se han hecho sugerencias de homosexualidad, y yo no tengo nada que ver con ese tipo de asuntos ... En él hay obscenidades, hay desnudos, y además (esto es lo más grave) se sugiere la pornografía y el sexo ... yo temo que todo esto pueda comprometerme personalmente, que la gente pueda creerme cómplice del film ... frente a la pornografía considero aceptable la labor del censor ... yo trato de no ser obsceno, de escribir y pensar en forma decorosa, no me gustaría saber que la gente malinterpreta todo y me juzga vinculado a la película de Christensen.[62]

As we have seen, it was true that Borges generally opposed obscenity and pornography in literature (and, by extension, art) and that decorum usually guided his treatment of sex. It was also a fact that throughout most of his life, he had avoided the topic of homosexuality and usually disapproved of it in literature. But there his sincerity stopped. Because in the specific case of "La intrusa" it was not true, as we have seen, that he had not made "sugerencias de homosexualidad." Similarly, while he usually worked (as he did in this text) to create the conditions for a multiplicity of interpretations, now he denounced Christensen's gay reading as a "versión distorsionada." How to explain these contradictions? There were aesthetic, political, and ultimately, professional factors that may explain his inconsistencies. When it came to the treatment of sex and homosexuality by a director like Christensen, there was an enormous distance between the very explicit language of cinema and

---

60 Aguilary and Jelicié, *Borges va*, chapter 9 and Balderston, "Dialéctica," 68–69.
61 Aguilar and Jelicié, *Borges va*, 124–25.
62 Borges, *TR3*, 301–2.

Borges's own indirect and highly allusive expression. This distance became visible not only in the scenes of nudity and sex but also in the straight-forward display of the epigraph: the director did not just cite the passage but at the beginning of the film he fully quoted the verses, making clear what the biblical story (and Borges) were talking about. In other words, what Borges seems to have conceived as a low-risk literary operation in a text was magnified by the big screen and ended up looking like an embarrassing "exposé." As his friend Ulyses Petit de Murat said when he attended a preview of the movie: cinema made Borges "más carnal."[63] This bothered him not only because of his aesthetic differences with Christensen but because he was concerned about the impact that the more accessible language of the movie could have on his reputation and, ultimately, on his standing as a literary figure: he said "yo temo que todo esto pueda comprometerme personalmente, que la gente pueda creerme cómplice del film," and that he would not like to find out that "la gente malinterpreta todo y me juzga vinculado a la película." Thus, confronted with the situation of either supporting a government that still aroused his sympathies or backing an aesthetically unsatisfying movie that openly addressed a question that disturbed him and that could taint his reputation, he chose the former. Moreover, we could even consider the possibility that he saw the controversy initiated by the government as an opportunity to de facto cancel his decision of giving Christensen the rights to the story. It is in this controversial context and as part of his reaction to a filmic interpretation of his work, then, that we have to read his 1981 comments on his own short story.

63 Quoted in Aguilar and Jelicié, *Borges va*, 125.

# Conclusions

The point of departure for this book has been the extended, but in my opinion questionable, view among readers of Borges of an absence of desire and sex in his literature, a commonly accepted reading that, when assessed against the evidence contained in a significant portion of his the texts, I found unconvincing. Until now Borges has been largely considered an asexual author but in the preceding pages I have shown, I hope, that sexuality was a major preoccupation for him, both as a reader and as a writer.

I have read Borges biographically, as others have done before, but I have proposed a different relationship between his sexual biography and his literary experience. While the most common readings, perhaps unaware of the frequent invisibility of sexuality in his texts, have understood that there was a negative relationship between his literature and his sexual biography, that is, that because of the conflictive relationship with his own sexuality he could not read, think, or write about sex, in this book I show that Borges's sexuality was the point of departure for parts of his oeuvre and that he himself thought that his sexual impotence could be one of the legitimate interpretive key for his literature, as he believed was also the case for other authors such as Edgar Allan Poe or the Argentine poet Almafuerte.

Borges's sexuality was a preoccupation that guided part of his readings. I have shown that he was a curious and ardent reader of erotic literature, an aspect of his literary experience that, to the best of my knowledge, had not been systematically explored before. As we have seen Borges was interested, among others, in texts that recreated and reflected on the sex act and lived through their erotic imagination: while some of them got him sexually aroused others could help him make sense, for example, of his own visit to a brothel. But equally important, being the derivative writer par excellence of the twentieth century, the study of the erotic shelves of his library gave us the opportunity to look at the relationship between his sexuality and his own writings and see how some of his readings worked as technical models and sources for his own texts and, ultimately, shaped his oeuvre. The exploration of Borges's erotic library allowed "to discover" authors such as Rossetti, Swinburne, Fernández Moreno, or Cheikh Nefzaoui, whose works had not being studied in relation to his literature, while it also opened another perspective to reevaluate his reading of works such as *The Book of the Thousand Nights and a Night* or Schopenhauer's *The World as Will and Representation*, which have been repeatedly considered in relation to his literature but whose erotic layers had escaped Borges's scholars before.

The writing of this book has also given me the opportunity to reflect on the ways and challenges of studying Borges. As an historian engaged in a literary inquiry I have taken the liberty of listening to creative writers, whose views on the production and explication of literature are, paradoxically, often absent from literary studies. Equipped with their critical reflections on how to read and explicate texts, I have explored relevant literary questions while employing a historical method that relies on evidence and, in the process, made the case again for the convergence of history and literature.

As I said in the introduction, this study has been possible only now because of the enormous amount of material by Borges or related to him that has been made available in the last 15 years and that was unknown or inaccessible to previous generations of scholars. However, and in spite of the new documents and information produced, major challenges remain: for example, while known manuscripts of short stories such as "Tlön, Uqbar, Orbis Tertius" or "Emma Zunz" allow to know the variants of sentences, wordings, and images that Borges tried, when it comes to literary influences and the light they could shed on questions such as the evolution of the form of the story and the overall intent of the author, these documents say little beyond what we can find in the published texts. Therefore, another necessary (and complementary) way to study some of these important questions is to become familiar with the range of literary sources that Borges fed on. That is, we will need to continue to rely in the old method of reading what the author read. Given the vastness of Borges's literary sources and the variety of genres, disciplines, languages, and cultural traditions that they comprise, this will always be a demanding task. In this respect, recent and path breaking studies of his marginalia have been a great contribution that support this research strategy; yet, even this type of studies cannot replace the reading of Borges's sources because his annotations highlight only part of his readings (Borges frequently makes references to books and passages that he did not annotate) and, more obvious and important, the student of Borges cannot make fully sense of the annotated passage unless she becomes familiar with the whole text and sometimes even with the oeuvre of the author read by Borges.

This is a method that has been tried countless times on Borges and many other authors and we may think we are past it. However, some of the evidence presented in this work, such as the facts that after more than half a century of Borges criticism his erotic shelves remained unread or that specialists have overlooked the ubiquity of the Stoic doctrine in his oeuvre, show that Borges's library is less known than we might think and that we need to continue to extensively probe his literary influences. Moreover, current institutional developments will make this approach unavoidable. In 2017 the International

Foundation Jorge Luis Borges announced that it was in the process of digitizing more than 2,000 books that belonged to Borges, while the National Library of Argentina acquired Adolfo Bioy Casares's and Silvina Ocampo's personal book collection comprised of 17,000 volumes, which Borges also used. While both events mean a great opportunity for specialists they also call for the necessity of knowing well this enormous corpus of readings. Thus, given the sheer number of books, their interdisciplinary complexity (poetry, mathematics, theology, philosophy, etc.), and the multiple languages in which they are written, the reading of what Borges read will be one of the "new" and major challenges that Borges scholars will confront in the future.

# Works Cited

Aguilar, Gonzalo. "¿Por qué Borges es nuestro único clásico universal?," *Clarín, Revista Ñ,* June 14, 2011.
Aguilar, Gonzalo and Emiliano Jelicié. *Borges va al cine.* Buenos Aires: Libraria, 2010.
Aizenberg, Edna. *Borges, el tejedor del Aleph y otros ensayos.* Madrid: Iberoamericana, 1997.
Almafuerte. *Obras completas.* Buenos Aires: Claridad, 2003.
Almeida, Iván. "De Borges a Schopenhauer," *Variaciones Borges* 17 (2004), 103–41.
Anderson Imbert, Enrique. "Encuesta de la revista Megáfono," in *Antiborges.* Ed. Martín Lafforgue. Buenos Aires: Vergara, 1999, 27–30.
Apollodorus. *The Library.* With an English translation by Sir James George Frazer. London: William Heinemann, 1921.
*Arabian Nights, The. Tales from a Thousand and One Nights.* Trans. and preface by Richard Burton, with an introduction by A. S. Byatt. New York: Modern Library, 2001.
Augustine, Saint. *City of God.* New York: Penguin, 2003.
Balderston, Daniel. "'Beatriz Viterbo c'est moi': Angular Vision in Estela Canto's *Borges a Contraluz*," *Variaciones Borges* 1 (1996), 133–39.
———. "Detalles circunstanciales: sobre dos borradores de 'El escritor argentino y la tradición'," *La Biblioteca* 13 (2013), 32–45.
———. "El pudor de la historia." *El deseo, enorme cicatriz luminosa: Ensayos sobre homosexualidades latinoamericanas.* Rosario: Beatriz Viterbo editora, 2004, 17–33.
———. *Innumerables relaciones: cómo leer con Borges.* Santa Fe: Universidad Nacional del Litoral, 2010.
———. "La dialéctica fecal: el pánico homosexual y el origen de la escritura en Borges." *Borges: realidades y simulacros.* Buenos Aires: Editorial Biblos, 2000, 59–76.
———. "Una lógica simbólica: manuscritos de Jorge Luis Borges en la Biblioteca Nacional." *Borges, el mismo, otro.* Buenos Aires: Biblioteca Nacional, 2016, 13–18.

Bate, Jonathan. "Libidinous laureate of satyrs," *Times Literary Supplement*, July 10, 2009, 14–15.
Baudelaire, Charles. *Correspondance*. Paris: Gallimard, 2000.
———. *Les fleurs du mal*. Notes Dominique Carlat. Paris: Gallimard, 2004.
———. *Écrits sur la littérature*. Paris: Le Livre de Poche, 2005.
Bergero, Adriana. *Intersecting Tango: Cultural Geographies of Buenos Aires, 1900–1930*. Pittsburgh: University of Pittsburgh Press, 2008.
Bernstein, Richard. *The East, The West, and Sex: A History of Erotic Encounters*. New York: Alfred Knopf, 2009.
Bioy Casares, Adolfo. *Borges*. Madrid: Destino, 2007.
Blasi, Alberto. "Guiraldes: vida y escritura," in Ricardo Guiraldes, *Don Segundo Sombra*. Ed. Paul Verdevoye. Paris: Colección Archivos, 1988, 237–70.
Boccanera, Jorge. *La pasión de los poetas: La historia detrás de los poemas de amor*. Buenos Aires: Alfaguara, 2002.
Borges, Jorge Guillermo. *El caudillo*. Buenos Aires: Academia Argentina de Letras, 1989.
———. *La senda*. Pittsburgh: Borges Center, 2016.
Borges, Jorge Luis. "An Autobiographical Essay," in *Critical Essays on Jorge Luis Borges*. Ed. Jaime Alazraki. Boston: Hall and Co., 1987, 21–55.
———. *Borges at Eighty: Conversations*. Ed. Willie Barnstone. Bloomington: Indiana University Press, 1982.
———. *Borges, el mismo, otro*. Buenos Aires: Biblioteca Nacional, 2016.
———. *Borges en El Hogar, 1935–1958*. Buenos Aires: Emecé, 2000.
———. *Borges, libros y lecturas*. Eds. Laura Rosato and Germán Alvarez. Buenos Aires: Biblioteca Nacional, 2010.
———. *Borges on Writing*. Eds. N. T. Di Giovanni, D. Halpern, and Frank MacShane. New York: Allen Lane, 1973.
———. *Borges para millones*. Ed. Fernando Godoy. Buenos Aires: Corregidor, 1978.
———. *Borges Profesor: Curso de literatura inglesa en la universidad de Buenos Aires*. Eds. Martín Arias and Martín Hadis. Buenos Aires: Emecé, 2000.
———. *Cartas del fervor: correspondencia con Maurice Abramowicz y Jacobo Sureda (1919–1928)*. Edited with prologue and notes by Joaquín Marco, Carlos García, and Cristóbal Pera. Barcelona: Emecé, 1999.
———. *Cuaderno San Martín*. Buenos Aires: Cuadernos del Plata, 1929.
———. *Deux Fictions: "Tlön, Uqbar, Orbis Tertius" et "El Sur."* Ed. Michel Lafon. Geneva: Fondation Martin Bodmer, 2010.
———. *Discusión*. Buenos Aires: Gleizer, 1932.
———. *Doctor Brodie's Report*. Trans. by N. T. Di Giovanni in collaboration with the author. New York: Dutton, 1972.
———. *El círculo secreto. Prólogos y notas*. Buenos Aires: Emecé, 2003.
———. *El matrero*. Buenos Aires: Barros Merino, 1972.
———. *El idioma de los argentinos*. Madrid: Alianza, 1999.
———. *El tamaño de mi esperanza*. Madrid: Alianza, 1995.
———. *El tango: cuatro conferencias*. Buenos Aires: Sudamericana, 2016.
———. "Emma Zunz," typescript of first draft. University of Texas (Austin), Harry Ransom Center, Jorge Luis Borges Collection, container 1.6, ms-0453.

———. *Fervor de Buenos Aires*. Buenos Aires: Imprenta Serantes, 1923. [Edición de autor, sin foliación.]
———. *Inquisiciones*. Madrid: Alianza, 1998.
———. *Introducción a la literatura norteamericana*. Buenos Aires: Editorial Columba, 1967.
———. *Jorge Luis Borges en Sur, 1931–1980*. Buenos Aires: Emecé, 1999.
———. *Jorge Luis Borges: Conversations*. Ed. Richard Burgin. Jackson: University Press of Mississippi, 1998.
———. "La secta del Fénix." Manuscript in private collection.
———. *Libro de sueños*. Buenos Aires: Random House Mondadori, 2013.
———. *Luna de enfrente*. Buenos Aires: Editorial Proa, 1925.
———. *Obras completas*. 4 vols. Buenos Aires and Barcelona: Emecé. 1974–96.
———. *Obras completas*. 3 vols. Critical edition annotated by Rolando Costa Picazo and Irma Zángara. Buenos Aires: Emecé, 2009–11.
———. *Obras completas en colaboración*. Buenos Aires: Emecé, 1979.
———. *Oeuvres Completes*. Ed. Jean-Pierre Bernes. Paris: Gallimard, 2010.
———. *Poemas [1922–1943]*. Buenos Aires: Losada, 1943.
———. *Selected Poems (1923–1967)*. Edited with an introduction and notes by Norman T. Di Giovanni. New York: Delacorte Press, 1972.
———. *Textos recosbrados (1919–1929)*. Barcelona: Emecé, 1997.
———. *Textos recobrados (1931–1955)*. Buenos Aires: Emecé, 2001.
———. *Textos recobrados (1956–1986)*. Buenos Aires: Emecé, 2003.
———. *This Craft of Verse*. Cambridge: Harvard University Press, 2000.
Borges, Jorge Luis and Silvina Bullrich (eds.). *El compadrito*. Buenos Aires: Emecé, 2000.
Borges, Jorge Luis, Silvina Ocampo, and Adolfo Bioy Casares. *Antología Poética Argentina*. Buenos Aires: Sudamericana, 1941.
Brodie, Fawn M. *The Devil Drives: A Life of Sir Richard Burton*. New York: Norton, 1967.
Burns, Robert. *Selected Letters of Robert Burns*. Edited and with an introduction by DeLancey Ferguson. Oxford: Oxford University Press, 1953.
Burton, Robert. *The Anatomy of Melancholy*. Introduction by William Gass. New York: New York Review of Books, 2001.
Byatt, A. S. *Passions of the Mind*. New York: Vintage, 1993.
Cajero Vázquez, Antonio. *Palimsestos del joven Borges: escrituras y reescrituras de Fervor de Buenos Aires (1923)*. San Luis Potosí: El Colegio de San Luis, 2013.
———. "Para la lectura de Fervor de Buenos Aires." *Fervor crítico por Borges*. Ed. Rafael Olea Franco. México: El Colegio de México, 2006, 13–34.
Cane Carrasco, James. "'Unity for the Defense of Culture': the AIAPE and the Cultural Politics of Argentine Antifascisme, 1935–1943," *Hispanic American Historical Review* 77:3 (1997), 443–82.
Canto, Estela. "Jorge Luis Borges: *El Aleph*," SUR, XXVII, 180, October 1949, 93–98.
———. *Borges a contraluz*. Madrid: Espasa-Calpe, 1989.
Carriego, Evaristo. *Obra completa de Evaristo Carriego*. Ed. Marcela Ciruzzi. Buenos Aires: Corregidor, 1999.

Carrizo, Antonio. *Borges, el memorioso: conversaciones de Jorge Luis Borges con Antonio Carrizo*. Buenos Aires: Fondo de Cultura Económica, 1982.
Cernuda, Luis. *Obra completa. Vol.2*. Eds. Derek Harris and Luis Maristany. Madrid: Ediciones Siruela, 2002.
Charbonnier, Georges. *Entretiens avec Jorge Luis Borges*. Paris: Gallimard, 1967.
Christ, Ronald. *The Narrow Act*. New York: New York University Press, 1968.
Cicerón. *Sobre la amistad. Sobre la vejez*. Intro., translation, and notes by Jorge Mainero. Buenos Aires: Losada, 2005.
Cortázar, Julio. *Clases de literatura: Berkeley, 1980*. Buenos Aires: Alfaguara, 2013.
Cortínez, Carlos and Gonzalo Sobejano, "Borges discusses Hispanic Literature," in *Borges, the Poet*. Ed. Carlos Cortínez. Fayeteville: The University of Arkansas Press, 1986, 33–63.
Darío, Rubén. *Los raros*. Buenos Aires: Espasa-Calpe, 1952.
———. *Poesía*. Caracas: Biblioteca Ayacucho, 1985.
De la Fuente, Ariel. "Lecturas eróticas de Borges," *Jornadas Internacionales Borges lector en la Biblioteca Nacional: Conferencias Plenarias, Buenos Aires, 24, 25 y 26 de agosto de 2011*. Buenos Aires: Ediciones Biblioteca Nacional, 2013, 25–32.
———. "Desire and Sex in Borges's Poetry on the Arrabal," *Variaciones Borges* 35 (2013), 217–39.
———. "Conjectures on Some Literary Sources of Jorge Luis Borges' 'Poema Conjetural,'" *Bulletin of Spanish Studies*, vol.XCI, 3, 2014, 399–417.
Del Mazo, Marcelo. *Los vencidos, segunda serie (El amor en la calle)*. Buenos Aires: Editorial Argentina, 1910.
Delvau, Alfred. *Dictionnaire Érotique Moderne* (2 vols.). Paris: La Bourdonnaye, 2014.
Des Cars, Laurence. *The Pre-Raphaelites: Romance and Realism*. London: Thames and Hudson, 2000.
*Destiempo*. Buenos Aires, 1936–37 (3 issues).
Di Giovanni, Norman Thomas. *Georgie and Elsa: Jorge Luis Borges and His Wife: The Untold Story*. London: The Friday Project, 2014.
Dobry, Edgardo. *Una profecía del pasado: Lugones y la invención del 'linaje de Hércules.'* Buenos Aires: Fondo de Cultura Económica, 2010.
Doll, Ramón. "Discusiones con Borges," in *Antiborges*. Ed. Martín Lafforgue. Buenos Aires: Vergara, 1999, 31–41.
Donne, John. *The Complete English Poems*. Ed. A. J. Smith. New York: Penguin, 1971.
Dreyfus, Laurence. *Wagner and the Erotic Impulse*. Cambridge: Harvard University Press, 2010.
Echeverría, Esteban. *La cautiva/ El matadero*. Ed. Sandra Gasparini. Buenos Aires: Ediciones Colihue, 2004.
Eliacheff, Caroline. "Inceste maternel: l'amour en plus," *Liberation*, July 26, 2004.
Eliacheff, Caroline and Natalie Heinich. *Mères-filles: une relation a trois*. Paris: Albin Michel, 2002.
———. "Étendre la notion d'inceste: exclusion du tiers et binarisation du ternaire," *A Contrario* 2005/1 (vol.3), 5–13.

Eliot, T. S. *Selected Essays, 1917–1932*. New York: Harcourt, 1932.
———. "The Three Voices of Poetry." *On Poetry and Poets*. New York: Farrar, Straus, and Giroux, 2009, 96–112.
Ferrer, Christian. *Barón Biza: el inmoralista*. Edición definitiva. Buenos Aires: Sudamericana, 2016.
Fernández Moreno, Baldomero. *Antología Poética, 1915–1940*. Buenos Aires: Espasa-Calpe, 1941.
———. *Elegía de la alondra: poemas inéditos*. Selected and prefaced by Mario Benedetti. Buenos Aires: Seix Barral, 1998.
———. *Las iniciales del misal*. Buenos Aires: José Tragant, 1915.
Fine, Ruth. "Villa Urquiza o la impronta de un silencio en la poesía de Borges." *Borges poeta*. Ed. Alfonso de Toro. Hildesheim: Georg Olms Verlag, 2010, 209–20.
Fishburn, Evelyn. "Traces of the Thousand and One Nights in Borges," *Variaciones Borges* 17 (2004), 143–58.
Fitzgerald, Donna. "Borges, Woman, and Postcolonial History," *Romance Studies* 24:3 (2006), 227–39.
FitzGerald, Edward. *The Rubáiyát of Omar Khayyám*. Ed. Christopher Decker. Charlottesville: University Press of Virginia, 1997.
Flaubert, Gustave. *Correspondance*. Paris: Gallimard, 1998.
Fuller, John. *Who is Ozymandias? and other Puzzles in Poetry*. London: Chatto and Windus, 2011.
Gamerro, Carlos. "Borges lector," in *Borges lector*. Buenos Aires: Biblioteca Nacional, 2010, 12–17.
———. "Borges y los anglosajones," *Variaciones Borges* 28 (2009), 27–41.
García, Carlos. *El jóven Borges, poeta (1919–1930)*. Buenos Aires: Corregidor, 2000.
———. "Borges y Hélene von Stummer. Un temprano amor desconocido o la traducción que quizás no fue (I and II)," *El trujamán* (Centro Virtual Cervantes), April 14 and April 25, 2005.
Gibson, Ian. *The Erotomaniac: The Secret Life of Henry Spencer Ashbee*. London: Faber and Faber, 2001.
Ginzburg, Carlo. "Clues: Roots of an Evidential Paradigm," in *Clues, Myths, and the Historical Method*. Baltimore: John Hopkins University Press, 1989, 96–125.
Goldar, Ernesto. *La "mala vida."* Buenos Aires: Centro Editor de América Latina, 1971.
Goldaracena, Rita. "Las inhibiciones del joven Borges: El psicoanalista Kohan Miller habla del autor de 'Ficciones' como paciente, sus conflictos personales y amorosos." *El País*. Madrid, 23 de diciembre, 1990.
Goujon, Jean-Paul. *Anthologie de la poesie erotique francaise*. Paris: Fayard, 2004.
Gracia, Jorge. *Painting Borges: Philosophy Interpreting Art Interpreting Literature*. Albany: SUNY Press, 2012.
Grafton, Anthony. *The Footnote: A Curious History*. Cambridge: Harvard University Press, 1997.
Greco, Martín. "El crisol del fascismo. Alberto Hidalgo en la década del 30," in *Alberto Hidalgo, el genio del desprecio: materiales para su estudio*. Ed. Alvaro Sarco. Lima: Talleres tipográficos, 2006, 335–81.

Guerriero, Leila. *Plano Americano*. Santiago: Ediciones Universidad Diego Portales, 2013.
Hall, J. B. "The David and Jonathan of the *orillas*; or, how did she die and could they forget her in Morón? Some Thoughts on Borges's 'La intrusa,'" *Journal of Iberian and Latin American Studies* 13:1 (2007), 11–23.
Harding, James E. *The Love of David and Jonathan: Ideology, Text, Reception*. Durham: Taylor and Francis.
Heinich, Nathalie. "L'inceste du deuxième type et les avatars du symbolique." *Critique* 583 (1995), 940–51.
Helft, Nicolás. *Borges, postales de una biografía*. Buenos Aires: Emecé: 2013.
Hidalgo, Alberto. *Diario de mi sentimiento (1922–1936)*. Buenos Aires: Edición privada, 1937.
Holmes, John. *Dante Gabriel Rossetti and the Late Victorian Sonnet Sequence: Sexuality, Belief, and the Self*. Aldershot: Ashgate, 2005.
Hyam, Ronald. *Empire and Sexuality: the British Experience*. Manchester: Manchester University Press, 1991.
Irwin, Robert. *The Arabian Nights: A Companion*. London: Tauris Parke, 2008.
Iverach, Lisa and Ronald Rapee. "Social Anxiety Disorder and Stuttering: Current Status and Future Directions," *Journal of Fluency Disorders* 40 (2014), 69–82.
Iverach, Lisa, Ross Menzies, Sue O'Brian, Ann Packman, and Mark Onslow. "Anxiety and Stuttering: Continuing to Explore a Complex Relationship," *American Journal of Speech-Language Pathology* 20 (2011), 221–32.
James, Henry. *The Aspern Papers and Other Stories*. Oxford: Oxford World's Classics, 1983.
———. *Selected Tales*. New York: Penguin Classics, 2001.
Keats, John. *The Major Works*. Oxford: Oxford University Press, 1990.
Kennedy, Philip. "Borges and the Missing Pages of the *Nights*," in *Scherezade's Children: Global Encounters with the Arabian Nights*. Eds. Philip Kennedy and Marina Warner. New York: NYU Press, 195–217.
Kilito, Abdelfattah. *L'œil et l'aiguille: essai sur les mille et une nuits*. Paris: Éditions La découverte, 1992.
———. *Dites-moi le songe*. Actes Sud, 2010.
*King James Bible, with Apocrypha*. Intro. and notes by R. Carroll and S. Prickett. Oxford: Oxford University Press, 2008.
Kipling, Rudyard. *Something of Myself*. Cambridge: Cambridge University Press, 1991.
Lanza, Silverio. *Páginas escogidas e inéditas. In memorian y epílogo por Ramón Gómez de la Serna*. Madrid: Biblioteca Nueva, 1918.
Latino, Simón. *Antología de la poesia sexual: de Rubén Darío a hoy*. Buenos Aires: CS Ediciones, 2006 [1959].
Lefere, Robin. "Fervor de Buenos Aires en contextos," *Variaciones Borges* 19 (2005), 209–26.
Lehman, David (ed.). *The Best American Erotic Poems from 1800 to the Present*. New York: Scribner, 2008.
Lehmann-Nitsche, Robert (Víctor Borde). *Textos eróticos del Río de la Plata*.

Trans. Juan Alfredo Tomasini, intro. Julián Cáceres Freire, and notes by Enríque Del Valle. Buenos Aires: Librería Clásica, 1981.

Leone, Leah, "La novela cautiva: Borges y la traducción de *Orlando*," *Variaciones Borges* 25 (2008), 223–36.

———. "An Inventory of Masculinities: Borges in Denevi's Enciclopedia secreta de una familia argentina," *Variaciones Borges* 39 (2015), 159–80.

*Les Mille et Une Nuits*, 3 vols. Traduction d'Antoine Galland. Paris: Flammarion, 2004.

Levine, Suzanne Jill. "Borges on Translation," *The Cambridge Companion to Jorge Luis Borges*. Ed. Edwin Williamson. Cambridge: Cambridge University Press, 2013, 43–55.

Linares, Gabriel. *Un juego de espejos que se desplazan: Jorge Luis Borges y el monólogo dramático*. Mexico City: El Colegio de México, 2011.

Lucretius. *The Nature of Things*. Trans. by A.E. Stallings. New York: Penguin, 2007.

Ludmer, Josefina. *El cuerpo del delito: un manual*. Buenos Aires: Perfil Libros, 1999.

Lugones, Leopoldo. *Antología poética*. Prologue and selection by Jorge Luis Borges. Madrid: Alianza, 1982.

———. *Obras poéticas completas*. Intro. Pedro Miguel Obligado. Madrid: Aguilar, 1959.

Maison de Victor Hugo. *Éros Hugo: Entre pudeur et excès*. Paris: Maison de Victor Hugo, 2015.

Malla, Kalyana. *Ananga Ranga. The Hindu Art of Love*. Trans. and annotated by F. F. Arbuthnot and Richard F. Burton. New York: Medical Press of New York, 1964.

Mallarmé, Stéphane. *Poésies*. Ed. and introduction by Bertrand Marchal. Yves Bonnefoy. Paris: Gallimard, 1992.

Marcus Aurelius. *Meditations*. Oxford: Oxford University Press, 2011.

Marechal, Leopoldo. *Adán Buenosayres*. Buenos Aires: Editorial Sudamericana, [1948] 1970.

Martínez, Guillermo. *Borges y la matemática*. Buenos Aires: Seix Barral, 2007.

Martínez Estrada, Ezequiel. *Muerte y transfiguración de Martín Fierro: ensayo de interpretación de la vida argentina*. Rosario: Beatriz Viterbo, 2005.

Mastronardi, Carlos. *Borges*. Buenos Aires: Academia Argentina de Letras, 2007.

Matamoros, Blas. "Yo y el otro: Eros y Tánatos, masculino y femenino," *Variaciones Borges* 9 (2000), 221–26.

McLaren, Angus. *Impotence: A Cultural History*. Chicago: University of Chicago Press, 2007.

Melo, Adrián. *Historia de la literatura gay en Argentina: representaciones sociales de la homosexualidad masculina en la ficción literaria*. Buenos Aires: Lea ediciones, 2011.

Miceli, Marcelo. *Sexo y letras: erotismo y lujuria en la literatura argentina*. Buenos Aires: Ediciones pausa, 2007.

Milton, John. *Paradise Lost*. Ed. Gordon Teskey. New York: Norton Critical Editions, 2005.

Mitford, A. B. *Tales of Old Japan*. Vermont: Charles Tuttle, 1966.

Montaigne, Michel de. *Les Essais*. Paris: Gallimard, 2002.
Monteleone, Jorge. "La invención de la ciudad: Evaristo Carriego y Baldomero Fernández Moreno." *La crisis de las formas*. Ed. Alfredo Rubione. Buenos Aires: Emecé, 2006, 205–35.
———. *200 años de poesía argentina*. Selección y prólogo de Jorge Monteleone. Buenos Aires: Alfaguara, 2010.
Muldoon, Paul. *The End of the Poem: Oxford Lectures*. New York: Farrar, Straus, and Giroux, 2006.
Nabokov, Vladimir. *Lectures on Literature*. Introduction by John Updike. New York: Harcourt, 1982.
Naouri, Aldo. "Un incest sans passage à l'acte: la relation mère-enfant." In *De l'inceste*. Eds. Françoise Héritier, Boris Cyrulnik, Aldo Naouri, Dominique Vrignaud, and Margarita Xanthakou. Paris: Odile Jacob, 1994, 71–128.
Nefzaoui, Cheikh. *The Perfumed Garden of the Cheikh Nefzaoui: A Manual of Arabian Erotology*. Trans. by Sir Richard Burton with an Introduction by Mary S. Lovell. New York: Signet Classics, 1999.
Núñez-Faraco, Humberto. "The Theme of Lovesickness in 'El Zahir,'" *Variaciones Borges* 14 (2002), 115–55.
Olea Franco, Rafael. "La verdadera primera poesía de Borges." *Borges poeta*. Ed. Alfonso de Toro. Hildesheim: Georg Olms Verlag, 2010, 37–53.
Ortega, Julio and Del Río Parra, Elena, eds. *'El Aleph' de Jorge Luis Borges. Edición crítica y facsimilar*. México: El Colegio de México, 2001.
*Oxford Classical Dictionary*, second edition. Eds. N. Hammond and H. Scullard. Oxford: Oxford University Press, 1979.
Pauls, Alan. *El factor Borges*. Barcelona: Anagrama. 2004.
Pauvert, Jean-Jacques. *Anthologie historique des lectures érotiques*, 5 vols. Paris: Stock, 1995–2001.
Pérez Marcilla, Francisco. "El canto de Borges o el propósito canónico de su traducción de 'Song of Myself,'" *Variaciones Borges* 41 (2016), 79–92.
Poe, Edgar Allan. *Poetry, Tales, and Selected Essays*. Eds. P. Quinn and G. R. Thompson. New York: Library of America, College Edition, 1996.
Portogalo, José. *Los pájaros ciegos y otros poemas*. Buenos Aires: Centro Editor de América Latina, 1968.
———. *Tumulto*. Buenos Aires: Ediciones Imán, 1935.
Pound, Ezra. *Literary Essays of Ezra Pound*. New York: New Directions, 1968.
Prose, Francine. *Reading Like a Writer*. New York: Harper Collins, 2006.
Provencio, Pedro (ed.). *Antología de la poesía erótica española e hispanoamericana*. Mexico: Edaf, 2003.
Pyñeiro, Juan Carlos. *Ficcionalidad e ideología en trece relatos de Jorge Luis Borges*. Stockholms: Universitet Stockholms, 2000.
*Revista Multicolor de los Sábados (1933-1934)*. Edición completa en CD-ROM, a cargo de Nicolás Helft. Buenos Aires: Fondo nacional de las Artes, 1999.
Rice, Edward. *Captain Sir Richard Francis Burton*. New York: Scribner's, 1990.
Richardson, Joanna. *Verlaine: A Biography*. New York: Viking, 1971.
Rodríguez Monegal, Emir. *Jorge Luis Borges, a Literary Biography*. New York: Dutton, 1979.
Roger, Sarah. "Apuntes sobre Jorge Guillermo Borges," in Jorge Guillermo

Borges. *La senda*. Introduction and notes by Daniel Balderston and Sarah Roger. Pittsburgh: Borges Center, University of Pittsburgh, 2016, 89–107.
Rossetti, Dante Gabriel. *Collected Poetry and Prose*. Ed. Jerome McGann. New Haven: Yale University Press, 2003.
———. *The Poetical Works of Dante Gabriel Rossetti*. Intro. by William M. Rossetti. New York: Thomas Crowell, 1890.
Russell, Bertrand. *The History of Western Philosophy*. New York: Simon and Schuster, 1972.
Sarlo, Beatriz. *Borges, un escritor en la orillas*. Buenos Aires: Ariel, 1995.
———. *La pasión y la excepción*. Buenos Aires: Siglo XXI, 2003.
———. "Orillero y ultraísta." *Escritos sobre literatura Argentina*. Buenos Aires: Siglo XXI, 2007, 149–59.
Sarmiento, Domingo F. *Facundo*. Ed. Noé Jitrik. Caracas: Biblioteca Ayacucho, 1977.
Schifino, Martin. "Slow Nightfall," *Times Literary Supplement*, January 21, 2011: 3–5.
Schopenhauer, Arthur. *The World as Will and Representation* (2 vols.). Trans. E. F. J. Payne. New York: Dover, 1969.
Seneca. *Dialogues and Essays*. Oxford: Oxford University Press, 2008.
———. *Letters on Ethics*. Trans. with an introduction and commentary by M. Graver and A. Long. Chicago: University of Chicago Press, 2015.
———. *Moral Essays* (vol.3, De Beneficiis). Cambridge: Loeb Classical Library, 1935.
———. *Selected Letters*. Oxford: Oxford University Press, 2010.
Sorrentino, Fernando. "Travesuras Borgeanas." *La Nación*, Buenos Aires, May 23, 1999, sección cultura, 4.
———. *Siete conversaciones con Borges*. Buenos Aires: Losada, 2007.
Stavans, Ilan and Jorge Gracia. *Thirteen Ways of Looking at Latino Art*. Durham: Duke University Press, 2014.
Stevenson, Robert Louis. *Selected Letters*. New Haven: Yale University Press, 2001.
Swinburne, Algernon Charles. *Poems and Ballads and Atalanta in Calydon*. London: Penguin Classics, 2000.
———. *Selected Poems*. Ed. L. M. Findlay. New York: Routledge, 2002.
Thalasso, Adolphe (ed.). *Anthologie de l'Amour Asiatique*. Paris: Mercure, 1907.
*The Book of the Thousand Nights and a Night*. 17 vols. Trans. and annotated by Richard F. Burton. Printed by the Burton Club for private subscribers only.
*The New Oxford Annotated Bible with the Apocrypha*. The New Revised Standard Version (third edition). Ed. Michael Coogan. Oxford: Oxford University Press, 2001.
Ugalde, Sergio. "Mito e historia. La poetización de Buenos Aires." *Fervor crítico por Borges*. Ed. Rafael Olea Franco. México: El Colegio de México, 2006, 35–52.
Vaccaro, Alejandro. *Borges: vida y literatura*. Buenos Aires: Edhasa, 2006.
Valéry, Paul. *Varieté* (I–V). Paris: Galllimard, 1924–1944.
Vatsyayana. *Kamasutra*. Trans. by Wendy Doniger and Sudhir Kakar. Oxford: Oxford University Press, 2002.

———. *The Kama Sutra of Vatsyayana*. Trans. by Sir Richard Burton and F. F. Arbuthnot. New York: Berkeley Books, 1966.
Vázquez, María Esther. *Borges, esplendor y derrota*. Barcelona: Tusquets, 1999.
Vendler, Helen. *Wallace Stevens: Words Chosen Out of Desire*. Cambridge: Harvard Universsity Press, 1984.
Verlaine, Paul. *Oeuvres Poétiques Completes*. Eds. Jacques Borel and Y. G. Le Dantec. Paris: Gallimard, 1962.
Vezzetti, Hugo. *Aventuras de Freud en el país de los Argentinos*. Buenos Aires: Paidós, 1996.
Vilariño, Idea. *Poesía completa*. Barcelona: Lumen, 2016.
Villena, Miguel Ángel. "'Borges tenía un matrimonio con su madre' afirma el biógrafo Vaccaro," *El País*, Madrid, March 27, 1997.
Virgil. *The Aeneid*. Trans. by R. Fagles and with an introduction by Bernard Knox. New York: Penguin, 2006.
Voltaire. *Correspondance choisie*. Paris: Livre de Poche, 1997.
Waisman, Sergio. *Borges and Translation*. Lewisburg: Bucknell University Press, 2005.
Wells, Stanley. *Shakespeare, Sex, and Love*. Oxford: Oxford University Press, 2010.
Wilde, Oscar. *Complete Works of Oscar Wilde*. London: Collins, 1966.
Williams, Gordon. *Shakespeare's Sexual Language: a Glossary*. New York: Continuum, 2006.
Williamson, Edwin. *Borges, a Life*. New York: Viking, 2004.
——— (ed.) *The Cambridge Companion to Jorge Luis Borges*. Cambridge: Cambridge University Press, 2013.
Willson, Patricia. *La constelación del Sur: traductores y traducciones en la literatura argentina del siglo XX*. Buenos Aires: Siglo XXI, 2004.
Wilson, Jason. "Borges and Buenos Aires (and Brothels)," *Donaire* 13 (December 1999), 47–54.
———. *Jorge Luis Borges*. London: Reaktion Books, 2006.
Woscoboinik, Julio. *El secreto de Borges: indagación psicoanalítica de su obra*. Buenos Aires: Editorial Trieb, 1988.
———. *El secreto de Borges: indagación psicoanalítica de su obra*. Segunda edición, corregida y aumentada. Buenos Aires: Grupo Editor Latinoamericano, 1991.
Wright, Thomas. *The Life of Sir Richard Burton*. 2 vols. New York: Burt Franklin, 1968.
Wyndham, Diana. "Versemaking and Lovemaking—W.B. Yeats' 'Strange Second Puberty': Norman Hare and the Steinach Rejuvenation Second Operation," *Journal of History of the Behavioral Sciences* 39:1 (2003), 25–50.
Yates, Donald. "Behind Borges and I," *Modern Fiction Studies* 19:3 (1973), 317–24.
Yeats, William Butler. *The Collected Works of W.B. Yeats*, vol. 1 (The Poems). Ed. Richard Finneran. New York: Scribner, 1997.
Young, Julian. *Schopenhauer*. London: Routledge, 2006.
Zambrano, María. *Pensamiento y poesía en la vida española*. Madrid: Endymion, 1996.

# Index

Aguilar, Gonzalo 6
Aguilar, Gonzalo and Emiliano Jelicié 173
Agustini, Delmira
  *Los cálices vacíos* 51
Aisenberg, Edna 174
Almafuerte 1, 2, 36, 59, 141, 143–44, 147, 164, 186, 206
  "El abismo" 143
  "El misionero" 186
Anderson Imbert, Enrique 25, 26
anormalidad 34
*Arabian Nights* 42, 53
  see also *The Book of the Thousand Nights and a Night*
*Arrabal* 129
Ashbee, H. S. 73
Astete Millán, Elsa 22, 29, 196

Balderston, Daniel 5, 12, 34, 52, 188, 200
Banchs, Enrique 148
  *La urna* 148
Barón Biza, Raúl 16
  *El derecho de matar* 16
Baudelaire, Charles 13, 64, 74, 142
  "La fin de la journée" 142
  "Les promesses d'une visage" 63
Bianco, José 203
Bioy Casares, Adolfo 4, 22, 32, 34, 54, 55, 56, 58, 60, 61, 63, 65, 105, 150, 158, 177, 189, 197, 201, 208
  *Borges* 6

Boccanera, Jorge 9, 10
Boileau, Nicolas 36, 141, 143
*Book of the Thousand Nights and a Night* 43, 45
Borges Center (University of Pittsburgh) 6
Borges, Jorge Luis
  autobiography in literature 35–36, 37–38
  bisexuality 33
  casual sex 28–29
  criticism as investigation 9
  desire 5, 27, 134, 138–39, 142, 164–70
  erotic poetry 41
  Father (Jorge Guillermo Borges) 22, 23, 24, 29, 30, 32, 58, 59, 60, 73, 85, 160, 170–71
    *El caudillo* 170–71
  Grandmother 159, 160–61
  homophobia 34, 100–3
  homosexuality 32, 33, 34, 100–3, 197–205
    see also sodomía; pederastia; perversión; anormalidad
  homosexual panic 34, 103
  incest 69–70, 106–8
  incest of a second type 30, 191–91
  lectures 7
  Mother (Leonor Acevedo de Borges) 29, 30–32, 153, 162, 174, 177
  orgasm 55, 72, 76

platonic incest 31–32
sex act 39–40, 45
sexual impotence 1, 2, 19, 22–24,
    32, 36, 104–5, 143–44
  critical reception of his work
    25–27
  homosexuality 32
  stigmatization 24–25, 26, 27
  writing 27
sexual initiation 22–24
sexually transmitted diseases 28
stuttering 19–22, 24
  social anxiety disorder 19–22, 24
suicidal thoughts 21
suicide (attempt) 159
time 116, 118, 120
venal sex 28–29, 136–37, 139–40
women (asymmetrical
  relationships) 31–32, 79–80,
  170–72
women (objectification of) 194–96
Works
    "Arrabal en que pesa el campo"
      39, 127, 137–40, 195
    Biblioteca Personal 53
    "Casa Elena" 39, 43, 195
    Cercanías 95
    "Cuando la ficción vive en la
      ficción" 105
    Discusión 44
    "Edgar Alan Poe" 1–3
    El Aleph 175, 179
    "El amenazado" 34, 39, 42–43,
      70, 75, 99, 119, 122–23
    "El congreso" 55, 70, 71, 72,
      76, 145
    "El escritor argentino y la
      tradición" 148
    "El evangelio según Marcos"
      194
    "El guardián de los libros"
      37–38
    "El incesto" 70, 106–7, 168
    "El incivil maestro de
      ceremonias Kotsuké No
      Suké" 157, 174, 175, 179–81,
      183, 184

"El indigno" 26, 33
El libro de arena 163
"El mapa secreto" 140–41
"El otro" 48
"El otro duelo" 121
"El Paseo de Julio" 39, 129–31,
    139
"El tamaño de mi esperanza"
    134
El tango (book) 149
"El tango" (poem) 190
"El Zahir" 105
"Elogio de la sombra" 141
"Emma Zunz" 5, 66, 69, 130,
    145, chapter 8, 207
"Endimión en Latmos" 5, 23,
    39, 55, 72, 75–80, 168
Evaristo Carriego 44
Fervor de Buenos Aires 132, 135,
    141
"Himno al mar" 76
"Historia de la eternidad" 109,
    115–19, 124–28
Historia de la noche 75, 78
Historia universal de la infamia
    180
"Hombre de la esquina rosada"
    155, 171
"Insomnio" 167
"Jacinto Chiclana" 196
"Juan Muraña" 145
Judería 73
"Junio, 1968" 35–38
"La casa de Asterión" 77
"La doctrina de los ciclos" 165
"La espera" (poem) 39, 119,
    122, 123
"La espera" (short story) 121–22
"La génesis de 'El Cuervo' de
    Poe" 8
"La intrusa" 5, 30, 34, 39, 60,
    145, chapter 9
"La lírica argentina
    contemporánea" 59
"La noche cíclica" 165–70
"La noche de los dones" 39, 55,
    72, 76, 162, 163, 170, 195, 196

"La secta del Fénix" 5, 26–27, 39, 43, 70, 109–15, 135, 168
"La señora mayor" 70
"La viuda Ching, pirata" 155
"Las calles" 135
*Libro de sueños* 107
"Los traductores de las 1001 Noches" 86–87, 89–93, 94, 98, 100
"Milonga de dos hermanos" 190
"Milonga del forastero" 196
"Nuestras imposibilidades" 34, 99–103
"Otro poema de los dones" 150, 162
*Para las seis cuerdas* 151
"Paréntesis pasional" 39, 195
"Pedro Salvadores" 5, 145, 155–57, 174, 175, 184
"Pierre Menard, autor del Quijote" 8
"Poema conjetural" 53, 72
*Poemas [1922–1943]* 165
"Profesión de fe literaria" 38, 41–42, 79
"Sábados" 132, 136
"Séneca en las orillas" 149, 164
"Sí a la censura" 204
"Sobre Oscar Wilde" 52
"Talismanes" 99, 123–24
"Tlön, Uqbar, Orbis Tertius" 45, 207
"Tres versiones de Judas" 186
"Ulrica" 39, 43, 80, 145, 163, 170, 194, 196
"'ultimo sol en Villa Ortúzar" 137, 138
"Un destino" 155, 165
"Un escolio" 77–78
"Un lector" 12
"Variación" 160
"Veinticinco de agosto, 1983" 159
"Versos de catorce" 137, 142
"Villa Urquiza" (Revista *Alfar*) 39, 57, 95, 131–37, 138, 195
"Villa Urquiza" (*Fervor de Buenos Aires*) 132, 135, 136

Co-edited with Bioy Casares and Silvina Ocampo
*Antología poética argentina* 60
Co-edited with Bioy Casares
*Destiempo* 61
H. Bustos Domeq (co-authored with Bioy Casares)
*Crónicas de H. Bustos Domeq* 202
"El signo" 89, 96
Trans. "Historia de los dos que soñaron" 92
Borges, Norah 30, 154, 155, 156, 161, 162, 170
Browning, Robert 53
Bullrich, Silvina 29, 164, 170
*La redoma del primer ángel* 164, 170
Burns, Robert 8, 10
Burton, Francis Richard 43–44, 73, chapter 4, 119
*The Book of the Thousand Nights and a Night* 85, 86–103, 109, 124–26, 127, 207
"Terminal Essay" 99–103
Burton, Robert
*The Anatomy of Melancholy* 166–67

Cain and Abel 189–91
Canto, Estela 1, 4, 21, 22, 27, 29, 31, 33, 34, 42, 48, 49, 52, 67, 69, 80, 81, 83, 130–31, 171, 175, 188, 189, 192, 193, 194, 195, 197, 198, 200, 203
Carlyle, Thomas 1, 2, 36, 143
Carriego, Evaristo 44, 58, 59, 143
"La queja" 137
Carroll, Lewis
*Alice in Wonderland* 46
Castrato 96
censorship 14–16
self-censorship 14–15
Cernuda, Luis 73, 74
Christ, Ronald 112, 114, 115
Christensen, Carlos Hugo 188, 203–5

Cicero
  *On Friendship* 147
Coleridge, Samuel 46
condoms 95
Confucius 181
Conselheiro, Antonio 185–86
Cortázar, Julio 14
  *Rayuela* 14
courage 146, 150, 152–57, 171, 175, 177, 184
cyclical time 165–67

Dante 53, 64
  *Divina Comedia* 43
Darío, Rubén 51, 64
  "Propósito primaveral" 72
David and Jonathan 187–88, 191, 198–203
death 157–60
de León, Fray Luis 64, 150
del Campo, Estanislao
  *Fausto* 148
Del Mazo 53, 58–60
  "Incontaminado" 59, 191
  *Los vencidos* 58, 107, 191
Delvau, Alfred
  *Dictionnaire erótique moderne* 95
De Quincey, Thomas 46
desire 5, 27
destiny 146, 177, 195–96
*Dias de odio* (movie) 178
Dickinson, Emily 46, 51
Di Giovanni, Norman T. 22
Doll, Ramón 25, 26
Donne, John
  "The Ecstasy" 17
  "Love's Progress" 63

Echeverría, Esteban
  "El matadero" 147, 153
  "La cautiva" 153, 154, 158–59
Eliot, T. S. 10
  *The Waste Land* 40
Epictetus 147, 153, 164

female sexual preferences 91, 98
Fernández, Macedonio 58, 59

Fernández de Andrada, Andrés 150
Fernández Moreno, Baldomero 42, 53, 60–64, 206
  *Antología, 1915–1940* 61
  *Elegía de la alondra* 61
  *Las iniciales del misal* 62
  *Libro de Sara* 61
  "Roja inicial" 62–64, 117, 134
  "Soneto de los amantes" 61
Fitzgerald, Donna 188
FitzGerald, Edward
  *The Rubáiyát of Omar Khayyám* 130
Flaubert, Gustave 8, 84
Freud, Sigmund 110, 114
Fuller, John 8, 9

Galland, Antoine
  *Les mille et une nuits* 89–92
Gamerro, Carlos 53–54, 181
Gibbon, Edward 46, 52
Gide, André 46
gifts ("dones") 160–62
Ginzburg, Carlo 13, 107
Girondo, Oliverio
  "Milonga" 144
Goujon, Jean Paul 40
Gracia, Jorge 10, 137
Guerrero, Concepción 131, 135, 136, 164
Guerrero, Margot 29
Güiraldes, Ricardo 20, 159–60

Harding, James 199
Hernández, José 147
  *El gaucho Martín Fierro* 150, 164, 186, 191, 202
Hernández, Juan José 203
Hidalgo, Alberto 20, 24, 25
  and anti-Semitism 25
homosexuality 5
Hudson, William H. 151
Hugo, Victor 64

Ibarra, Néstor 55
incest 5, 106–8
incest of the second type 59
Ingenieros, Cecilia 29, 175, 184

James, Henry 8
  "The Aspern Papers" 13
Jesus Christ 158
Johnson, Samuel 52
Judith 175–78, 184
Jurado, Alicia 29
justice 174, 178, 179–85

Kant, Immanuel 36
Keats, John 76, 77, 199
  "Endymion" 76, 77
Kilito, Abdelfattah 11
kissing techniques 97
Kodama, María 29
Kohan Miller, Miguel 1, 19, 20, 21, 22, 24, 27, 36, 48
Kropotkin 143

Lafon, Michel 12
Lange, Haydée 131
Lange, Norah 29, 131
langue verte 97
Lawrence, D. H.
  *Lady Chatterley's Lover* 41
Lawrence, T. E. 147
Lehmann-Nitsche, Robert
  *Textos eróticos del Río de la Plata* 102
Louys, Pierre 40
Lucano 150
Lucretius
  *The Nature of Things* 118
Ludmer, Josefina 173
Lugones, Leopoldo 50, 54–58, 60, 72, 94, 119, 134
  "Alma venturosa" 57–58
  "Delectación morosa" 54–55, 58, 72, 95
  *Libro de los paisajes* 60
  *Los crepúsculos del jardín* 54
  "Los doce gozos" 54, 57
  *Lunario sentimental* 54, 134
  "Oceánida" 56

Machen, Arthur 45
male sexual impotence 7, 32, 104–5
male sexual potency 91

Malla, Kalyana
  *Ananga Ranga: The Hindu Art of Love* 88, 93, 99
Mallarmé, Stéphane 64, 139
Manrique, Jorge 150, 151
Marcus Aurelius 149, 152, 160
  *Meditations* 160
Martínez Estrada, Ezequiel 60
  *Muerte y transfiguración de Martín Fierro* 202
Martinto, Domingo
  "Divagando" 133
Mastronardi, Carlos 128, 151, 160, 164, 201
Melo, Adrian 188, 200
Melville, Herman 46
Mitford, A. B. 181
  *Tales of Old Japan* 180
Montaigne, Michel de 49, 109, 119–24, 146, 147, 149, 154, 155, 156, 157, 158, 159, 171, 176, 177, 184
  *Les essais* 119–24, 147, 152
Moore, George 36
Moreira, Juan 44
Muldoon, Paul 11, 12, 126

Nabokov, Vladimir 7, 8, 9
Nefzaoui, Sheikh 53, 206
  *The Perfumed Garden* 85, 103–8
Nietzsche, Friedrich 110, 114, 166

Ocampo, Silvina 60, 63, 208
Ocampo, Victoria 148, 155, 161, 162, 165, 170
Olea Franco, Rafael 129
Olivari, Nicolás 144
Ovid 126

Paredes, Nicolás 161
pederastia/pederasty 34, 99, 202
perversión 34, 36
Petit de Murat, Ulyses 205
Peyrou, Manuel 28
Pezzoni, Enrique 203
Plato 125, 126

Poe, Edgar Alan 1, 36, 46–47, 206
  Auguste Dupin 9
  "The Murders in the Rue
    Morgue" 9, 38
  "The Philosophy of Composition" 8
Portogalo, José 139, 140
  *Tumulto* 139
Pound, Ezra 74
Prose, Francine 8, 12, 55
psychology 7
punishment 174, 179, 181–85
Pythagoras 166

Quevedo, Francisco de 147, 150

revenge 174, 178, 179–85
Rimbaud, Arthur 64
Rossetti, Christina 51
Rossetti, Dante Gabriel 6, 40, 41, 51,
    53, 67–72, 73, 119, 206
  erotic poetry 67–68
  "Inclusiveness" 67, 68–69, 70
  "Jenny" 72
  "Nuptial Sleep" 42, 70–72
  "Supreme Surrender" 71
  *The House of Life* 68, 70
  "The Kiss" 70, 71
Ruskin, John 36, 143

Sade, Marquis de 73
San Juan de la Cruz 41, 53
Sarlo, Beatriz 129, 144, 173, 188
Sarmiento, Domingo F.
  *Facundo* 147
Schopenhauer, Arthur 45, 53, 69,
    109–15, 135, 141, 142, 182–85, 207
  *The World as Will and
    Representation* 82–83, 109–15,
    135, 142, 207
Seneca 146, 148, 149, 150, 152, 153,
    154, 157, 158, 161, 162, 163, 164,
    176, 182, 185
  "Consolation to Helvia" 151
  "Consolation to Marcia" 151
  *De Beneficiis* 160, 162, 163
  "On Anger" 182
  "On Providence" 177

Seurat, Georges 13
sex act 5, 22, 23, 27, 91, 109–15
sex, casual 5, 28, 29
sex, venal 5, 24, 28, 29
sexual techniques 96, 98
Shakespeare 36, 45, 47, 121, 154,
    186
Shaw, George Bernard 146–47
Socrates 149, 158
sodomía 34, 100
speech pathology 7
stoicism 120, chapter 7, 175, 207
Storni, Alfonsina 51
Swift, Jonathan 1, 2, 36, 52, 143
Swinburne, Algernon 3, 53, 72–81,
    108, 115, 168, 206
  "Aholibah" 74, 126–27
  "Anactoria" 74, 75
  "Ave Atque Vale" 74
  "Dolores" 74, 75
  "Hermaphroditus" 74
  "Love and Sleep" 77
  "On the Russian Persecution of
    the Jews" 73
  *Poems and Ballads* 73, 80
  "The White Czar" 75
  "To Victor Hugo" 75

Tiempo, César
  *Clara Beter* 144

Vaccaro, Alejandro 31
*Variaciones Borges* 6
Vatsyayana 88
  *The Kama Sutra* 88, 126
Vázquez, María Esther 27–28, 135,
    164
Vendler, Helen 10
Verlaine, Paul 33, 51, 64–67
  *Femmes* 65
  "Green" 65
  *Hombres* 65
  *Poèmes saturniens* 65
  *Romances sans paroles* 65
  "Vœu" 65–66, 79
Vilariño, Idea 15
  "El amor" 15

Virtue 146, 176, 177, 185–86
Voltaire 52
von Stummer, Helen 30

Wagner, Richard 114
Walter
 *My Private Life* 40–41, 73
Watts, George Frederic
 "The Minotaur" 77
Whitman, Walt 41, 51–52, 63
Wilde, Eduardo 142

Wilde, Oscar 52–53, 198
 "The Ballad of Reading Gaol" 52
 "The Harlot's House" 52
Williamson, Edwin 5, 173, 188
Woscoboinik, Julio 5, 67, 80, 172, 173

Yates, Donald 23
Yeats, William B. 81–83, 115, 119
 "Leda and the Swan" 81–83

Zenner, Wally 29